MILITARY ENGINEERING.
(PART IV.)

MINING AND DEMOLITIONS.

GENERAL STAFF, WAR OFFICE, 1910.
(Reprinted, 1915, with Amendments to 1912 inclusive.)

The Naval & Military Press Ltd

Published by

The Naval & Military Press Ltd
Unit 5 Riverside, Brambleside
Bellbrook Industrial Estate
Uckfield, East Sussex
TN22 1QQ England

Tel: +44 (0)1825 749494

www.naval-military-press.com
www.nmarchive.com

In reprinting in facsimile from the original, any imperfections are inevitably reproduced and the quality may fall short of modern type and cartographic standards.

CONTENTS.

PART IV.—MINING AND DEMOLITIONS.

	PAGE
SECTION 1.—SUBTERRANEAN WARFARE	1
SECTION 2.—SHAFTS AND GALLERIES	7
General Description	7
Lining for Shafts and Galleries	7
Shafts and Galleries without Lining ...	9
Shafts with Cases	9
Galleries with Cases	11
Shafts with Frames and Sheeting	13
Galleries ,, ,, ...	14
Inclined Galleries	15
Returns	16
Great Galleries	16
Men and Tools for Shafts and Galleries ...	17
Bored Mines	18
SECTION 3.—COUNTERMINES	19
General System of Countermines	19
Countershaft Mines	21
SECTION 4.—VENTILATION AND LIGHTING OF GALLERIES ...	22
Rotary Blower	22
,, Fan	23
Apparatus for Breathing in Foul Atmospheres	23
Denayrouze Respirator	23
Applegarth Aérophore	24
Lighting of Mines	25
SECTION 5.—CHARGES AND EFFECTS OF MINES	26
Definitions of Terms and action of Mines ...	26
Rules for Calculating Charges	27
SECTION 6.—PREPARING MINES FOR FIRING	30
Loading	32
Tamping	32

CONTENTS

	PAGE
SECTION 7.—FIRING POWDER CHARGES WITHOUT ELECTRICITY	35
Safety Fuze	35
Substitutes for Safety Fuze	35
Instantaneous Fuze	35
Substitutes for Instantaneous Fuze	36
Arrangement of Fuze and Charge	36
Joints between Fuzes	37
Protection of Fuzes	38
Means of Lighting	38
Precautions in the use of Fuzes	38
Failure of Charges to Explode	39
SECTION 8.—FIRING CHARGES BY ELECTRICITY	40
Electricity when used for Firing Charges	40
Description of Electric Fuzes and Detonators	41
Description of Firing Apparatus, viz.:—	
Exploders	45
Batteries	46
Description of Covered Wires and Cables	47
" of Earths	48
" of Testing and Jointing Box and its Contents	48
List of Tools for Soldering Joints	52
Various arrangements of Circuits described	52
Grouping of Fuzes or Detonators	53
Jointing Wires	54
Necessity for Testing Stores	55
Inserting Fuzes or Detonators into Charges	56
Fixing Connecting Wires into Charges	57
Safety precautions	57
Estimating number of Fuzes or Detonators that can be fired by Exploder or Battery, and detail of Firing operations	58
Testing	60
Summary of procedure in preparing Charges for Firing by Electricity	66
Use of Strange Apparatus on Service	67
Electric-contact System of Land Mines	68
SECTION 9.—BORING AND BLASTING	70
Action of Extended Charges	70
Position of Bore Holes	70
Boring Tools	73
Method of Hand-Boring	75
Loading Bore-Holes	76
Splitting Stone	77
Calculation of Charges	78

		PAGE
SECTION 10.—EXPLOSIVES		81
	Guncotton	83
	Preparing Charges for Firing	89
	Nitro-Glycerine	90
	Dynamite	91
	„ No. 1	92
	„ No. 2	94
	Blasting Gelatine	94
	Gelatine Dynamite	95
	Nitro-benzole Explosives	95
	Picric Powders	96
	Cordite	97
	Other Explosives	97
	Fulminates	97
SECTION 11.—DEMOLITIONS WITH GUNPOWDER		98
	Deliberate Demolition of Walls, Buildings, and Revetments by Gunpowder	98
	Deliberate Demolition of Bridges by Gunpowder	102
	Hasty Demolitions with Gunpowder	108
SECTION 12.—DEMOLITIONS WITH GUNCOTTON		113
	Charges for Hasty Demolitions	122
	Demolitions by other High Explosives	123
SECTION 13.—DEMOLITION OF RAILWAYS		124
SECTION 14.—DEMOLITION OF TELEGRAPH LINES		133

APPENDIX I.

TESTS FOR EXPLOSIVES ... 135

Plates I.–XXXIX. following Appendix.

LIST OF PLATES.

Part IV.—MINING AND DEMOLITIONS.

I.—Mining Cases and Frames.
II.—Mining Tools.
III.—Shafts and Galleries.
IV.—Curb Shafts.
V.—Verifying Direction of a Gallery, &c.
VI.—Breaking out one Gallery from another.
VII.—Inclined Galleries, &c.
VIII.—Great Gallery.
IX.—Countermines.
X.—Ventilation of Mines
XI.—Apparatus for Breathing in Foul Atmospheres.
XII.—Firing Mines.
XIII.—Fuses.
XIV.—Field Service Fuzes and Detonators.
XV.—Electric Fuzes and Detonators.
XVI.— „   „   „   Naval Service.
XVII.—Cells Electric Dry " E."
XVIII.—Wires Electric Covered.
XIX.—Key Contact Mark IV; Galvanometer, Vertical, 3-coil, Mark II, and Resistance Coil, 100 Ohms.
XX.—Galvanometer, Vertical, 3-coil, Mark II.
XXI.—Pull Circuit Closer.
XXII.—Arrangement of Circuits.
XXIII.—Jointing Wires; arrangement of Fuzes in charges.

XXIV.—Line of Electro-contact Land Mines.

XXV.—Firing Mines with Battery, including firing by Successive Contacts.

XXVI.—Cable and Circuit Tests.

XXVII.—Exploder, Dynamo Electric Quantity, Mark V.

XXVIII.—Cliff Roads. Boring and Blasting—Position of Boreholes.

XXIX.—Boring and Blasting—Position of Boreholes.

XXX.—Boring and Blasting.

XXXI.—Dynamite Charges and Railway Demolition.

XXXII.—Demolition of Revetments.

XXXIII.—   ,,   of Buildings and Bridges.

XXXIV.—Preparing Charges.

XXXV.—Demolition of Revetments with Counterforts.

XXXVI.—Demolition of Iron Girder Bridges.

XXXVII.—   ,,   with Guncotton

XXXVIII.—Girders—Clear span 40 ft., 60 ft., and 75 ft.

XXXIX.—Girder—Clear span 30 ft., and formula for demolition of same.

MILITARY ENGINEERING.

PART IV.

MINING AND DEMOLITIONS.

SECTION 1.—SUBTERRANEAN WARFARE.

1. In all kinds of fortress warfare of which we have hitherto had experience, it has frequently happened that the besieger has had to carry on his advance below the ground, either because the fire of the fortress was still unsubdued, or because he had reason to believe that the besieged would endeavour to check his advance above ground by means of countermines. The recent example of a siege—that of Port Arthur—only serves to confirm the fact that subterranean warfare may have to be employed in similar cases in the future, and further to emphasize the necessity for the training in peace time of special troops for this service. Mining was made use of by the Japanese, but only to a small extent, and only when they discovered that without its assistance the capture of the forts was impossible. It seems probable that, if the Japanese had made greater use of mining on an organized plan, the final capture of the fortress would have been in no way delayed, and the enormous losses caused by the disastrous attempts at assault would have been avoided. The Russians also made very little use of countermining, of which they gave such a splendid example during the siege of Sebastopol 50 years previously. Owing to the small amount of mining and countermining done, to its improvised nature and to the apparent lack of coherent system in its application, the siege of Port Arthur throws little light on the subject as compared with that of Sebastopol. Neither the Japanese nor the Russians had an adequate armament of modern siege artillery, and it is impossible to say what new methods of attack may follow the improvements in artillery that have marked the opening of the 20th century. It is quite safe, however, to assume that mining will still have its rôle and, from time to time, its opportunities. Whether the occasion for the use of military mining arises suddenly, finding both sides unprovided with suitable material, or whether it occurs in a regular siege, where the attack may have all the

mechanical resources of the period at command, and the defence a complete system of countermine galleries, the general principles governing the action of both sides will be the same as they have been hitherto.

As regards the actual processes of mining, the only changes to be anticipated are the development of the use of rapid boring tools, and of high explosives for special purposes.

At all times subterranean warfare is a tedious operation to the attacker, but he has much in his favour, so that he should, sooner or later, gain ground, and the only object at which the besieged aims is, as at all other periods of the siege, to delay the advance as long as possible.

In no species of warfare is a clear cool head, combined with decisive and energetic action, more required than in the conduct of operations of this nature.

Comparison of the advantages of besieged and besieger.

2. The besieger, by using *large* charges, ruptures the countermines at a great distance and forms crafters, which act as cover to his advance. He has but little anxiety as to the amount of damage he may cause to his own galleries. The besieged would also like to produce ruptures at a great distance to the galleries of the attack by using large charges, but the fear of forming craters, and of destroying his own galleries, ties him down to small charges only. The besieger therefore can use charges of any size, whereas the besieged is compelled to use only comparatively small charges.

The besieger can, in cases of emergency, fire increased charges with little or no tamping, and thereby save time—the besieged would never dare to do so. On the other hand, the besieger generally loses much time, and gives a corresponding advantage to the defence, by being obliged continually to start a new system of shafts and galleries from each set of craters. As the besieged generally has his countermines constructed beforehand, he is ready to branch out in any direction to meet the attack.

Organization of working parties.

3. As soon as a resort to subterranean warfare has been determined on by either the attack or defence, special working parties are detailed for these operations, and the direction of the works placed under an officer of R.E.—"*the Controller of Mines*"—who is charged under the direction of the Chief Engineer with forming his project of attack or defence, with the necessary requisitions for men, tools, &c.

Under the controller are other officers for specially superintending the mining operations; one of whom is detailed to keep the plans, correcting, and adding to them from time to time—a most important duty, as, without accurate plans, the controller of a subterranean warfare is like a man fighting in a fog.

The number of men (if possible, all R.E.) employed, depends entirely on the nature of the work, and is based on the detail shown in para. 32. Great care should be taken in selecting men for listening purposes, and the controller himself should be the principal listener.

Working in the galleries is very irksome, and the reliefs should never exceed six hours; the officers relieving each other at half-time. In' the later stages, more particularly on the side of the defence, extra strong reliefs are necessary, as at that time opportunities for action occur which may fail entirely if labour is wanting.

At all times the senior officer on duty with the working parties should be given latitude in his powers of action, for in this species of warfare the success of an operation often depends on a resolution rapidly conceived, and as rapidly put into execution. In urgent cases therefore the senior officer on the spot, when the controller is absent, should be ready to take the responsibility of actually putting into execution any measures he may consider necessary, reporting what he has done to the controller.

4. In order to insure accuracy in the keeping of the plans, every effort must be made at starting to have certain fixed points, whose level and position have been thoroughly determined, and which should be so selected that from them observations over the whole field of operations may be taken. All sentries should be specially warned to report anything they note, from which the position of the enemy may be fixed by observation on the plans. *Keeping of plans.*

The theodolite, compass, and sextant may be used for fixing points. In the galleries, a theodolite with shortened legs is most useful, as the compass is there very unreliable. Instruments for purposes of observations should always be kept under cover close to the field of operations.

5. The besieger will not take to subterranean warfare until he is absolutely obliged to do so. If he has reason to suppose that the ground in which he is to operate is countermined, he will, before determining on his attack, make every effort to gain a knowledge of the whereabouts of these countermines, and he should then arrange his system of attack so as to embrace the whole front of the portion attacked, either by direct galleries, or by side galleries thrown out for listening purposes. All through his attack he must carefully avoid the temptation to contract his front, and so allow the besieged to concentrate all his resistance against him. On a small front he should make the general depth of his galleries at least equal to the estimated depth of the countermines, and at distances apart about three times this depth. *General system of attack by galleries.*

He should commence the heads of his direct galleries of attack from a line as nearly as possible parallel to the extremities of the countermines so that he may arrive within striking distance of them all at about the same time. To effect this he will sink shafts or inclined galleries (the choice depending on the supposed distance to the countermines) from one of the most advanced trenches. He will use every endeavour to prevent the enemy from discovering their whereabouts, and even by deception to mislead him.*

When the galleries reach a depth at least equal to that of the countermines, they are continued at the same depth until the countermine galleries are believed to be well within reach. Overcharged mines (*see* para. 61), are then prepared and fired at the heads of the galleries, if possible, simultaneously. The craters formed by these mines should be at such distance apart as not to fill each other up, and at the same time near enough to form a fairly continuous line of cover.

Before firing these mines, the besieger must have everything in readiness :—

1. For occupying the craters immediately after firing the mines and intrenching himself in them.

2. For forming communications, covered or open, from the trenches to the craters, which may be helped by intermediate explosions simultaneous with the overcharged mines.

3. For constructing a certain number of positions for the guards told off to protect the craters against sorties.

These three points require particular attention, as there is always an unavoidable check to the further advance of the besieger after forming craters. It is now that the besieged knows the exact position of his adversary, and he will make every effort to advance to points from which he can only be driven back with difficulty.

From the new lodgments in the craters the besieger continues his advance as before, by means of shafts and galleries, or more rarely by inclined galleries. Very often he will find that, however quickly he recommences his advance after forming craters, the besieged has forestalled him, and has managed to surround him. His best chance then is to sink shafts only partially lined in order to place charges to be fired hastily with little or no tamping; or else, he may endeavour to lodge charges by boring, and so break through the countermines. He can rarely attain his end without suffering more or less heavy loss; but too much prudence and circumspection at this point for the sake of avoiding loss, is fatal to his chance of success. Sooner or later he must push his way forward, and so drive the besieged back.

<small>Hasty shafts.</small>

<small>General system of defence by galleries.</small>

6. As has been stated above subterranean warfare is a most tedious operation to the besieger, and therefore the besieged should endeavour to make him take to mining as early as possible. As soon as it is evident that he has done so, every endeavour must be made to push forward the countermines at the particular point attacked, so as to meet and check the besieger. The rules as to their depth and distance apart are the same as those for permanent galleries. (Paras. 35 and 41.)

---

* The earth excavated from the galleries is very apt to point out the entrance to the different galleries, and it should, therefore, either be scattered or taken to some point not opposite the entrance.

As soon as it is calculated that the two opposing parties are approaching near to one another, listening for the enemy must be resorted to, and for this purpose it is advisable that all work should be suspended at *irregular* intervals, for some five minutes, and the doors of communication closed, in order that experienced listeners may try to discover the locality of the attack from the head of the countermines.

As this true judgment of distance is a point of the utmost importance in mine-warfare, practice in listening is essential, and every effort should be made in peace operations to train the sense of hearing in this respect. From the results of the experiments during the Siege Manœuvres of 1907, it would appear that an unpractised listener had little difficulty in detecting "direction" and could estimate distances not exceeding 10 feet with fair accuracy. Beyond 10 feet, however, an unpractised listener was most unreliable. Correct estimation appeared to be a matter of chance. No regular error of over or under estimation was apparent, and great difficulty was experienced in appreciating the relative distances of sound, but the general tendency of the inexperienced listeners was to underestimate the distance.

A few records by an experienced civilian miner were obtained during the manœuvres and the results showed an ability to estimate correctly, quite beyond the powers of an unpractised listener.

It is however much better to come into actual collision with the enemy's miner, than to explode a charge at a distance greater than the line of least resistance (L.L.R.), which is the distance from the centre of the charge to the ground surface.

The points guiding the besieged are:—

1. To hold on to every inch of ground as long as possible, endeavouring to meet and check the enemy's advance by destroying his galleries, poisoning the ground with noxious gases, &c. (*e.g.*, Sebastopol).

2. To avoid making craters which could give cover to the besieger, and yet to destroy his lodgments above ground.

As soon as the besieger has fired his mines (which the besieged should try to compel him to do as early as possible), the defence must strain every nerve to prevent him from getting under ground again; and it is at this point of attack that an energetic defender can best show his powers of resistance. The position of the craters must be accurately fixed on the plans, and the direction of the galleries altered as may be required, so as to embrace them in front and on the flanks.

Every effort must be made at the same time to delay the occupation of the craters by the besiegers; all available artillery fire should be turned upon them, hand grenades poured into them, and frequent sorties made against them.

The great danger to be feared is from hasty shafts formed by the besieger (*see* para. 8). To meet these in time, the besieged may resort to the use of bored mines (*see* para. 33), and so place a charge in advance of the head of his countermines.

Exploration after explosions.

7. The exploration of the mines after an explosion should be put off as long as possible, consistently with not delaying or affecting the operations.

In exploring, an officer having a life line secured round his chest should lead the way, a N.C.O. should follow about 5 yards in rear, holding the life line, and men should be placed about every 20 or 30 yards along the line to pass messages, &c. The men should be ordered to maintain perfect silence, to keep their heads as high as possible, and to be on the look-out to pass orders. The words used, may be "*advance*," "*pay out*," "*hold on*," "*retire*," "*pull back gently*." In the event of a man having to be hauled out by means of a life line, it should be done very slowly. An officer or a N.C.O. should always remain at the entrance to the mine with two or three men in readiness to act as circumstances may require.

Attack by shaft mines.

8. Where the defence above ground is weak, "*shaft mines*" may be employed as follows :—

A trench of a **T** form (the head of the **T** being nearest to the place) is constructed by flying trenchwork at nightfall. Along the head of the **T**-head circular shafts are sunk at 2-*lined intervals* (*see* para. 61), without frames or casing. When they are loaded they are tamped by throwing down earth, so that the whole may be ready for firing by daybreak. In order to ensure the connection of the craters, larger charges than usual are used. When the charges are fired, the head of the **T** is converted into a lodgment, the stalk acting as a communication to the trenches.

Final result of subterranean warfare.

9. The final result of subterranean warfare is, as a rule, that the besieger drives back the defender, and arrives at the counter scarp of the fort.

From this point he has two courses open :—

(1) To blow in the counterscarp wall with large charges and so fill up the ditch as to render an assault practicable.
(2) To continue mining through the counterscarp wall across the ditch and beneath the parapet. To blow up the parapet with large charges and so lay the fort open to assault.

In either case every endeavour must be made to destroy the flank defences of the ditch before assault. (The siege of Port Arthur affords examples of both methods.) When the ditch is narrow the first method is preferable, but with a wide ditch the second is necessary.

For the charges required, and the usual position of such charges, *see* paras. 234 and 248.

Section 2.—SHAFTS AND GALLERIES.

General Description.

10. Military mining differs essentially from the mining practised in civil life in that the latter is usually carried on at greater depths and often in hard rock, whilst the former is mostly carried on within a few feet of the surface, seldom in hard rock, and generally in soil so wanting in tenacity as to require the support of wooden linings. Moreover, the question of drainage, frequently of great difficulty in civil mines, seldom gives trouble in military mining.

Military mining would nearly always be carried out by manual labour. When the amount of labour available is large and the reliefs can therefore be made as short as required, no mechanical excavator has hitherto been found so suitable as the pick and shovel. Any variations in the nature of the ground which would not affect manual labour would necessitate change of power, tools and cutters if machines were used, and thus cause delay.

11. Military mines, as used in the field, comprise shafts and galleries as follows :— *(Shafts and galleries.)*

1. *Shafts* used for vertical descent only.
2. *Common galleries.*
3. *Branch galleries.*

The common galleries are usually used for horizontal and inclined passages, the branch or smaller size being only used in extension of the common galleries.

The smaller the gallery is, the less lining is necessary and less excavation has to be done, but owing to the cramped space for working in and for removal of material, it does not follow that the rate of progress is always quicker.

4. *Great galleries.* These are large enough to give passage to a gun, and have been used for the descent into the ditch in the latter stages of a systematic attack on a fortress. It is doubtful whether in modern wars any occasion for their use will arise.

Lining for Shafts and Galleries.

12. Shafts and galleries may be lined, either by means of *cases*, set close together or at open order, or by means of *sheeting* supported at intervals by *frames*. (Pl. I.) *(Lining for shafts and galleries.)*

In cases, and frames for galleries, the pieces which are laid on the ground are termed *groundsills*, the side pieces *stanchions* and the upper pieces *topsills*. In frames for shafts the end pieces are termed *rails* or *end rails*, and the side pieces *stiles*.

Dimensions of frames and cases.

13. The dimensions of the frames and cases are as follows (*see* Pl. I):—

Description of gallery, &c.	Size of cases.				Size of frames.				Thickness of sheeting planks.	
	In the clear.		Over all.		In the clear.		Over all.			
	Height.	Width.	Height.	Width.	Height.	Width.	Height.	Width.	Top.	Side.
	ft. in.	ft. in.	ft. in.	ft. in.	ft. in.	ft. in.	ft. in.	ft. in.	in.	in.
Great gallery ...	6 6	6 8	7 2	7 4	...	...	...	...	...	...
Common gallery ...	5 6	2 0	5 10	2 4	4 10	2 0	5 4	2 7	2	1½
Branch gallery ...	4 0	2 0	4 4	2 4	3 6	2 0	4 0	2 7	2	1 or 1½
Shaft	4 4	2 0	4 4	2 4	4 0	2 0	4 7	2 7	2	2

Cases and frames are articles of store, and are made of sound fir. The dowels are of oak, and the fillets of elm.

Pl. I, Fig. 1, shows the case used for shafts and branch galleries; it is provided with two sets of hand holes, which form a ladder when used in a shaft.

Fig. 2 shows a common gallery case.

Fig. 3 shows a branch gallery frame.

Fig. 4 shows the frame used for the top of a shaft; it is made with projecting *horns* to prevent it from falling down the shaft.

Fig. 5 shows a shaft frame.

Fig. 6 shows a common gallery frame.

The sheeting (Fig. 7) is generally made in 5 feet lengths, 11 inches wide and 2 inches thick, having one end bevelled for about 6 inches, thus admitting of the frames being placed at intervals of about 4 feet.

Cases form a much better lining for shafts and galleries than frames and sheeting, as they are more easily placed, are stronger, and with the same amount of excavation give a greater clear width and height; but in ordinary soil they take up more timber.

Tools and appliances

14. The shafts and galleries, in which the miner has to work, being small, special picks and shovels, of the dimensions shown in Pl. II, Figs. 1 and 2, are provided. In addition, the miner requires a *push-pick* (Pl. II, Fig. 3) for loosening the earth in the angles behind the cases, previously to getting in a new case.

The *miner's truck* (Pl. II, Fig. 6) is used for drawing the earth from the end of the gallery to the bottom of the shaft. Wheel guides for the truck should be laid on the floor of the gallery. (Pl. II, Fig. 7.)

The earth is raised to the surface either in the truck or in a *miner's bucket* (Pl. II, Fig. 5), made of canvas, attached to two ropes, and drawn up by two men.

It saves time to draw up the full truck to the top of the shaft, instead of transferring the contents into buckets at the bottom. An arrangement for doing this can be made with a windlass at the top.

Shafts and Galleries without Lining.

15. When shafts of moderate depth are intended for hasty explosions, wood lining may frequently be dispensed with. When the soil is favourable, such as chalk or hard gravel, shafts 20 or 30 feet in depth may stand for several weeks without support. Shafts and galleries without lining.

In excavating shafts, where woodwork is not to be used, an elliptical section is decidedly the best. The dimensions of the axes should be the same as those of an ordinary shaft, viz., 4 feet by 2 feet; and two gauges corresponding with the two axes of the ellipse must be provided to guide the miner in the size of his excavation. A rectangle marked on the ground, having its angles rounded off, makes a good section for a shaft. (Pl. III, Fig. 3.) Shafts.

In soil so tenacious as to allow of galleries being excavated safely without the use of woodwork, the miner may adopt the section shown in Pl. 3, Fig. 4. This is the best shape that can be adopted for temporary galleries, or branches intended for immediate explosion. But if the galleries are to stand for any length of time, it is better to form their tops in the form of a semicircular or pointed arch, as there is then undoubtedly much less risk of their giving way than if cut flat. The miner must in this case be provided with gauges, and the arch should be shaped to a template. (Pl. 3, Fig. 5.) Galleries.

Shafts with Cases.

16. A party consisting of one non-commissioned officer and four sappers is detailed for each shaft. They commence operations by levelling the ground 6 feet square around the intended position of the shaft. Shafts with cases.

The first case is laid together on the ground, in the position of the proposed shaft, with its longer sides parallel to the direction of the gallery that is to be driven from the bottom of the shaft. The ground is then marked round the case, and the case removed. The earth within the marked space is excavated to a depth of 1 foot; the case is then place in the excavation with its upper edge level with the ground, and earth rammed in all round its sides.

In placing each succeeding case, the ground must be excavated for one side first, then for one end, next for the other side, and lastly for the remaining end, placing each piece singly, and cutting away no more earth than is necessary. But in order that the last end may be put in, it is necessary that a wedge-shaped recess should be cut away behind it, into which it

B

may be pushed. It is then drawn forward to its proper position, so that its mortice fits on to the tenon of the side piece (Pl. 3, Fig. 1). The earth remaining is then excavated from the middle, and the next case got in in the same manner, taking care to make the wedge-shaped recesses on opposite ends of the shaft, as otherwise there would be a hollow behind the cases all down one side, which would give no support to the cases on that side. It is advisable to fill up these spaces with sods, &c., pushed up from below.

In soft soil it will be advisable to nail battens at intervals to the cases, in order to keep them from slipping down.

When the ground is firm and good the shaft can be dug by simply excavating to the depth of one case at a time, letting the excavation be a little deeper at the centre, for convenience of standing and working when placing the cases. This must not be attempted except in good soil.

The cases must be all flush with one another on the inside, and close together. In this way the shaft is continued to the required depth. When it is intended to break out a gallery the ends of the lowest cases (five for a branch gallery (Pl. 3, Fig. 1), seven for a common gallery) are omitted; the sides of the shaft being there kept from closing in by end pieces of cases (which must not be allowed to slip into their usual places) or by means of battens 2 feet 4 inches long. This width allows of a gallery being driven.

In shafts in good soil that will stand without much support, the cases can be placed at intervals of 2 or 3 feet, the shaft being made 4 feet by 2 feet in the clear, and the cases let into the sides and ends 2 inches. For tools required, *see* para. 32.

Sinking shafts with curbs.   17. In ordinary soil the following methods of sinking shafts with curbs may be adopted with advantage.

The frame a, b, c, d (Pl. 4) is fixed as in sinking a shaft with frames and sheeting (para. 23), its inside dimensions in the clear being the same as those from out to out of the cases; 12 to 18 inches of earth are removed from the inside of the frame and the curb dropped in, the curb being an ordinary case, with triangular fillets of wood secured into the corners; 12 more inches of earth are then excavated and the curb allowed to drop down; a second case is put together and dropped in on top of the curb.

The sinking of the shaft proceeds by excavating depths of 12 inches at a time, the curb being kept up by means of ropes attached to pickets while the excavation is going on, cases being added at the top as required.

The rate of progress is twice as fast as that of an ordinary shaft sunk with cases, and a better shaft is the result; there are no hollows necessary at alternate sides to enable the end to be fitted on the tenon: and all chance of cases slipping is avoided.

If, owing to bad work, the cases get jammed, the ordinary method can then be resorted to.

To break out a gallery it is only necessary to excavate 3 inches extra in rear of the last 5 or 7 end pieces, so that they can be easily removed, a gallery case 4 inches in width being fixed at the bottom to take the thrust of the side pieces.

Galleries with Cases.

18. Before commencing a gallery, its centre line is marked at the bottom of the shaft by pickets, their positions being determined by plummets let down from two points in a straight edge placed over the mouth of the shaft, in the proper direction. (Pl. 5, Fig. 1.) Commencing the gallery.

Before the battens or ends are removed from between the sides of the shaft cases, a case must be temporarily set up in the shafts (Pl. 3, Fig. 1), (or better, uprights of about 3 inches by 2 inches, strutted at top and bottom) close to them, to take the thrust of the sides. The end pieces or battens can then be removed.

The first case of the gallery (Pl. 3, Fig. 1) should be placed with its inner edge flush with the inside of the shaft, so that the sides of the shaft may have a bearing against it, and be prevented from collapsing when the temporary case is removed. Just enough earth is excavated to allow the groundsill to be placed; grooves are next cut for the stanchions, and lastly, the topsill is got in by cutting a wedge-shaped recess above the top of one stanchion, into which it is pushed and then drawn down to its proper position, with its mortice on the tenon of the stanchion.

No more earth must be cut away above the topsill than is absolutely necessary. The object of placing the various pieces of the case in the grooves, and leaving the earth solid in the centre, is, that it may be afterwards picked down on to the groundsill, whence it is more easily removed than from the floor of the gallery before the groundsill is placed.

The temporary case is now removed, and the last *complete* case of the shaft supported by wedges or pickets, driven over the topsill of the first gallery case. The succeeding cases of the gallery are placed in a similar manner, the recesses for the placing of the topsills being right and left alternately. Cases at open order.

Common and branch galleries are driven in the same way.

In galleries in good soil, the cases need not be at close order. If sheeting be not available, they may be placed at alternate central intervals of 2 feet 7 inches and 4 feet 7 inches, laying alternately a couple of topsills and a couple of stanchions over the intervening spaces, resting on the topsills of the regular cases, with bearings of 4 inches at either end.

19. When the gallery has proceeded for some distance its direction may be verified and corrected with accuracy in the following Verifying direction of a gallery.

12   SHAFTS AND GALLERIES.   PART IV.

way (Pl. 5, Fig. 1) :—Lay a straight edge over the centre of the shaft, and from it hang two plummets with lines sufficiently long for the plummets to just clear the bottom of the shaft; then, standing at the surface of the ground, line these plummets accurately in the required direction of the gallery; and, by means of a third plummet held at the end of the gallery and lined with the help of a light on the two at the bottom of the shaft, determine a point in the true direction of the gallery and mark it with accuracy on the groundsill of the gallery.

Changing direction of a gallery.

20. In changing direction of a gallery the change must be made gradually, fitting the cases close together at one side, and leaving intervals at the other. (Pl. 5, Fig. 3.)

If the soil be very bad, pieces of wood must be driven in between the cases at the openings, to support the earth.

When the direction of a gallery is to be changed and its new direction has to be set off accurately, the angle to be made with the old direction should be carefully set off above ground by means of a field level, and some profile battens should be nailed at the required angle (Pl. 5, Fig. 2). The centre line of the old direction having been carefully marked on the groundsills, the template should then be taken below and applied to it, thus giving the required new direction. It is not easy to use the field level for setting off angles in the gallery of a mine.

Breaking out one gallery from another (with cases).

21. In breaking out one gallery from another (Pl. 6, Fig. 1), the stanchions must be taken out to form the opening for the new gallery, and the topsill of the stanchions strutted up 2 inches above their former level. These stanchions being removed, an excavation is made perpendicular to the old gallery, and a case is put up (2 inches of the width of its groundsill having been previously sawn off) with its inner edge flush with the inside of the old gallery, so that its topsill may support the topsills of the old gallery.

The temporary struts may now be removed, and the gallery proceeded with, any change of direction or diminution of size being made after the first case has been placed.

Working party.

22. The party required to sink a shaft, and drive the first 4 feet of a gallery from it, consists of one non-commissioned officer and four men; one man works at the bottom of the shaft, or head of the gallery, and is relieved as soon as he has placed one complete case, and excavated the earth it contains; two draw up the earth in a miner's bucket, and the fourth removes it, scattering it, if necessary for concealment, on the surrounding surface. One of the men employed in raising the earth relieves the man in the shaft, who, on coming up to the surface, distributes the earth as it accumulates, the man previously employed in this duty assisting to raise the earth.

The gallery having advanced 4 feet from the bottom of the shaft, an additional man will be required to move the earth from the gallery in a miner's truck, and attach the rope for hoisting the truck up the shaft.

After the gallery has advanced another 20 feet, an additional man must be added to move the earth from the head of the gallery to the bottom of the shaft, and so on for every other 20 feet.

For rate of advance and tools, *see* para. 32.

Time, tools, &c.

Shafts with Frames and Sheeting.

23. The depth to the floor of the gallery being known, it is necessary to determine the distances to be left between the frames. To find this, let us suppose that a branch gallery is to be driven from the bottom of a shaft 20 feet 11 inches deep. (Pl. 3, Fig. 2.) The height of the gallery from the floor to the top of the topsill (the stanchions being sunk 2 inches into the floor) is ... ... 3ft. 8in.

Sinking shafts with frames and sheeting.

Thickness of top sheeting of gallery	0 „ 2 „
Part of bevel of sheeting of shaft, say	0 „ 4 „
Thickness of shaft frame next above the gallery	0 „ 4 „
Total	4 ft. 6 in.

The top, therefore, of the frame next above the gallery must be 4 feet 6 inches from the bottom of the shaft, which being subtracted from 20 feet 11 inches, there remain 16 feet 5 inches. The frames should then be placed at three intervals of 4 feet 1 inch, and one of 4 feet 2 inches, for the last. The length of the lowest set of sheeting planks is found by adding the thickness of one frame and an overlap of 2 inches to the height of 4 feet 6 inches, making 5 feet. The ground being levelled, &c., as already described for commencing a shaft with cases, the top frame (*i.e.*, the one provided with horns, Pl. 4, Fig. 1) is placed on the surface, the ground is marked round it, and a vertical pit excavated, 2 or 3 feet deep; small trenches for the horns of the frame are made, so that they may be flush with the ground. The top frame is placed perfectly level in all directions, and the excavation continued to the level of the bottom of the next frame; then an ordinary shaft frame is placed, and made to correspond exactly with the top frame in position.

Grooves are cut for the sheeting planks, which are then pushed down, bevelled faces next to the earth, until the tops rest against the top frame, and the bevelled ends against the second frame, but wedged out 2 inches from it, so as to allow the next pieces of sheeting to be forced down. After each frame is placed it must be supported in position by wooden battens or ropes fastened to the sides of the frame above. If battens are used, they are best placed near the angles and nailed to the sides. The shaft is then proceeded with, care being taken to see that the extreme dimensions of the frame are not exceeded. When the third frame has been placed, other sheeting planks are driven. displacing the wedges.

The frame next above the top of the intended gallery being in position, and the sheeting placed, the excavation is continued to the level of the floor of the gallery, and a frame placed at the bottom of the shaft, and grooves cut for a single thickness of sheeting only; this sheeting, as before shown, must be 5 feet long, and is placed only on three sides of the shaft, leaving that side clear on which the gallery is to be commenced.

Two breadths of sheeting are usually sufficient for each side of a shaft, and one for each end. If regularly cut stuff cannot be obtained, the sheeting may consist of any planks procurable, cut into convenient lengths.

Galleries with Frames and Sheeting.

Commencing the gallery.

24. The centre line of the gallery is marked as before, para. 18. An excavation is made in its direction about 1 or 2 feet long, and the first gallery frame fixed with great accuracy, letting the stanchions their own depth into the sides of the excavation, sinking their feet about 2 inches into the floor of the gallery, and using no groundsill (Pl. 3, Fig 2). After placing the frame, the excavation is continued for 4 feet, the position of the second frame is then determined by stretching a line over the two pickets or marks, and driving a third picket, or marking a third point, in the same direction near the head of the gallery.

The stanchions are set upright on either side of the gallery, and their position is marked with the push-pick. They are then removed and the earth is cut out in the spaces marked to such a depth that the inner sides of the stanchions may be flush with the sides of the gallery. Their feet are sunk 2 inches into the ground, unless groundsills are used. The topsill is then put on, taking care that its under side is at the proper level with reference to that of the topsill of the first frame. This must be ascertained by the field level. The top sheeting planks are pushed over the first frame, with their bevelled ends upwards and foremost, until they rest also upon the topsill of the second frame; they are then separated from the frame by wedges, to make room for the next set of top sheeting. It will be necessary in bad soil to fix the two first frames at an interval of about 2 feet, and to use short pieces of sheeting over them. Sheeting for the sides is also required in bad soil, and groundsills to keep the feet of the stanchions from being forced in. The groundsills should be sunk their own depth in the floor.

Use of a false frame.

25. When there appears to be a risk of the soil falling in, the sheeting must be introduced as soon as possible and pushed forward as the man excavates, so that he may always be protected. When it is required to do this for a greater distance than a foot or two, a temporary frame, called a false frame, is used to support the projecting ends of the sheeting (Pl. 6, Figs. 3, 4 and 5). The height of this frame is 2 inches less than that of a regular gallery frame, but the width remains the same. The topsill is of hard

wood with rounded edges. The method of using it is as follows:—After an ordinary gallery frame has been fixed the false frame is set up in front of it and placed on hard wood wedges so constructed as to give the top sheeting the required splay at the position of the ordinary gallery frame to be next set up. These wedges are 5 feet long and 6 inches broad, tapering from $\frac{1}{4}$ inch to 2 inches, and are cut into five sections of 1 foot each. The thinnest section is placed first under the false frame, and the others in succession as the frame moves forward. Other wedges are used between the stanchions and side sheeting in order to leave room for the insertion of the next lengths of sheeting. Grooves are next cut for the sheeting, which is driven forward *never more than a foot beyond the false frame*.

The earth is then excavated and the false frame moved forward by striking it with a maul, first a few inches at the top, and then at the bottom alternately, great care being taken not to knock the groundsill from under the stanchions, and thus allow the sides to fall in. In this way the movement may be effected with great regularity; an ordinary frame being erected behind the false frame whenever the latter has advanced as far to the front as the sheeting will allow.

26. Galleries in bad soil should be carried on without interruption.

The detail of men for shafts and galleries with frames and sheeting is the same as in para. 22, the only difference being that a man who has not to fix a frame excavates 2 feet instead of 1 foot. For tools and rate of advance, *see* para. 32.

Men, time, &c.

27. In breaking out one gallery from another, an excavation is made in the required direction, and the frames set up as usual, a short piece of sheeting being placed, if necessary, on the sheeting in the first frame and on that in the old gallery. (Pl. 6, Fig. 2.)

Breaking out one gallery from another (with frames).

Inclined Galleries.

28. An *inclined gallery* is executed in a similar manner to a horizontal one, the inclination being verified by the field level. The stanchions in inclined galleries are placed at right angles to the slope, which should never exceed one in two. In Pl. 7, Fig. 2, is shown an inclined gallery with cases at close order, and in Fig. 1 a similar gallery with frames and sheeting.

Inclined galleries.

With frames and sheeting, the distance between each frame is measured along the slope, so that the same sheeting answers for both horizontal and inclined galleries. On first placing the frames, the stanchions should be set a little more backward at the top than the proper angle of inclination, for in driving the sheeting they will afterwards be forced forward an inch or two.

In driving inclined galleries, precautions must be taken to prevent the trucks from running down the incline and injuring the workmen.

Returns.

Returns. 29. Galleries, about 3 feet long, called *returns*, should be broken out in the usual way, at right angles to the mine gallery, and at intervals of 30 feet along it, for the reception of the empty trucks going up to the mine head, while the loaded trucks pass them on their way to the bottom of the shaft or mouth of the gallery.

Great Galleries.

Great galleries for descent into ditches. 30. Great galleries might possibly be required for the descent into the ditch of a fort, and are made with a slope not greater than one in four, depending on the distance from the ditch at which they are commenced, and the level which it is required to reach. They should meet the counterscarp of a wet ditch 1 foot above the highest water level; and that of a dry ditch about 4 feet 6 inches below its bottom, if it is to be sapped across; if otherwise, on a level with its bottom.

Great gallery with cases. Great gallery cases (Fig. 1, Pl. 8) are 6 feet 8 inches wide, and 6 feet 6 inches high in the clear; the groundsills are 3 inches, stanchions 4 inches and topsills 5 inches thick, by 11 inches wide. The feet of the stanchions are prevented from collapsing by blocks of elm 7 inches wide and 2 inches thick, fixed down on each sill, 4 inches from the ends, which also serve as guides to prevent the axles of guns striking the stanchions. The clear interval between the blocks is 5 feet 6 inches. The tenons at the top of the stanchions are 2 inches long, and fit into mortices which are only cut $2\frac{1}{4}$ inches into the lower sides of the topsills. There are handholes on each side of the stanchions 1 foot from the top.

The first case is got in by simply excavating the earth to a distance of 1 foot, setting up the case complete, and pushing it into the excavation. (Pl. 8, Figs. 1 and 2.) In placing the next and following cases, two wooden crutches are used (Pl. 8, Fig. 3), the shanks or feet of which rest on the groundsill of the case already placed, whilst the head of each crutch, being 2 feet long, projects about a foot in front of the topsill of the last case. An excavation is made, large enough to admit the topsill of the next case, which is laid on the projecting ends of the crutches, and being supported by them, prevents the earth over the roof of the gallery from falling whilst the excavation is continued to admit the remainder of the new case. The groundsill is then placed; and next the stanchions, one after another, the bottom of each behind the cleat on the groundsill, and the head driven back until the tenon is opposite the mortice in the topsill, which then falls down into its place. The crutches are then taken down and the earth in the centre is cut away, and removed in wheelbarrows, when the operation is repeated for the next case. As a precaution against the cases slipping forward, especially when working in very loose

SEC. 2.   SHAFTS AND GALLERIES.   17

soil, it is advisable to carry a double rope entirely round the
stanchions on each side, secured to a holdfast, and racked up
by a Spanish windlass; the rope being shifted after each
stanchion is put in, the stanchion last placed being wedged or
strutted up meanwhile. This is also a convenient way of
guarding against accidents, when, for instructional purposes,
cases are withdrawn.

In Pl. 8, Fig. 3, a crutch is shown: the head is made Crutch.
movable on the shank, and is secured by a chain tie. The fore
part of the head is 2 inches higher than the back, in order that
each new topsill in succession may stand at first somewhat
higher than its final level, so as to clear the tenons of the
stanchions. The crutch is steadied and tightened up by a
wedge, driven into a groove in a box called a *shoe*, placed under
its foot.

31. In commencing a great gallery from a sap, it is necessary Commencing
to deepen the trench to 7 or 8 feet (Figs. 1 and 2, Pl. 8). The a great gallery
first gallery case can then be at once placed. Great care is from a sap.
required in placing the cases until the topsills are at a depth of
3 feet or more below the surface of the ground.

A common gallery may often be substituted for a great
gallery, recesses 1 foot deep and 2 feet wide being made on each
side, at 4 feet interval. These are made by using two cases
with special top and ground sills, 4 feet 4 inches long. When
material has to be passed down the gallery, it is done by men
standing in these recesses.

Men and Tools for Shafts and Galleries.

32. The following table gives the detail of men, tools, &c., Time, men,
for galleries and shafts, with cases or frames:— and tools for
galleries and
shafts.

Description of Gallery, &c.	Dimensions in the clear with cases.		Men R.E.			Tools.											Rate of advance‡ Inches per hour.		
	Height.	Width.	N.C. Officers.	Sappers.	Axes, pick.	Picks, miners, 4½ lb.	Picks, push.	Shovels, R.E.	Shovels, miners'.	Trucks, miners'.	Levels, P.S., 4 ft.	Rods, measuring, common 6ft.	Lines, tracing.	Mauls, G.S.	Buckets, miners.	Ladder, rope, miners.	Barrows, wheel, entrenching.	Blowers, rotary.	In earth.	In brickwork.	In masonry.
	ft. in.	ft. in.																			
Great gallery ..	6 6	6 8	1	12*	4	2	2	8	..	..	1	1	1	1	..	..	..	4	..	12	..	..
Common gallery	5 6	2 0	1	4††	..	1	1	2	1	1†	1	1	1	1	1	..	1		16	6	..
Branch gallery ..	4 0	2 0	1	4††	..	1	1	2	1	1†	1	1	1	1	1	..	1		24	6	1½
Shaft ..	4 0	2 0	1	4	..	1	1	2	1	..	1	1	1	1	1	..	..		{18 / 24}	6	2½

* The number of men given is that for the gallery only; four of them may be
infantry.
  † This number of men and trucks for galleries is that required when first commencing,
i.e., within the first 4 feet; beyond that distance an extra man and truck must be
added, and one more for every additional 20 feet the gallery advances.
  ‡ These rates can only be attained by thoroughly well-trained men, well practised
in this particular work; with recruits or men new to the work the rate of progress
will not exceed half that quoted above.

The length of reliefs is dependent on the nature of the soil and the difficulties to be contended with. During the Siege Manœuvres, 1907, a three hours' relief was found the most suitable. A longer relief than this is not recommended, but a two hours' relief will be sometimes found convenient.

Bored Mines.

Bored mines.   33. In easy soil much time may be gained by using "bored mines" at the head of the gallery. A hole is bored in the required direction, and a chamber formed at the end of it by exploding a small charge of high explosive. This chamber is then used for the reception of the mine charge.

Bored mines are specially useful for the defender, as the charges will necessarily be comparatively small.

When special tools are not available the tube well apparatus can be used for boring the hole, but it is noisy. A description of this apparatus is given in Military Engineering, Part V. The boring will have to be horizontal, or only slightly inclined, and in prolongation of a gallery on account of the length of the tubes. A wooden frame with two uprights should be made to carry the tubes, and the monkey must be worked by hand, one man on each side carrying it back and swinging it forward. The tubes should be kept well oiled. Thirty feet have been bored in medium soil in this way in 2 hours, including fixing up and withdrawing the apparatus.

The small charge to form the chamber must be some form of high explosive.

Assuming that only that portion of the chamber can be loaded which is below the level of the end of the borehole, charges of from 2 lbs. to 4 lbs. will give chambers in ordinary soil capable of holding from 400 to 900 lbs. of gunpowder.

It is not necessary to tamp either the chambering charge or the main charge. For the former a couple of filled sandbags should be placed at the mouth of the borehole, for the latter it is advisable to use about a dozen. In both cases it is well to withdraw the mining party behind the nearest turn in the gallery.

One method of loading the chamber is to use a long scoop at the end of a rod. The scoop is filled with the explosive to be used, passed up the borehole and turned half round, allowing the explosive to fall into the chamber. (The rods used for cleaning drains are suitable for the purpose of loading.)

In certain very exceptional cases boring machinery will have to be resorted to. A rock drill driven by an air compressor will be the best for the purpose, there are several patterns on the market. In the cramped space of a common gallery the rate of progress of these machines is slow, and they will only be resorted to when absolutely necessary.

Section 3.—COUNTERMINES.

34. The system of mines called *countermines*, formed for the close defence of a permanent fort, generally consists of galleries lined with masonry and constructed as part of the fortification. As such, they hardly come within the scope of this work, but a short description of the system is necessary in order to properly understand the details of subterranean warfare.

General System of Countermines.

35. Any system of countermines should extend as far to the front as possible, and should at the same time embrace the whole probable field of attack. The mines are usually placed under the glacis, in front of the principal salients of a work, and consist of a number of approximately parallel galleries, stretching out toward the front, connected with each other by lateral galleries, for purposes of communication and ventilation, though, as will be afterwards explained, these lateral galleries are not a necessary part of a system of countermines. The most advanced of the galleries are termed "*listening galleries*" or "*listeners*"— the nearer, "*galleries of communication*" and the transverse galleries, "*envelopes*." There are, in addition, what are known as "*branch galleries*" thrown out at any angle to the front from the listeners, and used partly for the same purpose as the listeners, but more particularly for the reception of defence powder charges, which may there be fired without doing damage to the main galleries. *[General system of countermines]*

36. Each "*listener*" should, if possible, have a separate "*gallery of communication*" to the ditch. *[Listeners.]*

37. The "*envelopes*" or lateral communications, to be effective, should occur at every 40 or 45 yards of the length of the main galleries, and in many systems an envelope connects up all the galleries at the point where the "*galleries of communication*" terminate and the "*listeners*" begin—where a change of dimensions in the size of the gallery occurs. *[Envelopes.]*

The envelope, when used, should be rather salient between any two galleries; as otherwise, in the close attack, it is apt to become a source of weakness to the besieged; for, presenting its side to the concussion of the enemy's charge, it is soon rendered untenable, and when blown in, is liable to form a long, open trench above ground, giving cover to the attack.

For this reason the envelope is often omitted in a permanent system of countermines, and its place supplied by short salient branches from the listeners, which form part of the permanent work, and which, while adapted for lodging charges, can also be connected up one with the other for purposes of communication and ventilation as required.

Magistral gallery.	38. As a base to the system of countermines, some *magistral gallery* is usually required, affording a general communication to all the galleries, and containing magazines and depôts for the service of the mines; and this gallery may be again connected with the main works by an underground communication; a counterscarp gallery will be found convenient for this purpose.
Length of galleries.	39. The length of the "*galleries of communication*" and "*listeners*" is limited by the expense of their construction, and the difficulty of ventilating their extremities beyond a certain point; otherwise, as at first stated, the farther out they extend the better. The extremities might be 200 feet from the ditch before the siege commenced, and be driven afterwards as far forward as the supply of fresh air admitted.
Distance apart of listeners.	40. The distance apart of the "*listeners*" (or advanced main galleries) in a system of countermines should be such as not to admit of the besieger passing between them without being heard from the branch galleries on one side cr the other. This distance therefore depends upon the length to which the branch galleries extend, but would probably be 30 or 40 yards. The maximum without branches should be about 25 yards.
Depth of countermines.	41. In determining the depth of the countermines, the various systems differ a great deal. The object aimed at is to keep the galleries so low that the besiegers cannot get below them, and at the same time they must be sufficiently near to the surface to allow of the besieged destroying with small charges lodgments above ground.

With this double object in view, in General Marescot's system, (one of the best), the main galleries fall gently towards the front to a depth of 30 or 40 feet below the surface of the ground, and that branch galleries run obliquely upward from them to the right and left leading to the mines, which are placed at various depths according to circumstances. The disadvantages in this system are that deep sloping galleries are always very difficult to ventilate and to work in: and it is not easy in an emergency to place a charge to destroy a lodgment. It, therefore, seems advisable to drive galleries and branches at some fixed depths, which shall be a medium between the two desiderata.

The maximum distance apart of the main listeners has been already fixed at from 90 to 120 feet, and it may be assumed that branches for mines are run out to the right and left of these main galleries (Pl. 9, Fig. 1). In order that these latter may not be destroyed by the explosion of the common mines, and yet that the circles of rupture may be tangential to one another, the radii of these circles must not be more than $22\frac{1}{2}$ to 30 feet (say 25 feet). A common mine (para. 61) would probably be the largest the defenders would dare to use (*see* para. 2). With such a mine the L.L.R. would be about $\frac{3}{5}$ of the radius of rupture (para. 61), or in this case $\frac{3}{5} \times 25$, say 15 feet; and something between this and 18 feet is usually fixed on for the depth of the main galleries.

Thus a good system would be—main listeners 90 to 120 feet apart and 15 feet deep, with branches at every 40 feet to the right and left (sloping up to a depth of 12 feet if deemed necessary), of such a length as to place the charges far enough away from the main listeners to prevent the possibility of the destruction of these galleries themselves.

42. Small depôts for storing tools, tamping, &c., are often formed by enlarging the galleries (Pl. 9, Fig. 2), and may be made with advantage at the juncture of each "*listener*" with its gallery of communication. Depôts.

There may also be a plate-iron loophole door at this junction (c, Pl. 9, Figs. 2 and 3) for defence in case the enemy should penetrate into the gallery, and also to cut off all outside noises whilst listening.

43. Returns, as described in para. 29, are generally formed in permanent countermines (g, Pl. 9, Fig. 2), to receive trucks, men, &c., and to allow others to pass. Returns.

44. Permanent air shafts (d, Pl. 9, Fig. 3) are often made in countermines, running up to the ground surface. They should be outside the listeners, or else fitted with tight-fitting stoppers, as otherwise noises above ground are heard; but, from the possibility of the enemy discovering their whereabouts, and pouring down water, inflammable oil, or explosives, they are a doubtful advantage. Air shafts.

45. The main galleries of a system of countermines, lined with masonry, should be about 6 feet, and the branch galleries 5 feet high, and both 3 feet wide. Dimensions of countermine galleries.

Grooves are sometimes made in the side walls (f f, Pl. 9, Fig. 2) to receive the ends of short timbers to form barriers or to strengthen the tamping, and cesspits sunk (e, Fig. 3) for drainage.

Countershaft Mines.

46. The besieger will probably try to destroy the main countermine galleries by means of "*shaft mines*" (para. 8). Countershaft mines.

To check this without destroying the countermine galleries *countershaft mines* are sometimes prepared beforehand at intervals along the main galleries. These are small chambers near the surface of the ground (k, Pl. 9, Fig. 3) which can be loaded from the main galleries through tubes.

Section 4.—VENTILATION AND LIGHTING OF GALLERIES.

General rules and precautions.

47. When mines are fired the gases which result from the explosion are apt to fill the galleries, though the charges may have been well tamped, and even to penetrate through cracks or fissures to adjoining galleries. These gases are very poisonous, and are the more dangerous because the miner may be unaware of their presence until he falls faint and insensible under their influence.

The breathing of the workmen and the fumes from candles also vitiate the air, so that a gallery should not be driven more than about 60 feet without providing the means of renewing the air in it.

Boring a hole for ventilation.

48. When circumstances permit, mines may be very effectually ventilated by boring a hole upward from the gallery to the surface of the ground. When an earth borer is available the shaft can be simply bored up from the top of the gallery by using the borer as an auger. In using a borer great care must be taken that the end does not appear above ground, and so intimate to the enemy the position of the gallery. When no special borer is at hand, the shaft can be made from below by using cases, and working upwards by a long-handled push-pick, keeping the upper portion of the shaft conical, and protecting the worker from falling earth and stones, by a removable shield of planks resting on the top of the cases.

Ordinary rectangular shafts with cases may be used in good soil, but circular shafts with circular frames and sheeting are better for this purpose.

Artificial ventilation.

49. When the galleries have to be driven to any great length, or when gases resulting from an explosion are suspected to exist, air must be forced in in large quantities. For this purpose, either a pipe of small diameter with air at high pressure, or tubes of larger diameter with air at low pressure, can be used, either manual labour, steam, or electrical power being employed to propel the air.

Rotary Blower.

Rotary blower.

50. For high pressure the "*Blower, Rotary, Mark IV.*," answers. It can be worked by two men. Vulcanised indiarubber hose with an outside stiffening of coiled wire, made in different lengths with metal union, should be used.

The bellows of any medium-sized portable forge can be fairly well used for this purpose.

Rotary Fan.

51. For low pressure a rotary fan (Pl. 10, Fig. 1), worked by two men and provided with multiplying gear, can be used;* the tube or hose should be about 3 or 4 inches in diameter, and if hose is used means must be provided for keeping it distended. Such a hose will give a strong current of air up to a distance of 200 feet along a gallery. *Rotary fan.*

For turning corners, hose with distending rings placed close together, or lined with a coil of wire must be used.

The hose must be provided in various lengths, and with unions, and must be fixed up in the galleries by spunyarn lashings, tied on outside so as not to choke up, or constrict it. The lashings should be fastened to nails driven in either top corner of the gallery.

Apparatus for Breathing in Foul Atmospheres.

52. For entering shafts or galleries when filled with poisonous gas fumes or smoke, some apparatus is necessary.

The form of apparatus described in former editions of this book was the "Denayrouze Apparatus." This comprised— "The Respirator," "Low Pressure Apparatus," and "High Pressure Apparatus."

Where these exist, details of their use and construction can be found in previous editions of this book up to 1892. The apparatus now made are as follows :—

The Denayrouze Respirator,
The Applegarth Aérophore,

which take the place of the old low pressure and high pressure apparatus respectively.

Denayrouze Respirator.

53. This apparatus is for use when a man has to go for a comparatively short distance into a bad atmosphere which is not at a greater pressure than the outside air. The man sucks his own air through a tube; it is not pumped to him. *Denayrouze respirator.*

The parts of the apparatus consists of a tube, a valve-box, and a pair of eye protectors.

The tube is of gutta-percha 50 feet long, without joints or unions. It is $\frac{3}{4}$-inch interior diameter, with a coil of wire inside. One end of the tube is fitted with a valve-box, from which a short length of unwired tube leads; this has the mouth-piece on the end of it. *Tube.*

The valve-box is of tin, and has a valve composed of a double leaf of thin flat indiarubber, in the form of a flattened tube. This allows air to pass out of the tube, but none to come in; the breathed air is thus allowed to escape. (See Pl. 11, Fig. 2.) *Valve box.*

---

* As the work is hard, it would be advisable, where possible, to rig up the fan so as to be driven by the legs, like a bicycle.

Mouth-piece.	The mouth-piece (Pl. 11, Fig. 3) consists of a thin oval sheet of rubber, which is placed between the teeth and the lips, and two small blocks of rubber on it which are gripped by the teeth.
Eye protectors.	The eye protectors are a pair of glass goggles mounted in front of an inflatable indiarubber mask, which is worn over the upper part of the face and strapped behind the head. (See Pl. 11, Fig. 1.)
Method of wearing apparatus.	The mask should be strapped on and then inflated by a second person till the rubber sits close to the face round the eyes and the nose is tightly gripped between the projections of the mask.
	The eye protectors having been put on, the tubes should be attached to the body by buckling up the waist belt and shoulder strap above and below the valve-box, so that the valve-box lies in the centre of the back. The mouth-piece is inserted in the mouth, and the apparatus is ready for use.
	Care must be taken that the free end of the tube is in the fresh air, and cannot fall into the bad atmosphere.
Tube as life-line.	The tube is in itself strong enough to bear a man's weight, and can be used as a life-line; but where the necessity for this is anticipated, the tube should be strongly lashed to the man, as the belt attachment is weak.
Speaking through the tube.	The tube can be used as a speaking tube with a little practice. When the lungs are charged by sucking, the mouth-piece can be removed, and the end of the tube spoken into, care being taken to replace the mouth-piece before the breath is exhausted and inspiration takes place.
Limit of distance.	A man can work up to a distance of about 75 feet with the respirator with safety.

Applegarth Aérophore.

Aérophore.	54. This apparatus is for use when the distance is too great for the respirator to be used, or where the poisonous atmosphere is under pressure.
Parts.	It consists of a helmet, with a water and gas-proof jacket attached, lengths of tubing, and an air pump.
Helmet.	The helmet is somewhat similar to a diver's helmet. It is made of copper, and has a glass door in front which can be opened and shut. The inlet valve is at the top of the helmet, the air entering about the forehead, the tube being screwed on with a union joint behind. At the right of the helmet is the expiration valve, which is similar to that of the respirator. (See Pl. 11, Fig. 4.)
Jacket.	The jacket is made of waterproof material, tight round the waist and arms, and having a belt round the waist. (See Pl. 11, Fig. 4.)
	The tubing is indiarubber, lined with a spiral steel spring, and is supplied in lengths of 50 feet, with screw unions, the internal diameter is $\frac{3}{4}$-inch.
Pump.	The pump is a hand air pump of brass, the tube being attached at the bottom of the barrel by a screw union. (See Pl. 11, Fig. 5.)

SEC. 4.   VENTILATION AND LIGHTING OF GALLERIES.   25

The helmet and jacket being put on, and the waist belt drawn tight and the tube connected up to the pump and the helmet, and buckled to the waist belt, the wearer is ready to enter the bad atmosphere. To wear the jacket comfortably the soldier's serge or frock should be taken off. *Method of wearing apparatus.*

With this apparatus work can be done in a poisonous atmosphere at a distance of 200 feet from the pump. If work of a greater distance is required, a stronger pump is necessary than that usually supplied. *Limit of distance.*

The tube cannot be used for talking, owing to the pump being attached. *Talking through the tube.*

The tube is strong enough to be used as a life-line if it is firmly lashed to the waist. *Tube as life-line.*

55. Where it is necessary that a man should enter a deadly atmosphere without being connected by a tube with the outside, a Denayrouze High Pressure Aérophore can be used. This consists of a steel knapsack (air reservoir), air pump for charging the reservoir, pressure gauge, tube belt, &c. The knapsack being charged, a man can take with him a sufficient supply of air to last him half an hour. A special miner's lamp is also supplied with this.

Lighting of Mines.

56. Light can be supplied to mines, either by reflecting daylight or artificial light down the galleries by sheets of tin, &c., or by the use of lanterns, candles, or electric lamps. Sheets of tin have been effective up to 180 feet. *Lighting of mines.*

Candles fixed in miner's candlesticks (Pl. 2, Fig. 4) are convenient, as they can be readily fastened to the side or floor of the excavation. Care must be taken, however, that they do not set fire to the frames or cases. *Candles.*

When a mine is being loaded, no candle or other lights should be left burning in any of the galleries through which the powder has to be taken. They may be replaced after the powder has been brought in, and has been well covered with tamping.

57. Sheets of glass or zinc, covered with "*Paint, Balmain's luminous,*" emit sufficient light to enable the men who are loading a mine with powder to see what they are doing, and are absolutely safe. *Balmain's luminous paint.*

58. Experiments with portable incandescent electric lamps have been made, but so far no suitable pattern has been introduced into the service. Such a lamp must be capable of giving light for at least 8 hours, and a lamp provided with a small accumulator is the only pattern likely to fulfil this condition. Where, however, as in a fortress, steam power might be available, electric lighting could easily be arranged. *Electric lamps and electric power.*

C

Section 5.—CHARGES AND EFFECTS OF MINES.

General uses. 59. Mines are charges of explosive placed under the surface of the earth, the position and quantity of the charge depending on the object to be fulfilled, whether it be desired to produce a large crater at the surface (which may be useful as a shelter for troops) to damage the enemy's works, above or below ground, to blow down a revetment wall, &c.

Explosives used. 60. For most of these purposes, gunpowder (in the grained black varieties) is still the best explosive in common use. Its action in earth is less violent than that of high explosives, but almost equally extensive; and it gives off less poisonous fumes than gun-cotton, dynamite, picric acid, &c. Pebble and prism powders are not suitable for use in mines; their action is so slow that most of the gases of explosion have time to filter away through the earth.

Definitions of Terms and Action of Mines.

61. The effects of mines depend on the quantity of the explosive used, the depth of the charge below the surface, and the nature of the soil.

Action of a mine. The effect of the pressure of the gases formed by the explosion of the charge is, first to compress the earth around it into a hollow sphere, and then if the charge is strong enough, to burst outwards in the direction of least resistance, forming a hollow called a *crater*.

(*See* Pl. 12, Fig. 1.)

Craters. The crater is really an inverted cone, having its apex at the centre of the charge, and is partially filled up again by the falling back of the earth.

L.L.R. The shortest distance from the centre of the charge to the surface of the ground (OA) is called the *line of least resistance* [L.L.R.], and is always measured in feet.

Radius of crater. The radius of the circular opening on the surface of the ground (AB) is called the radius of the crater [r].

For any given value of L.L.R., r varies with the charge.

Radius of explosion. The line drawn from the centre of the charge to the edge of the crater is called the *radius of explosion* [OB].

Craters are classified as follows:—

A crater, the diameter of which equals the L.L.R. is called a *one-lined* crater. When the diameter is double the L.L.R. it is a *two-lined* crater, and so on.

Mines with reference to their craters. Mines are classified as follows:—

Mines charged to produce two-lined craters are called *common* mines; those more heavily charged, *overcharged* mines; those with smaller charges, *undercharged* mines; those with charges so small compared to their L.L.R. as to produce no craters, *camouflets*.

Mines are said to be at *one, two,* or *three-lined intervals* when the distance between their centres equals once, twice, or three times the L.L.R. when they have the same L.L.R., or, once, twice, or three times the mean of the L.L.Rs. when these are different.

Besides producing a crater at the surface, the effect of the explosion of a charge produces an internal commotion in the ground all round in its immediate neighbourhood.

<small>Underground effects of mines.</small>

The distance from the charge to which this commotion extends is called the *radius of rupture.*

Where no crater is formed by the explosion, this underground commotion is roughly limited to a sphere having its centre at the centre of the charge.

When a crater is formed the commotion extends to a greater distance horizontally than it does vertically, and the action is limited more by a spheroid or an ellipsoid, having for horizontal and vertical axes the horizontal and vertical radii of rupture respectively.

The consideration of the crater likely to be produced is important only with reference to whether cover above ground is desired or not.

The consideration of the radii of rupture is necessary with reference to (a) the destruction of the enemy's works underground; (b) the non-destruction of your own works underground.

Thus, to destroy a gallery the mine must be so placed that the gallery is well within the radius of rupture.

To avoid destroying a gallery it must be well beyond the radius of rupture.

Rules for Calculating Charges.

(See Pl. 12, Fig. 2.)

62. The quantity of powder to be used is always given in lbs., *in terms* of L.L.R.[3]

The following formulæ may be used for calculating the powder charges for mines and their radii of rupture.

Those for overcharged mines are not entirely reliable, as the experiments of which we have the details give such discordant results that only approximate rules can be framed.

In working by the calculated radii of rupture care should be taken to be well on the safe side either way until some experience of the local soil is gained.

If, l = L.L.R. in feet.
   r = radius of crater in feet.
   c = powder charge in pounds.
   s = a variable dependent on the nature of the soil.

<small>Formulæ for calculating charges.</small>

Then—

In a common mine ... ... $c = \frac{s}{10} l^3$.

In an overcharged or undercharged line $c = \frac{s}{10}\{l + \cdot 9 (r-l)\}^3$.

Hence if c' is the charge of an overcharged or undercharged mine, and c is the charge of a common mine having the same L.L.R. :—

$$c' = c \left(\cdot 9\frac{r}{l} + \cdot 1 \right)^3.$$

For calculating the charges for camouflets the formula for undercharged mines is of no use, as, there being no crater, $r = o$ and the expression becomes an absurdity.

Practically, any mine with a charge less than one-sixth of that of a common mine of the same L.L.R. has no crater and can be considered as a camouflet.

The values to be given to s are shown in the following table :—

Nature of soil.	Value of s.
Very light earth	0·80
Common earth	1·00
Hard sand	1·25
Earth mixed with stones	1·40
Clay mixed with loam	1·55
Inferior brickwork	1·66
Hard chalk	2
Rock, or good new brickwork	2·25
Very good old brickwork	2·50

Formulæ for calculating the radii of rupture.

Horizontal R.R. all mines.

63. For all classes of mines the *horizontal radius of rupture* in any soil depends on the charge, and is as follows :—

For common mines $= \frac{7}{4}l$ or $\frac{7}{4} \sqrt[3]{\frac{10c}{s}}$.

For overcharged mines $= \frac{7}{4} \sqrt[3]{\frac{10c}{s}}$ or $\frac{7}{4}\{l + \cdot 9 (r - l)\}$.

For undercharged mines $= \frac{7}{4} \sqrt[3]{\frac{10c}{s}}$ or $\frac{7}{4}\{l - \cdot 9 (l - r)\}$.

Vertical R.R. common mines.

The *vertical radius of rupture*

For a common mine $= \frac{7}{5}l$ or $\frac{7}{5} \sqrt[3]{\frac{10c}{s}}$.

For overcharged and undercharged mines the vertical radius of rupture does not keep this relation with the charge, the pressure in the vertical direction being influenced by the depth of the charge.

SEC. 5.   CHARGES AND EFFECTS OF MINES.

It has been found at Chatham that the earth is affected to a depth below the centre of the charge of $1\frac{2}{3}l$ with a 4-lined, $2l$ with a 5-lined and $2\frac{1}{4}l$ with a $7\frac{1}{2}$-lined crater, all of which are overcharged mines. For overcharged and undercharged mines the vertical radii of rupture can be found approximately by working out that for a common mine of the same charge. Overcharged and undercharged mines.

For camouflets the vertical and horizontal radii of rupture are about equal and may be taken to be equal to the horizontal radius of rupture of a common mine of the same charge. Camouflets.

As a rule, the vertical radius of rupture is not so important as the horizontal.

When arranging the position of a charge to destroy galleries, it should be remembered that owing to their shape they are weaker when attacked from the side than when attacked from above, below, or end on. Destruction of galleries.

64. The following deductions were made from experiments carried on in a soil weighing from 90 to 122 lbs. per cubic foot, and with L.L.R. of 6 feet; and they have been found to be accurate with much greater L.L.R. up to 3-lined craters:—

  (*a*.) To form lodgments in earth, endeavour to produce 3-lined craters at 2-lined intervals, but never with a L.L.R. of less than 6 feet.

  (*b*.) The effects of charges calculated to produce craters not greater than 3-lined, are nearly certain, but for mines with larger craters they are not so certain; it is therefore better to use a number of small charges to produce a certain effect, than to use one large one to produce it, the latter being very wasteful of powder.

65. The following table gives some details of other experiments:—

Place and date.	Explosive.	Charge in lbs.	L.L.R.	Crater.		Nature of soil.
				Diameter.	Depth.	
Chatham 1881	Gunpowder	900	15' 9"	48' × 43'	11' 0"	Unknown.
do. 1891	do.	1000	10' 4"	43' 6"	11' 3"	Unknown.
do. 1893	do.	1000	12' 0"	45' 6"	10' 7"	Clay loam.
do. do.	do.	1000	14' 0"	52' 0"	13' 0"	Sandy loam.
do. 1894	do.	800	14' 0"	53' 0"	13' 6"	do. do.
do. 1907	do.	200	7' 4"	23' 0"	4' 0"	Hard chalk.
do. do.	do.	414	8' 6"	29' 0"	6' 0"	do. do.
do. do.	do.	250	8' 0"	32' 0"	4' 3"	Soft chalk.
do. do.	Tonite	200	9' 0"	35' 6"	4' 9"	Hard chalk.

Section 6.—PREPARING MINES FOR FIRING.

The chamber

66. The position of the charge, and the quantity of powder to be used having been determined with reference to the effect to be produced, a recess or chamber is cut at right angles to the gallery. This recess need not be long, but merely out of the direct line of the shaft or gallery.

Care must be taken that it is of the most compact form, and only of sufficient size to hold the charge. (*See* table in para. 69.)

The position of the chamber, with reference to the bottom of the gallery, vertically, is usually determined by the length which it is considered necessary to give to the line of least resistance; but where no consideration of this kind prevails, it is better to put the chamber at the top of the gallery when electricity is to be used for firing the charge (*see* para. 94), and at, or near, the bottom, when fuze is to be used. (*See* paras. 78–87.)

* Cases or bags for the charge.

67. In dry soil, and when the mine is to be fired shortly after loading, the powder may be put into the chamber in bags containing about 50 lbs. each, some brushwood or straw having been previously put in to prevent the bags from coming directly into contact with the soil. In damp soil the outsides of the bags must be coated with a waterproof composition, or well greased, or tarred, or one or more boxes, made just large enough to contain the charge, may very well be used.

In very damp soil, tin or metal cases may be used; but a powder barrel, well payed over with hot pitch, and provided with an extra large bung, will be found to answer very well for this purpose.

Powder bags for mines liable to be flooded.

68. Bags to be used for mines liable to be flooded must be payed over with a waterproof composition made as follows :—
Beeswax, tallow, and pitch, in the proportion by weight of one part beeswax, one part tallow, and four parts pitch, are melted together over a slow fire, well stirred, but not allowed to boil.

The bags to contain the charges can be made of No. 1 sail canvas, with a canvas nozzle for loading and to receive the hose, fuze or wire.

The composition is applied as follows :—

The bags are first filled with dry sand, and payed over twice with the waterproof composition, the first coat being allowed to cool before the second is laid on. When the second coat is cold, some finely powdered chalk or whiting is shaken all over the bags, to prevent the composition from sticking to anything and thereby detaching itself from the canvas.

SEC. 6.   PREPARING MINES FOR FIRING.   31

The bags are then emptied of the sand and filled with the charges. The fuze is introduced when the bags are about one-third full, and the nozzles are carefully frapped round it with twine, spun yarn, or wire, drawn very tight, and passing some little way up the fuze above the nozzle. The charges are then ready for use.

The only indiarubber waterproof bags kept as articles of store are those inside the powder barrels to contain 100 lbs. *Waterproof bags for powder.*

Waterproof canvas bags for guncotton are service stores, and might be used where obtainable for gunpowder; they are in two sizes, 25, and 5 lbs.

Wood clamps with screws are issued with these bags for fastening them.

Leather bags to hold 50 lbs. of powder are an article of store, and could be used where obtainable. *Leather bags.*

69. A barrel of gunpowder contains 100 lbs. One pound of gunpowder measures 30 cubic inches. The following table gives the quantity of gunpowder that can be placed in cubes of various sizes:— *Space occupied by powder.*

Size of cube in inches.	Gun-powder in pounds.	Size of cube in inches.	Gun-powder in pounds.	Size of cube in inches.	Gun-powder in pounds.	Size of cube in inches.	Gun-powder in pounds.
1	0·03	19	228·63	37	1684·43	55	5545·83
2	0·26	20	266·06	38	1829·06	56	5853·86
3	0·9	21	308·7	39	1977·3	57	6173·1
4	2·13	22	354·63	40	2136·33	58	6503·73
5	4·16	23	402·56	41	2297·36	59	6845·96
6	7·2	24	460·8	42	2460·6	60	7200
7	11·43	25	520·83	43	2650·23	61	7566·03
8	17·06	26	585·86	44	2839·46	62	7944·26
9	24·3	27	656·13	45	3037·5	63	8334·9
10	33·33	28	731·73	46	3244·53	64	8738·13
11	44·36	29	812·96	47	3460·76	65	9154·16
12	57·6	30	900	48	3686·4	66	9583·2
13	73·23	31	993·03	49	3921·63	67	10025·43
14	91·46	32	1092·26	50	4166·66	68	10481·06
15	112·5	33	1107·9	51	4421·7	69	10950·3
16	136·53	34	1310·13	52	4686·93	70	11433·33
17	163·70	35	1429·16	53	4962·56	71	11930·36
18	194·4	36	1552·2	54	5248·8	72	12441·6

If a box be used, the height of the chamber must exceed the calculated height of the box by a few inches, to allow the powder to be poured in after the box is inside the chamber. The hole in the box should be 6 inches square and close to the front edge. *Box for powder charge.*

Loading.

Mode of conveying the charge to the chamber.

70. Whatever mode of loading the chamber be adopted, it must not be forgotten that the work has to be done in the absence of naked lights, and that the person loading is generally crouching down in a more or less constrained position. The utmost care must be taken in making up the charge outside the gallery, so that there shall be the least possible amount of work to be done inside the gallery itself.

The powder can generally be best taken along the galleries in a miner's truck, taking care that the truck is free from stones, flints, or any substance likely to strike a spark; or it can be placed in sand-bags, which are passed by men stationed in the gallery for the purpose.

Placing the charge in position.

As the success of the mine depends very much on the proper placing of the charge, it is desirable that the officer in immediate charge should place it with his own hands, and should himself ascertain that the insertion of the firing gear has been properly made, and that the wires, hose, or fuze, leading from the charge, are thoroughly protected from any chance of injury during the subsequent process of tamping.

Connecting fuze or wire.

Before proceeding with the tamping, the fuze, hose, or wires must be connected with the charge. The fuze need only be connected with one box or bag, as the explosion of the first will instantaneously ignite the powder in the remainder. With very large charges there should be more than one point of ignition.

Rate of loading.

At Chatham a mine was loaded with 1,000 lbs. powder placed in sand-bags, passed up a gallery 136 feet long by hand, and emptied into a box made to fit the powder chamber, in 30 minutes.

Tamping.

Tamping.

71. The tamping of mines consist in filling up the gallery with solid material, for a certain distance from the chamber, with the view of preventing the force of the explosion expending itself in the gallery, rather than in the direction in which the mine is required to act. The tamping should extend from the charge for a distance equal to at least $1\frac{1}{2}$ L.L.R. (or 2 L.L.R. for a 3-lined crater); and if the material used for forming the tamping be not heavy, or but loosely packed, this distance should never be less than 2 L.L.R.

For camouflets, if time allows, tamp to a distance of twice the calculated radius of rupture.

The materials usually employed in tamping consist of the earth which has been excavated in the formation of the gallery, sods, half-filled sand-bags, or indeed any heavy substance which may be at hand. If the soil be clay, it may be roughly moulded into bricks, which form an excellent material, and one with which the operation proceeds quickly. Tamping with sand-bags is, however, considered the most expeditious method.

It is often desirable to strengthen the tamping by pieces of timber, crossing each other diagonally, and with their ends securely jammed into the sides of the shaft or gallery.

It has been found that the proportionate value of tamping decreases with the increase of charge, under similar circumstances.

The operation of tamping is very liable to detection by the enemy; the cessation of the sound of the miner's pick, and the increased frequency of the noise made by the miner's truck passing up the gallery when that mode of conveying tamping material is used, suggest to a listener what is going on. *Precautions.*

It is therefore better, when secrecy is essential, to avoid using the truck for this purpose, and to continue the excavation at some part of the gallery near the head, so as to mislead listeners.

72. Tamping with earth is usually carried on by passing it up to the head of the gallery in trucks, or by men at short intervals who shovel it from one to the other. With sand-bags or sods, men at intervals of 6 feet or thereabouts, all facing the mouth of the gallery, can throw the materials between their legs to one another. *How carried out.*

The work of piling the bags at the head of the gallery is a severe task, and the strongest and best men should therefore be selected for it, in order to keep pace with the rate at which the material is passed up. A bricklayer best understands the style of work required.

Reliefs of 20 minutes are the best for the men at the head of the gallery.

73. When solid tamping such as sand-bags or sods is employed, much time has been saved, and still the same result obtained, by using the ordinary length of tamping, but with air spaces, *i.e.*, omissions of the tamping material at intervals along the length. Thus, 34 feet of tamping, with two separate air spaces, each 5 feet long in its length, has been found to act as well as though the whole length was solid, and much time was consequently gained. This gaining of time is occasionally of the utmost importance, but further experiments are required in order to determine the maximum amount of air spaces allowable. A mine tamped with air spaces, however, cannot be entered so soon after explosion as one tamped solid. *Tamping with air spaces.*

74. A special method of tamping with sand-bags has been practised, with a considerable saving of time in galleries which descend steeply, in the following manner:—Men are placed at intervals of 3 or 4 feet along the entire length of the gallery, sitting upright, and all facing towards one side of it. The first bags passed in are employed in building up the spaces between the men to about the level of their knees, so that the succeeding bags may be rolled by hand from one man's knees to those of the next, without the labour entailed in dropping and relifting the bags between each pair of men. Eventually those bags that *Tamping inclined galleries.*

34 PREPARING MINES FOR FIRING. PART IV.

have been employed to fill up the spaces between the men are withdrawn, and passed to the head of the gallery, commencing from the mouth, so as to complete the tamping.

75. A method of tamping practised with success during the Siege Manœuvres of 1907, is as follows:—

Rate of tamping.
Men are placed 6 feet apart, facing the exit, legs apart and trunk bent. They pass the bags backwards between their legs.

76. From recent experience the rate of tamping has been found to be about two hours for 15 feet of actual tamping (*i.e.*, exclusive of air spaces).

Proportion of sandbags.
77. The following is the proportion of full, three-quarter filled, half filled, and quarter filled bags found necessary:—

60 %	full.
?-10 %	three-quarter filled.
20 %	half filled.
10 %	quarter filled.

The partially filled bags must be tied up at the mouth, making it possible to fit them into interstices of any shape.

Section 7.—FIRING POWDER CHARGES WITHOUT ELECTRICITY.

78. In order that a mine may be fired with safety to the firers, some means by which the charge can be ignited from a distance are employed. This can be done electrically, or by means of fuzes designed for the purpose, without electricity.

Electricity gives the means of firing a charge at any moment, and also gives greater security, and should always be employed where possible. This is fully dealt with in Sec. 8.

The means of firing without electricity are as follows:—

Safety Fuze.

79. The service safety fuze, vocabularised as "*Fuze, Safety, No. 9*," and generally known as Bickford's, consists of flax, spun and twisted in the same manner as in twine-twisting and cord-making, with a column of fine gunpowder in the centre. The flax is covered with gutta-percha, and has an exterior coating of tape and varnish, which delays the oxidation of the gutta-percha. It is supplied in hermetically sealed tins, containing 8, 24, or 50 fathoms. *Safety fuze.*

Its rate of burning is, at the slowest, 1 yard in 105 seconds, and at the quickest 1 yard in 75 seconds. If the rate of burning is not known, it must be remembered that it *may* burn as fast as $2\frac{1}{2}$ feet per minute, and that the more the fuze is handled the quicker it burns. *Rate of burning.*

Practically the rate of burning can be taken as 2 feet per minute. It is stated by the manufacturers (Messrs. Bickford, Smith, and Co.) that this fuze will burn under water at a depth of 90 feet after 24 hours' immersion. It is coloured BLACK. *Colour.* (*See* Pl. 13, Fig. 1.)

Substitutes for Safety Fuze.

80. When safety fuze is not available, the following can be used:—Common powder moistened and pressed firmly into a tube. This burns at the rate of about 2 feet per minute. *Moist powder.*

(For precautions in the use of safety fuze, *see* para. 90.)

Instantaneous Fuze.

81. The service instantaneous fuze is vocabularised as "*Fuze, Instantaneous, Mk. III.*" *Instantaneous fuze.*

It consists of a strand of quickmatch enclosed in flax and several layers of waterproof tape, with a linen thread cross-snaking outside. It is just thin enough to fit into the shank of a No. 8 service detonator. (*See* para. 205.)

36   FIRING POWDER CHARGES WITHOUT ELECTRICITY.   PART IV.

Supply.
Rate of burning.
It is supplied in hermetically sealed tins containing 100 yards. It burns at the rate of 30 yards per second, or practically instantaneously. It will fire after 48 hours' immersion in water.

Colour.
It is coloured ORANGE.

Instantaneous fuze can be distinguished from other fuzes in the dark by feeling the thread snaking. (*See* Pl. 13, Fig. 2.)

Substitutes for Instantaneous Fuze.

Powder hose.
82. Powder hose is only used if instantaneous fuze is not available. It is made of strips of strong linen; the edges are turned over outwards and the double parts brought together and *serged*, by passing the needle alternately through the four thicknesses of stuff and back again over all.

For 1-inch hose 4-inch strips of stuff are required.

Powder hose is filled by means of copper funnels. A hose of about 20 feet long may be filled from the upper window of a house, but that is the greatest length which can be filled at one time. If a greater length is wanted, it must be filled in separate lengths and sewn together afterwards.

It burns at the rate of from 10 to 20 feet per second.

The following table gives the amount of powder required for different sized hose:—

Diameter of powder hose.	Weight of powder per yard of hose.			Weight of powder per 100 yards of hose.		
	lbs.	oz.	drs.	lbs.	oz.	drs.
One inch...	1	1	0	106	4	0
Three-quarters inch	0	9	12	60	15	0
Five-eighths inch	0	5	12	35	15	0
One-half inch	0	4	0	25	0	0
Three-eighths inch	0	1	8	9	6	0
One quarter inch	0	1	4	7	13	0
Three-tenths inch	0	0	10	3	14	8
One-twelfth inch	0	0	2	0	12	8

Arrangement of Fuze and Charge.

Safety fuze alone.
83. A charge can be fired by safety fuze alone, in which case one end of the fuze is placed in the charge, and the other end is lit.

This should be done wherever possible, as it obviates joints in fuzes, which always give chances of failure.

The end of the fuze to be placed in the charge should be so cut that the column of powder in the fuze is exposed. It is then inserted well into the centre of the powder. To prevent its accidental withdrawal by a jerk, the end should be knotted round a small stick or tied in a thumb knot.

The end of the fuze to be lit should be cut on the slant to expose as much of the column of powder as possible.

When the distance from the place of lighting to the charge is so great that the use of safety fuze alone would cause too long a delay, it must be used in conjunction with instantaneous fuze. This would nearly always be the case with mines. *Safety and instantaneous fuze.*

Instantaneous fuze can seldom be used alone, as its action is so quick that it does not allow time for the person lighting it to get under cover. To allow this time, a piece of safety fuze of sufficient length should be attached to the instantaneous fuze. *Instantaneous fuze alone.*

The end of the instantaneous fuze (or powder hose) in the charge should be placed as described for safety fuze. The end of the safety fuze to be lit as already described.

Powder charges can be fired by a No. 8 detonator, but no advantage is gained by so doing. *Detonator.*

Joints between Fuzes.

84. The joint between the safety and instantaneous fuzes can be made in the 3 following alternative ways :—(a) Both fuzes are cut on the slant so as to expose the quickmatch and powder column (Pl. 13, Fig. 1); these two surfaces are then spliced together with string, a little fine powder or quickmatch being placed between the surfaces (Pl. 13, Fig. 2). A small piece of wood can be used as a splint for the joint (Pl. 13, Fig. 3). The joint can be made waterproof by being wrapped round with indiarubber tape smeared with indiarubber solution at the ends, or, failing this, with ordinary tape smeared with tallow, which will last for a short time. (b) Place the ends of both fuzes in a small bag or box of powder, the quickmatch of the instantaneous fuze being bared for about 2 inches. (c) Cut a semi-circular nick in each fuze about 1 inch from the end. The fuzes are then superimposed and secured with a few diagonal turns of string (Pl. 16). *Joint between safety and instantaneous fuze.* *Another method.*

85. For firing several charges simultaneously, a small junction box (Pl. 13, Fig. 6) can be used, with a hole bored through the sides for each mine fuze and one for the safety fuze. The box is filled with powder, in which the ends of the fuzes, prepared as above, are buried (Pl. 13, Fig. 7). S is the safety fuze for lighting, I, I are the lengths of instantaneous fuze to the charges. These lengths must be exactly the same, laid with bends if necessary. It is very difficult to ensure simultaneous firing by the use of instantaneous fuze. *Joint for instantaneous charges.*

86. To join safety fuze and powder hose, the end of the safety fuze is inserted into the powder hose and well secured to prevent its withdrawal. The joint should be covered with moist clay to prevent sparks reaching the powder hose. *Joint between safety fuze and powder hose.*

Protection of Fuzes.

Fuzes. 87. Fuzes of both kinds are laid along the bottom corner of a gallery, and require no special protection during tamping. They will not be damaged unless battered by heavy stones. Instantaneous fuze when lying on the open ground should be weighted down with small stones to prevent its jumping.

Powder hose. 88. Powder hose being more fragile requires more protection. It is laid along the lower angle of the gallery, and should be carefully protected from injury by a casing of wood; failing wood, a casing of straw rope wrapped round the hose gives a certain amount of protection.

Casing tubes are best made from 1-inch plank, 3 inches wide. By cutting a groove in each piece, then fitting the two grooved pieces together with the hose between them, and lastly spiking the two pieces together with wooden spikes or small trenails a very efficient casing is formed.

A bamboo, split down the centre and with the joints removed, makes a very good casing.

Whatever kind of casing is used, great care must be taken that the hose is thoroughly protected at the corners of the galleries, otherwise it is sure to be broken and the mine will fail.

After powder hose has been laid it should be protected from the chance of accidental ignition by covering it with earth; this also helps to protect it from injury.

Means of Lighting.

Portfires. 89. Portfires are supplied for lighting safety fuze. A portfire burns at the rate of 1 inch per minute. It can be extinguished by knocking it against the boot with a sharp blow.

Slow-match. Slow-match, which answers the same purpose, can be made by steeping rope in a solution of saltpetre and limewater. When dry, it burns at the rate of 1 foot per hour.

Fuzees. Safety-fuze can be easily and quickly lighted with a fuzee, but it is very hard to light with an ordinary flame. When only ordinary matches are available, cut the fuze on the slant so as to expose the powder, and place the match head against the powder. Light this match either with another match or by striking the box on it.

Piece of quick-match. If it is desired to fire the fuze at any given moment, and no portfire is at hand, it is well to prepare it for firing by splitting the end, inserting a small piece of quick-match or flake of dry guncotton, and tying the latter in, so that the end projects. The quick-match or guncotton ignites instantly with an ordinary flame (Pl. 13, Figs. 4 and 5).

Precautions in the Use of Fuzes.

Old Fuze. 90. The rate of burning of safety-fuze varies with its age, and old fuze should be tested for rate of burning before use.

SEC. 7.   FIRING POWDER CHARGES WITHOUT ELECTRICITY.

It is also liable to deteriorate through age, especially abroad; Deterioration. in hot climates fuze should not be used which has been in store more than six months. Cheaper or locally purchased fuze should never be used where avoidable, as it cannot be relied on.

Accidents caused by old or inferior fuze are likely to occur as follows :—

Parts of the fuze composition may have become inert owing to moisture getting through the cover, or by deterioration from age. The fuze being lighted, the composition will burn as far as the faulty part, and then go out; but the jute wrapping round the composition may continue to smoulder till it passes the fault, when the composition will begin to burn again. This smouldering is so extremely slow that the impression is produced that the fuze has gone out.

Practically, the only safeguard against this is the use of service fuze, fresh and in good condition.

Failure of Charges to Explode.

91. If a missfire should occur and a charge fail to explode, the longest possible time should be allowed to elapse before the charge is approached. As a general rule, *at least* 30 minutes should be allowed from the time of lighting the fuze.

The charge should only be withdrawn or touched when it is absolutely necessary that this should be done, as the removal of the tamping and fuze often causes a smouldering fuze to start burning again and the explosion to take place.

92. *Blasting in Bore-holes.*—A missfire in a bore-hole will Bore-holes. hardly ever have to be withdrawn. It is best to leave the charge alone and proceed with other shots, having drowned the charge with water.

A powder charge, if it has to be withdrawn, should be drowned with water, and the tamping carefully picked out, water being poured into the hole the whole time.

A dynamite or guncotton charge should be treated similarly, great care being taken not to pull the fuze out with a jerk.

93. *Other Charges.*—Guncotton and dynamite charges, where Other not in inaccessible places, can best be "killed" by placing and charges. detonating a fresh charge close to them; this is safer than attempting to meddle with them.

For all charges, when they have to be withdrawn, the tamping should be carefully picked out, after being well wetted with water; if enough water is poured in, the withdrawal should be quite safe, but with a very large charge this waste of explosive may not be expedient.

Care must be taken that where a detonator is used, the fuze is not pulled or jerked during the untamping.

Iron or steel tools should not be used for taking out tamping Tools. when near a charge; pieces of wood should be used.

Section 8.—FIRING CHARGES BY ELECTRICITY.

Electricity, when used for firing charges.

94. To ensure success it is essential that the precautions and tests described in this section should be applied, and unless the necessary facilities for carrying these out are available it is doubtful whether electrical methods should be resorted to, but when the means are at hand, electricity should be used to fire charges in mines, or when covered by tamping, or when it is desirable to fire a number simultaneously.

In the demolition of large structures this is always a most important consideration. *The safety precautions detailed in para. 125 must in all such cases be adhered to.* Single charges, such as blasting charges, &c., in places accessible up to the last moment are more simply fired by other means.

95. For firing charges electrically there are provided—

Fuzes and detonators distinguished.

(*a.*) Electric fuzes, for firing charges of powder only, henceforward always called *fuzes* in this section of this book.

*(*b.*) Electric detonators, for firing charges of guncotton, dynamite, &c., henceforward always called *detonators* in this section of this book.

Fuzes are designed to start *combustion* and are not suitable for charges which require to be *detonated*.

Detonators, on the other hand, are unsuitable for powder charges, as the violence of the explosion is liable to scatter the grains without igniting them (*see*, however, Section X, para. 192).

Detonators can be distinguished from fuzes as they are furnished with metal tubes painted red. These tubes are filled with fulminate of mercury, and must on no account be bent, twisted, struck, heated, or trodden on ; nor must they be allowed to come into contact with strong acids.

Distinguishing marks for various services.

96. The heads of all service fuzes and detonators are painted white if provided with iridio-platinum wire bridges, yellow if with platinum-silver wire bridges. The colour of their shoulders denotes the service for which they are provided :—

    White for Field Service.
    Yellow for Naval Service.

Certain field service detonators intended for drill purposes only are also provided. The tubes of these are painted white and are empty.

Electric gun tubes are used in the Royal Navy, and also by the Royal Garrison Artillery, and might, should occasion arise, be used for firing charges in mines.

---

* Detonators can also be used for powder charges under certain conditions. *See* Section 10 of this book.

SEC. 8.   FIRING CHARGES BY ELECTRICITY.   **41**

  The general appearance and construction of the electric fuzes, Descriptions.
detonators, and gun tubes in use in the services are shown in
Pls. 15 and 16.
  Electrical details of these are set forth in the table on
page 42.
  No. 14 fuze consists of a cup of ebonite, having two insulated No. 14 fuze.
copper wires inserted into the cup head. These wires are held
$\frac{1}{4}$ inch apart, and are connected at the ends by a piece of fine
iridio-platinum wire (*vide* Table for details).
  The fine wire is wrapped round with a small piece of fleecy
guncotton, and the hollow of the cup is filled with mealed
powder, the end of the cup being closed with a metal cap.
  In firing, the current passes by the copper wires to the
iridio-platinum wire, which, having a high electrical resistance
per element of its length, is heated, and so ignites the fleecy
guncotton and explodes the fuze.
  These fuzes (No. 14) are painted white, and are used for firing
gunpowder. They are packed in white cylinders, containing
twenty-five.
  No. 13 detonator is similar electrically to No. 14 fuze, but it No. 13 detonator.
is provided with a metal tube containing (in the latest pattern)
43 grains of fulminate of mercury. It is used for firing high
explosives, and is inserted into the hole, provided for that purpose,
in the guncotton primer, exactly as in the case of the No. 8
detonator (*see* para. 205).
  The head and body of this detonator are painted white, but
the tube containing the fulminate is painted red (Pl. 15).
  These detonators are packed in cylinders (twenty-five in each),
the upper halves of which are painted white, the lower red.
  Drill detonators are nearly similar in construction and are Drill detonators.
quite similar in the colouring of their shoulders to the others,
but their tubes, which are painted white, contain no fulminate.
  No. 9 detonator is for naval service only. This detonator, Naval detonators, fuzes, and gun tubes.
the naval gun tube No. 10, the drill gun tube No. 11, and also
No. 19 naval disconnecting fuze differ electrically from the land
service fuzes and detonators in that their fuze-wires are made of
platinum silver. They are more sensitive than the land service
fuzes and detonators, but cannot be relied upon to fuze simultaneously when connected up in series.

D

Constants of Field, Naval and Artillery Service Fuzes, Tubes, and Detonators.

	Field Service. No. 13—Detonator. No. 20—Drill Detonator. No. 14—Fuze.	Naval and Artillery Service. No. 10—Gun Tube. No. 11—Drill Gun Tube. No. 9—Detonator. No. 19—Disconnecting Fuze, and all Vent-Sealing Tubes.
Material of bridge wire	Iridio-platinum	Platinum-silver
Weight " per yard	·45 grains.	·21 grains.
Length " "	·25 in.	·25 in.
Diameter " "	·0014 in.	·0014 in.
Resistance—cold (i.e., at about 60° Fahr.)	1·05 ohms	1·65 ohms
" when just hot enough to start ignition	1·3 "	...
" at fuzing point	2·6 "	2·9 ohms
Smallest current that can fire ...	·35 ampère	...
" " fuze...	·8 "	·48 ampère
" " to be calculated for to fire a charge	·8 "	...
" " duration of contact to be made when firing by battery and key	½ sec.	½ sec.
Largest safe testing current when testing charges	·05 ampère	...
Testing for over-sensitiveness:—		
Current to be used	·32 "	...
Duration of contact	4 sec.	...
Resistance when current is passing	1·3 ohms	...
Testing for under-sensitiveness:—		
Current to be used	·45 ampère	...
Duration of contact	4 sec.	...
Resistance when current is passing	1·47 ohms	...

SEC. 8.   FIRING CHARGES BY ELECTRICITY.   43

There are also in the naval and artillery services electric gun-tubes known as " vent-sealing tubes " (V, M, and R) for use with breech-loading guns; they are electrically similar to Nos. 10 and 11. As previously explained (para. 96), electric fuzes and detonators are fired by the thin wire bridge becoming heated by the passage of a current, and the amount of heat produced bears a definite relationship to the strength of the current.

97. It will be noticed on reference to the table on page 42 that the resistance of the bridge does not remain constant but increases with rise in temperature until the fuzing point is reached. This phenomenon has to be taken into account in calculating the current which may be expected under any given circumstances. *Firing current.*

The strength of a current is measured in " Amperes," and with a given resistance, depends directly on the amount of electrical pressure or E.M.F. available.

The least strength of current which will fire the various patterns of fuzes and detonators has been experimentally ascertained and recorded in the table on p. 42, but this figure must only be regarded as an average, and individual fuzes and detonators may vary as much as $30°/_0$ either way. In calculations it is necessary to ensure at least the normal current required to fuze.

In the case of a number of fuzes or detonators in series, if the current is of such strength that it requires several seconds for sufficient heat to be generated in the bridges of the fuzes or detonators, the most sensitive fuze or detonator will fire first and in so doing will probably cause the circuit to be broken at that point, thereby preventing the firing of the remainder of the series. To avoid this it is necessary that the current passing in the circuit shall be considerably greater than that required to *fire* only. It is for this reason principally that the current to be calculated for is that required to *fuze* the bridge wire; if the actual current is greater than this no harm is done. Experience shows that if the current is not less than the fuzing current, firing takes place practically instantaneously and moreover ignition always takes place to all intents and purposes instantaneously in all the fuzes or detonators of the series. This presupposes that there are no defective fuzes or detonators in the circuit and that the same current flows throughout the circuit. A fuze or detonator defective so far as its sensitiveness is concerned, due for example to damp composition, but intact as regards its electrical condition, would only cause that particular charge to fail. Conductors defective in insulation between the successive charges would allow some of the current to leak past the fuzes or detonators; and if the leakage was sufficiently serious, those fuzes or detonators might, quite likely, not fire before the circuit was broken by those that did fire.

The sensitiveness of a fuze or detonator is dependent upon the temperature at which the composition in contact with the bridge ignites; and for any given material used for the bridge it is also dependent for any given current upon the diameter and length of bridge and nature of the contacts to which the bridge is secured. The greater the diameter, the greater is the firing current required. The longer the bridge, within limits, the smaller the firing current, because the heat is not so freely conducted away by the contacts. The larger the contacts, the greater the firing current, because the large contacts radiate the heat. Uniformity in behaviour is attained by care in manufacture, every reasonable effort being taken to insure that fuzes or detonators of any one type are practically alike. Notwithstanding this care, small variations in sensitiveness do occur.

The composition becomes less sensitive with time, and there are unavoidable minute differences in the bridge itself.

Primary cells.   98. The electrical pressure or E.M.F. required to generate a current is obtained, under normal conditions, from

(a) Primary cells,

or (b) A Dynamo electric exploder.

Generally speaking, any type of primary cell may be utilised for firing charges electrically, the fundamental conditions being that the number and description of the available cells shall be suitable for generating the necessary current. It should be borne in mind that the current produced by a given battery is determined by the *total* resistance in circuit, which includes the internal resistance of the battery itself. When a considerable current is required, as in firing electrical fuzes, and the external resistance of leads, &c., is small, the internal resistance of the battery is a factor of great importance, and it can be shown that, under such conditions, if the internal resistance in ohms exceeds the E.M.F. in volts, it is practically impossible to obtain the necessary current whatever the number of cells joined in series.

A primary cell, therefore, to be suitable for firing charges electrically should have:—

(a) High E.M.F.

(b) Low internal resistance.

The E.M.F. depends principally on the nature of the elements of which it is composed, those most commonly used being:—

Zinc, Carbon, and Salammoniac.—E.M.F. about 1·5 volts, *e.g.*, Le Clanche and the numerous patterns of so called "Dry" cells.

Zinc, Copper and dilute Sulphuric Acid.—E.M.F. about 1 volt, *e.g.*, Daniells and Minotto cells.

Zinc, Platinum and Nitric Acid. E.M.F. about 1·9 volts, *e.g.*, Grove cells.

The internal resistance of a cell depends on so many circumstances that its value cannot be accurately arrived at without measurement. Generally speaking, with a given type of cell, the larger the cell the lower the internal resistance. It may be taken that for firing charges no cell is to be recommended whose internal resistance is more than 1 ohm.

SEC. 8. FIRING CHARGES BY ELECTRICITY. 45

The Grove cell, which was formerly extensively used for this purpose, but is now obsolete, has an E.M.F. of nearly two volts and an internal resistance of about 1 ohm. It is therefore capable of giving large currents, but is ill-adapted for field service owing to the strong acids employed in it and the consequent transport difficulties.

The same objections apply, in a modified degree, to all cells made up with liquid electrolyte, and the "Dry" cell has therefore been adopted for use in the field. "Dry" cells are of the Le Clanche type and have the Salammoniac solution in the form of a paste. As a rule the zinc element forms the containing vessel and the carbon rod is in the centre. On Plate 17 is illustrated the pattern of dry cell, which is at present the service cell for field telegraphs. The E.M.F. of dry cells may be taken as 1·5 volts and the Internal Resistance (I.R.) of the larger sizes should not exceed ·25 ohms.

Dry cells are apt to deteriorate in store, especially in hot and dry climates, and should never be used for firing charges without being previously tested. They will only recuperate to a limited extent, after heavy work, and when once exhausted, become useless and must be replaced by others.

The "O" size cell is obtainable in wood boxes containing 6 and 10 cells respectively and vocabularised as "Batteries," dry "O" "Six Cell" and ditto "Ten Cell."

Special care is necessary to avoid "short-circuiting" dry cells, *i.e.* joining the positive and negative terminals together without an appreciable resistance in circuit.

NOTE.—The Mark II pattern of dry cells are provided with two terminals, and a connecting cord with tabs is issued with each cell.

99. The present service exploder (Pl. 27) is vocabularised as "Exploder Dynamo, electric quantity Mark V." It only differs in unimportant details from the Mark IV pattern. It consists essentially of a small series wound dynamo of which F.F. are the field magnets, with pole pieces P.P. and armature M revolving between them. The field magnets and armature are wound with insulated wire, and the latter is provided with a two part commutator and caused to revolve by means of a pinion which engages with the rack R, but is provided with a free wheel arrangement which ensures that the armature is only rotated on the downward stroke. *Dynamo exploder.*

The two field magnet coils are normally connected in series through the contact K (see diagram of connections). When using the exploder the handle is first pulled up as far as it will go, and the line wires may then be connected to the terminals.

There is always some residual magnetism in the field magnets and as the armature revolves on the downward stroke of the handle it generates a current which still further excites them, until at the bottom of the stroke the maximum E.M.F. is developed. The contact at K is now broken by the end of the rack depressing the spring, and the current flows through the external circuit.

It should be noted that the maximum effect is produced at the moment of breaking contact at K, and that the rack should be made to descend as swiftly and smoothly as possible.

With batteries it is chemical energy which is converted into electrical energy, but with the dynamo-electric exploder it is mechanical energy which is thus converted and the portability, durability and compactness of such a machine renders it superior in many respects to batteries for firing charges electrically.

100. In addition to primary batteries and the service exploder the possibility of using other sources of electrical energy should not be overlooked. Of these, the secondary cell or accumulator, especially the portable variety, offers ideal advantages owing to its high E.M.F. (2·0 volts when charged) and negligible internal resistance. With the extended use of electricity in field operations the portable accumulator is likely to be more generally available in the future.

In default of an exploder any small dynamo may be made to serve, the fundamental condition being very similar to that in the case of primary battery, *i.e.* that it must be capable of furnishing sufficient current to the external circuit.

Whatever source of energy is utilised, a complete conducting path must be provided from it through the fuzes or detonators and back again. Insulated wire will generally be available for this purpose.

FIRING CHARGES BY ELECTRICITY.

DETAILS OF INSULATED WIRES AND CABLES IN THE SERVICE WHICH MAY BE AVAILABLE FOR FIRING CHARGES ELECTRICALLY.

Vocabulary Number.	Wires, electric.				Cables, electric.			
	*S.11 Mk. I.	*S.11 Mk. II.	S.3.† Mk. I.	E.2. Mk. I.	C.1	D.5. Mk. IV.	E.1. Mk. II.	J.5.
No. of strands in conductor { Copper	3	3	1	7	3	5	6	7
Steel	0	0	0	0	0	14	1	0
Diameter of each strand in inches	·028	·028	·064	·028	·028	·012	·02	·048
Nearest S.W.G.	22	22	16	22	22	30	25	18
Resistance of whole conductor per 100 yards at 60° F......ohms	1·35	1·35	·768	·6	1·35	3·58	1·43	·193
Nature of insulating material	V.I.R.	V.I.R.	V.I.R.	V.I.R.	V.I.R.	V.I.R.	V.I.R.	V.I.R.
Nature of covering	P.T.	C.C. P.W.	P.T. B.	B.	P.T.	B.	B.	P.T. B.
Outside diameter of covering	·175	·19	·204	·32	·35	·145	·175	·35
Weight per 1,000 yards ....lbs.	71	60	85	170	334	48	57	290

(1.) V.I.R. = Vulcanised India-rubber. P.T. = India-rubber or primed tape. C.C. = Cotton-covered. P.W. = Paraffin waxed. B. = Boiled and coated with compound.
(2.) D_4 is armoured with 18 galvanised steel wires, each ·035 in. diameter and then braided.
(3.) Of the above wires S_{11} is used for connections of instruments and for electric lighting purposes. E_1 is for main connections in heavy demolitions. C_1 is a Field telegraph cable for river crossings. D_4 is a Service pattern of Field telegraph cable. It is not well suited for demolition work on account of its high C.R. E_1 is specially designed for Field service demolition equipments. S_2 and J_5 are E.L. Cable.

* Both of these wires are obsolescent and are replaced by S.11 Mark III.   † Being replaced by S 3 Mark II.

101. Plate 18 and the table on p. 47 show several of the covered wires and cables used by the Royal Engineers for various purposes. Those most likely to be available for firing charges electrically are S_{11} E_2 D_4 and E_1.

D_4 is not very suitable on account of its high conductivity resistance (C.R.). In default of service wires and cables any insulated copper wire of not less than 16 S.W.G. may be used, provided the insulation is good enough for the conditions under which it is to be used. In dry weather and on dry ground, a very lightly insulated or even bare conductor might be used for the whole circuit, if great care is taken to avoid the wires being "short-circuited," *i.e.* allowed to make contact with each other, and if good conductors are employed.

On an emergency an uninsulated conductor may be used for the "Return" wire in any situation, but in that case the insulated conductor should be above suspicion.

Weight and bulk being always important considerations, and the lower the C.R. and the higher the I.R. the heavier and more bulky become insulated conductors, care should be taken to select wires and cables which are not unduly in excess of requirements in those respects.

For ordinary work a C.R. of 1·5 ohms per 100 yards will suffice, while the standard of I.R. should be such that the I.R. of the actual firing circuit shall not be less than 1,000 ohms.

Earths.

102. On account of the high resistance of ordinary earths, it will, as a rule, only be possible to complete wire fuze circuits with earths in the sea or salt lakes. The earth connections when used should be made either with clean metal plates, at least 6 inches square, soldered to the leads, the joint being protected from the action of the salt water, or with a long length of bare wire.

The earth pipe employed in field telegraph equipments makes a good earth. The pointed end section of a Norton's tube well driven into moist ground and kept filled with water will also make a good earth.

Though probably a somewhat remote contingency, a firing circuit made up with earths is liable to be exploded by atmospheric discharges.

Testing and jointing box.

103. *The Testing and Jointing Box* issued with field equipments is a tin box in a leather cover, measuring $14'' \times 8'' \times 5\frac{1}{2}''$ outside; its weight is 12 lbs. 3 ozs., and it holds all materials, instruments, and tools for testing and jointing (except soldering).

Its contents are as follows:—

For testing
- 1 box of "firing" resistance coils (100 ohms).
- 1 three-coil galvanometer.
- 1 cell electric dry "E."
- 2 reels (metal) with X_{11} ·0014 in. iridio-platinum wire (4 dwts).
- 1 chamois leather.
- 1 box of plate powder.

SEC. 8.   FIRING CHARGES BY ELECTRICITY.

For jointing.
{ 1 pair 5-inch side-cutting pliers.
2 tubes of india-rubber solution.
4 cylinders of india-rubber tape.
½ lb. cotton waste.

104. The *firing resistance coils* (vocabularized as "coils Resistance resistance 100 ohms") are made of thicker wire than ordinary coils (100 resistance coils, so as not to be damaged by the comparatively ohms). large currents passed through them. They are arranged (Pl. 19) so as to be easily connected up as a Wheatstone's bridge; they are also furnished with clips ¼ inch apart for holding the iridio-platinum wire used in the fusion test, which will be explained hereafter.

They are graduated from $\frac{1}{20}$ ohm to 100 ohms, ascending by the fraction of $\frac{1}{20}$ ohm.

The resistances from 1 to 100 are worked in the ordinary way, by plugging and unplugging.

The fractions of an unit 1 to 20 are introduced into the circuit by a wandering plug to which the lead completing the circuit is attached, and which is shifted to the hole marked to the required number of $\frac{1}{20}$ths.

When used as a Wheatstone's bridge the connections are perhaps more clearly shown in the figure below than in the plan in Pl. 19.

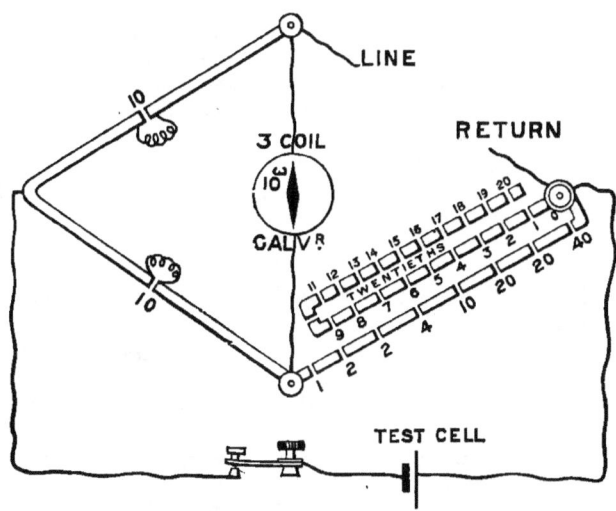

Fig. 1.

It will be noted that the key is placed in the battery circuit, and that the galvanometer is always in circuit. When testing a circuit containing earths this may be a disadvantage, in which case another key should be obtained and inserted in the galvanometer circuit, or failing that the battery and galvanometer may be interchanged.

Cleanliness of the pegs and other contact points is essential, especially in measuring small resistances. The two 10 ohm bridge coils must only be unplugged when using the box as a Wheatstone's bridge, as they are liable to be damaged by passing heavy currents through them.

105. Pl. 20 shows the external appearance of the 3 coil galvanometer and Fig. 2, Pl. 19, the diagram of connections. As its name implies it has three coils, the bobbins of which are wound to 2, 10, and 1,000 ohms respectively, either of which can be brought into circuit at will by means of the brass peg. The end of all the coils is connected to one terminal, the others being connected each to its respective brass block. Hinged flaps are fixed on each side of the case, on the inside of which are provided paper forms for calibration purposes. The bobbins are hollow and a small magnetised needle is pivotted vertically so as to swing in the hollow space, the magnetic field being strongest in the interior of the coils. An external pointer is fixed to the same axis as the needle and is weighted so that the latter is normally retained in a vertical position. A small arm with a bent end is provided by means of which the pointer may be deflected to any required degree and retained in that position.

The deflection corresponding to any given current depends primarily on the strength of the magnetic needle, and as the latter tends to lose its magnetism with lapse of time, the instrument, even if originally accurately calibrated should not be relied on for absolute *measurements* of current and E.M.F. It may, however, be used for *comparisons* between different currents and E.M.F.

The 1,000ω coil is mainly useful for :—

(a) Comparing and indicating small currents up to ·005 ampere.
(b) Comparing E.M.F.'s and P.D's.
(c) Comparing high resistances.

The 10ω ohm coil is chiefly used with the Wheatstone's bridge.
The 2ω ohm coil is used for :—

(1) Comparing and indicating current from about ·05 to 1 ampere.
(2) For comparing small resistances and for continuity testing.

The deflections on a galvanometer of this type are not in a simple arithmetical proportion to the currents providing those deflections. It may however be assumed that between 0° and 20° the deflections are roughly so proportional.

The 1,000ω coil is used for roughly ascertaining the insulation resistance of a circuit, since if this is high it is only the 1,000ω coil which will indicate the small current passing through it.

SEC. 8.   FIRING CHARGES BY ELECTRICITY.   51

The 2ω coil is mostly used simply as a current indicator or detector, but it is also useful for comparing the internal resistance of cells. If two cells give practically the same deflection on the $1{,}000\omega$ coil, but one gives a markedly smaller one on the 2ω coil, the latter will have the higher internal resistance. If one of the cells is known to be in good order, it can be used as a standard in this way to ascertain the condition of other cells.

When testing with the 2ω coil, or under any conditions which require current, the contacts should be short to avoid polarising the test cell or battery.

The best way to manage this is to watch which way the needle throws at the first contact, and then by means of the bent arm move the pointer to the position it may be expected to take up when the current passes. Make short contacts and adjust the pointer until a kick can just be perceived.

106. The "Cell electric, dry, E," illustrated on Pl. 17 is for testing purposes. It is a special form of dry cell similar to the Obach pattern but provided with a resistance coil which brings the total internal resistance up to 12 ohms, this obviating the possibility of anything but a very small current being sent out by it under any circumstances. Its E.M.F. is $1\cdot5$ volts.

107. The *iridio-platinum wire* in the testing and jointing box is Fuze or of exactly the same composition and diameter as that used in detonator the construction of the Field Service fuzes and detonators. wire.

Its diameter is, as before stated, $0\cdot0014$ inch, and its weight per yard is $0\cdot45$ grain.

It is issued on *metal* reels containing about 2 dwts., *i.e.*, 48 grains.

This wire is known in the service as "Wire, electric, X_{11}," and costs about £13 per ounce (troy), that is to say, nearly $3d.$ per yard. Economy should therefore be exercised in its use.

Pieces of card cut $\frac{1}{2}$ inch wide may be used for wrapping Cards for one or more turns of fuze wire on to facilitate the wire being fuze wire. inserted in the clips of the firing coils. These $\frac{1}{2}$-inch strips should

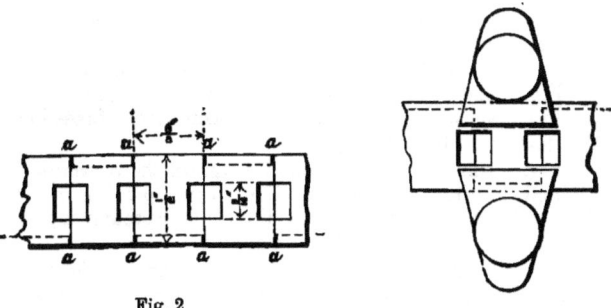

Fig. 2

Fig. 3.

be perforated with square holes $\frac{3}{16}$ inch wide and $\frac{3}{8}$ inch apart centre to centre, as shown in Fig. 2. Small slits are made at *a*, *a*, &c., and the wire wound on as shown. Fig. 3 shows how the strips are placed in the clips when two wires are to be fuzed. If more than two wires are to be fuzed the wire must be wound on accordingly. Unless the cards be perforated the results obtained are not reliable. Unless used in this way a great waste of fuze wire may take place.

Cleaning materials.

108. The *chamois leather* and *plate powder* are used for keeping the plugs and terminals of the firing coils clean.

India-rubber solution and tape.

109. *India-rubber solution* being liable to dry up should be kept well covered up to prevent evaporation. It is issued in ",squeezer tubes" to ensure economy in its use. *India-rubber tape* when left exposed to the atmosphere also dries up, and gets hard and useless; it should also therefore be kept covered up, and if possible in water.

Pliers and knife.

110. A pair of *side-cutting pliers* is almost a necessity for jointing work ; so also is a *sharp knife* for removing the insulation of covered wires. Every sapper is supposed to carry a knife.

Tools for soldering joints.

111. When joints have to be soldered the following stores are necessary :—

      Pot, fire, tinman's (or telegraph mechanic's).
      Files, bastard, half-round, 8-inch.
      Iron, soldering, tinman's (or jointer's).
      Resin, black.
      Salammoniac, lump.
      Solder, tinman's.
      Zinc chloride solution.
      Lamp, blow, spirit.
      Methylated spirit.
      Wick, common.

Various arrangements of circuits.

112. Circuits for firing fuzes or detonators may be arranged in several ways. Pl. 22, Fig. 1, shows a simple metallic circuit with one fuze and one battery.

Fig. 2 shows a similar circuit with separate earths instead of a return wire.

Fig. 3 shows another similar circuit with a bare or uncovered wire used as a return, and this wire earthed at each end. The resistance of such a return wire, if well earthed, is very low.

Fig. 4 shows 9 fuzes *in series* with an exploder.
Fig. 5 shows 5 fuzes *in divided*, with a battery.
Fig. 6 shows a *series* of 5 mines, each with 2 fuzes *in divided*, and joined up to a battery.

Fig. 7 shows 3 *groups* each of 4 mines, the 3 groups being in divided circuit, and the 4 mines in each group being in series with 2 fuzes in series in each mine ; the whole system being connected to cells connected in divided (or parallel).

113. Seeing that the service exploder cannot under any circumstances be relied on to furnish more current than is required to fire one fuze or detonator, it follows that when it is used *all* fuzes

or detonators must be connected *in series*. A full explanation of the reasons for this rule is outside the scope of this book. It should, however, be borne in mind that when a certain current flows in a circuit it has the same strength at every point in that circuit, and therefore if the current is strong enough to fire *one* fuze it must be strong enough to fire all other fuzes connected in *series* with it. The *maximum* current obtainable from the exploder is limited by other considerations, and though it may be able to give say ·8 amperes through 100 ohms external resistance, it does not follow that it will give 1·6 amperes through even a negligible external resistance. Whether two or only one fuze or detonator is placed in each charge depends upon circumstances. If the maximum permissible resistance of the circuit is not exceeded, two per charge should be used to lessen the chance of failure, leaving out of consideration causes of failure which are independent of the number used in each charge, such as the premature firing of an over-sensitive fuze and the resulting disconnection of the circuit before the others have fired.

With dry cells also, and Le Clanché cells generally, the maximum current which should be taken out of them is only sufficient to allow the fuzes or detonators to be connected up in series, unless the cells themselves are joined up in parallel. The effect of joining up two cells or batteries in parallel (*i.e.* + terminals, and — terminals respectively joined together) is to halve their internal resistance while the E.M.F. is unaltered, thus rendering it possible to get a larger current in the external circuit.

114. The theoretically *best grouping* of fuzes and detonators and batteries for large demolitions requires considerable calculation and is of little or no practical value. If powerful cells of low internal resistance, such as the Grove, or accumulators, are to be used, the charges may be divided into groups and connected in parallel, as in Fig. 5, Pl. 22. Care must be taken to ensure that no fuze or detonator gets less than the prescribed firing current and matters will be greatly simplified if all branches on divided circuit are made of equal or nearly equal resistance. <small>Grouping of fuzes or detonators.</small>

The advantage of this method is that the premature explosion of one charge does not cause failure of the rest as may happen if all are in series, but on the other hand connecting all detonators and fuzes in series has the following practical advantages :—

 (1) The connections are easier to make and there is consequently less chance of error.

 (2) The C.R. of the circuit is more easily calculated. This may be of importance where actual measurements cannot be made.

 (3) Faults are more easily located.

Connecting pairs of fuzes.	115. Pl. 23, Figs. 7 and 8, show the method of connecting pairs of fuzes "in divided" and "in series" respectively. The wire attached to fuzes and detonators should not be untwisted.
Care required in jointing.	116. Great care is necessary in jointing the wires used in all electric circuits, and especially in firing circuits in which it is so important to keep down the resistance; defective jointing being a common source of failure in firing mines by electricity.
Jointing wires.	117. To joint insulated wires:—

Strip off the insulation 2 inches, and clean the conductor thoroughly by scraping with the *back* of a knife; take great care not to *nick* the wires. Cross the wires at right angles as shown in Pl. 23, Fig. 1, and then bend them round each other as shown in Figs. 2, 3 and 4. With each end make three or four complete and close turns; cut off the spare ends and pinch them close in with the nose of the pliers.

In jointing stranded wires, each strand should be cleaned thoroughly; the wrapping round of the ends is then best done with the strand spread out flat and not twisted up.

Pl. 23, Fig. 6, shows the commencement of a three-way joint with single strand conductors. With many-stranded conductors such a joint is usually formed by placing two of the stranded conducters side by side, and then twisting them up with the remaining stranded conductor, as if forming a two-way joint.

By a series of three-way joints any number of conductors can be joined.

Soldering the joint with acid or chloride. 118. If time admit the joint may now be soldered. To solder a joint heat the soldering iron or "bolt" (really a piece of copper set in an iron stem) in the fire until it will make a stick of solder run freely when applied to it. Rub one face of the bolt first with a bastard cut file, and then with a piece of lump salammoniac (or dip it quickly into a strong solution of salammoniac). The solder should now adhere to the cleaned surface of the iron and "tin" it.

Having previously sprinkled the joint with powdered resin* apply the tinned face of the hot bolt below the joint, melting a little solder on at the same time.

If the joint has been properly cleaned, and if the iron is hot enough (and it must not be too hot) the solder will *sweat* up through the joint.

The soldering should be done quickly to avoid injuring the insulation by the heat of the bolt.

The joint should then be washed and wiped with a rag or some waste.

Soldering joints with resin as flux. 119. All joints of covered wires soldered with acid, and even those soldered with pure chloride are apt to deteriorate unless subsequently washed with an alkaline solution. For this reason it is preferable to use *resin* as a flux. There is always

---

* The resin may also be conveniently applied in the form of a thin paste, made by dissolving it in spirits of wine.

some difficulty in getting men to solder with resin, but the only precaution really necessary to ensure success is that the joint must be kept entirely free from dirt and grease, which can be effected by using gloves or pieces of rag when twisting up the wires.

Fuzes and detonators should always be placed in safety boxes before making soldered joints on them.

120. If the joint is to be under water or in wet soil the insulation must be made thoroughly waterproof and as homogeneous as possible. To do this the protective covering should be removed and the rubber exposed for about three-quarters of an inch on both sides of the joint. The last quarter of an inch of the insulation is then tapered as shown in Fig. 5. A six-inch length of rubber tape with the ends tapered is slightly warmed, stretched, and wrapped around the joint, commencing about half-way up the tapered portion on one side and terminating at the top of the tapered portion on the other. Each turn should overlap about half its predecessor. The first layer of tape and the bare rubber is now smeared with india-rubber solution and the tape wrapped on in successive layers until used up. Each layer should extend a little further up each side of the joint than its predecessor and solution be applied to each layer before the next is wound on. The tape should be stretched as it is applied. Under no circumstances must solution be applied to the bare conductor.

A joint can be quickly and effectively insulated by passing over one of the ends of the wires previously to making the joint a piece of $\frac{3}{8}$-inch india-rubber tubing, then slipping the tubing over the joint when made and tying the ends tightly to the insulation of the wire or cable on each side of the joint with twine or with fine wire. A piece of india-rubber tubing so secured is a very good addition to any joint, and is specially useful when a joint is going into deep water, or is intended to last for many weeks.

If neither india-rubber tape nor tubing are available a fairly good insulating covering may be formed by slitting the insulation of a spare piece of wire longitudinally, removing it and applying two such pieces of sufficient length to the joint so as to overlap one another, and then binding them firmly together and to the covering of the jointed wire with twine, or even fine wire from a strand of the spare wire.

121. It should always be remembered that the joint is the weak part of the circuit. A joint should therefore never be made at any point, such as the mouth of the bag containing the charge, where the wire is especially liable to be bent when handling the charge. *Joint's weak places.*

122. Before a circuit is connected up all the stores to be used should be tested (*see* paras. 132–148). *Necessary to test stores.*

After the connections have been made the complete circuit must also be tested (*see* paras. 149, 150).

The *safety precautions* detailed in para. 125 must be strictly adhered to.

Inserting the fuzes or detonators into the charge.

123. The fuzes or detonators having been connected with the line wires, should be inserted into the charge as follows :—

If the charge be of gunpowder, contained in bags, fill a bag one-third full (Pl. 23, Fig. 9), insert the fuzes, and while holding them in place, fill up the bags with gunpowder; give a slack of about half a foot to the wires inside the bag, and then lash up the mouth of the bag and the wires passing out through it very firmly with 10 or 12 turns of spun yarn.

Then take two or three turns with a rope round the outside of the bag, knotting it up like a bundle, and attach to it a piece of any light line about 4 fathoms long (Pl. 23, Fig. 10).

Let this last-mentioned rope be drawn tight and seize to it, at intervals of 2 feet 6 inches, the line and return wires, keeping them quite slack as shown in Fig. 10. In this way, any strain or tension incurred during tamping or placing in position is taken by the light line and not by the line wires.

If the charge is to be loaded in a chamber at the end of the gallery of a mine, the wires should be neatly coiled down, and the coil held together by a couple of stops of spun yarn put on with draw knots. The charge bag with the coil of wires can then be carried to the head of the mine·without fear of injury to the connections.

If the ground in which the charge is placed is liable to be flooded, and the vulcanized india-rubber bags (*see* para. 68) provided for holding charges under water are used, the fuzes should be inserted in the same way as described above, but the mouth of the bag, instead of being lashed, should be closed by a clamp consisting of two pieces of hard wood drawn together by screw bolts and provided with grooves to give passage to the line and return wires. Clamps for this purpose are articles of equipment.

The mouth of the bag, before being pressed together by the clamps, is made waterproof by being smeared over on the inside with india-rubber solution.

Whatever mode of placing the charge be adopted, care must be taken that no pull on the wires outside the charge can come on the fuzes or on the jointing of the fuzes to the line wires.

When gun-cotton is used, proceed as follows, viz. : first insert the rectifier in the hole in the primer disc and withdraw it, taking care not to separate the layers of the gun-cotton in the act. Then insert the detonator tube, paying special attention to this part of the process; on the one hand, no force is to be applied, and, on the other, the tube should not fit loosely. If it does, it should be wrapped round with paper round its entire length before insertion ; it should then be lashed to the disc by string or spun yarn, so as to make sure that the detonator does not slip out of the disc.

When a large charge of gun-cotton is fired, the primer should be lashed firmly into a bundle with the detonators well in the centre.

124. The charge having been placed in the chamber, the wires should be fixed up along either top corner of the gallery, taking particular care to avoid injuring the wires during the process of tamping. The wires should not be allowed to hang slack, but should be lashed to nails by spun yarn at intervals of about 5 to 8 feet. The practice of driving staples over covered wires should never be allowed. *Fixing connecting wires in mining.*

Branch circuits should be tested before tamping is commenced.

When a number of mines have to be fired together, and the galleries are long, it will generally be better to complete the tamping with only so much of the wires attached to the charge as will allow their ends to project a few feet beyond the tamping when completed. In this way there is little or no possibility of mistaking the different leads, as there would be if a number of wires were fixed up along the galleries.

The final connecting up can be done after the tamping has been finished.

Outside the galleries the wires leading to the firing station should be laid out along the ground at a distance of about a yard apart. *The wires outside the galleries.*

125. The following precautions are always to be observed in making tests, and preparing and firing charges:— *Safety precautions.*

1. When testing a detonator or fuze never attach a wire to either lead of the detonator or fuze until it is in a safety box. Detach both wires before removing it from safety box.

2. Never solder a lead to a detonator or fuze unless the latter is in a safety box.

3. Always hold a detonator or fuze pointing from you, and from others near.

4. Do not place detonators near strong acids.

5. Take care that no strain is put on the leads of a detonator or fuze, especially in making up a charge.

6. Any person attaching a lead to any detonator, fuze, or charge, is responsible for his own safety; in doing so he must therefore make a point of seeing that the far end of the lead is and remains disconnected while he is at work. If this is impossible a break should be made in the circuit at a safe distance from the explosive and within his view.

7. Put a N.C. officer in charge of the ends of the leads from the charges, with orders not to let them go out of his own hands, and to keep them insulated.

8. Ascertain that everyone is at a safe distance from the charges, in case of an accidental explosion, before and during the operation of testing any part or the whole of the complete circuit.

9. Do not bring up the firing apparatus before it is wanted.

10. If a battery is to be used for firing, first ascertain that the contact key, which you must know from actual examination really causes discontinuity when not depressed, has no wires attached to it, no loose wires or conductors near it, and has its safety block in place. Then connect one terminal of the firing key to the positive pole of the firing battery (*see* Pl. 25). The wire used for making this connection should be attached first to the terminal of the contact key and then its other end to the positive pole of the firing battery. When the time comes for firing, first connect one lead from the charges,—the insulated one if either is connected to earth,—to the other terminal of the contact key, and lastly attach the other lead from the charges to the negative pole of the firing battery just before removing the safety block and firing. Replace the safety block immediately after firing (*see* Pl. 19, Fig. 1).

11. Disconnect both leads from the firing instrument immediately after firing, and give them in charge of the N.C. officer, with similar orders to those in sub-head 7.

12. A single cell only will be used for testing fuzes and detonators and any part or the whole of the complete circuit; if a test cell is not available, any other cell may be used, sufficient resistance being added to ensure not more than $\frac{1}{10}$ ampère being sent through even one fuze on short circuit.

Number of fuzes or detonators limited by power of exploder or battery.

126. Before deciding upon the general arrangement of charges of fuzes or detonators and of the firing circuit it will be necessary to limit the number of fuzes or detonators to be fired simultaneously, so as to come within the power of the exploder or battery available. *See*, however, para. 130.

Estimating number of fuzes or detonators to be fired by exploder.

127. If it be intended to use an exploder:—

Fuzes or detonators to be fired by the exploder are always connected in series. If then it is required to fire a certain number of charges it will first be necessary to ascertain whether the exploder is strong enough to enable two fuzes, or detonators, to be put in each. To do so the exploder must be tested as laid down in para. 133, and the number of ohms through which it is capable of fuzing the standard wire must be ascertained. If the resistance of the fuzes, or detonators, at fuzing point and of the main leads is not greater than 80 per cent. of this, the exploder may be taken as strong enough: if it is greater, one fuze, or detonator, only can be put in each charge, or the number of charges must be reduced.

Example.

EXAMPLE.—It is required to fire with an exploder 15 charges through leads of resistance 6 ohms; the exploder is tested, and fuzes through 78 ohms. Putting two fuzes in series in each charge, the total resistance $= 2 \cdot 6 \times 2 \times 15 + 6 = 78 + 6 = 84$. The number of fuzes must be therefore reduced; if only one be put in each charge, the resistance will be $15 \times 2 \cdot 6 + 6 = 39 + 6 = 45$, which is well within the power of the exploder.

SEC. 8.   FIRING CHARGES BY ELECTRICITY.   59

If it cannot fire one fuze or detonator in each charge, the number of charges must be reduced, or a battery used. Having decided on the arrangement of the circuit, the testing of the fuzes or detonators, leads, earths, and the connecting up and testing of the circuit, &c., will proceed as hereafter described.

128. To fire charges with an exploder :— *Firing with exploder.*
Arrange the exploder so that the handle can be vigorously pressed down, arrange the circuit leads so that they may be readily attached to the terminals, but out of the way of the handle; then when the signal is given, attach both leads, pull up the handle and push it down smartly. Immediately after firing disconnect.

129. Calculations, as careful and precise as circumstances permit, should invariably be made in order to avoid arranging a circuit through which the firing apparatus available cannot pass the necessary current.

The calculations should, whenever possible, be subsequently checked by actual tests.

If it is intended to use a battery of the Le Clanché type with all fuzes or detonators connected in series the number of cells required is readily calculated :—

Let n = number of cells.
,, r = internal resistance of one cell.
,, e = E.M.F. of one cell.
,, c = current required to fuze.
,, R = total resistance of fuzes and leads.

then $C = \dfrac{n \times e}{n \times r + R}$

Taking the same conditions as in the previous example (para. 127) and putting $r = \cdot 25$ ohms
$e = 1 \cdot 5$ volts

we have $\cdot 8 = \dfrac{n \times 1 \cdot 5}{n \times \cdot 25 + 84}$

and $n = 51 \cdot 7$ or say 52 cells.

If such a number of cells were not available it would be necessary to reduce the number of charges or place only one fuze in each charge.

A rough rule with the Le Clanché type of cell is to allow two cells for every fuze or detonator and one cell for every "ohm" of resistance in leads and connections. Add 25 °/₀ to calculated results in all cases where it is impossible to ascertain by actual trial the resistance through which the battery will fuze the standard wire.

130. In the event of the battery power available being insufficient to fire the requisite number of charges, even with but one fuze or detonator in each, the device of firing by "successive" contacts may be resorted to. The object is, of course, whatever

apparatus is used, to explode all charges as nearly as possible simultaneously without polarising the battery, which should be capable of firing two groups simultaneously. Fig. 2, Pl. 25, shows one possible method, in which the wires from the various groups are connected to terminals or screws arranged on the arc of a circle and the battery wire to a revolving metal handle. The handle would be moved across the contacts with an uniform motion and at such a speed as would complete the operation in about one second.

Firing by battery.

131. When firing charges with a battery and contact key the connections should always be made in the order shown by the numbers in Pl. 25, Fig. 1, which is that prescribed in the safety precautions in para. 125.

If a contact key be not available, an ordinary Morse " single current key " as used for telegraphy will do fairly well, a slip of bone or hard wood being inserted in the front contact to take the place of the turn-buckle.

If no key is available, contact must be made by firmly pressing the loose end of the main lead on the free terminal of the battery, but the greatest care is necessary with improvised contact matters that the parts in contact shall be absolutely clean. In this connection it should be noted that the lacquered surfaces of terminals, &c., act as insulators.

Testing.

132. *Testing* may be divided into—

(1.) Testing the firing apparatus.
(2.)   „   fuzes or detonators.
(3.)   „   conducting wires.
(4.)   „   earths in cases where they are substituted for return wires.
(5.)   „   complete circuit after everything is ready for firing.

Operations 1, 2, and 3 are conducted under cover, 4 and 5 on the ground.

It is undesirable to lay down what is absolutely essential, but in every case a continuity test of the complete circuit should be taken, and the firing apparatus tested to see that it will fire through its calculated " hot " resistance.

Testing exploders.

133. If in good condition, exploders should fuze as follows :—

Mark V, one ·0014″ platinum wire through 100* ohms.
Mark I, one ·0014″   „   „   60   „

This test is carried out with the firing resistance coils connected up as shown in Pl. 19, Fig. 4.

The exploder should not be tried with a resistance it is unable to fuze through. A small resistance should therefore be tried first and gradually increased till the machine fails.

---

* In some cases this figure may be considerably exceeded.

It should at least be able to fuze through a resistance 25 per cent. greater than the calculated resistance of the circuit at fuzing point.

If no platinum wire is available, the exploder may be considered sufficiently powerful if it is able to *fire* a fuze or detonator through a calculated resistance 90 per cent. greater than the estimated resistance of the circuit at fuzing point.

134. If the exploder be found to be faulty, it must be examined as follows :—Short circuit the terminals—Raise and depress the handle as in the act of firing. There should be a distinct opposition to the down stroke and the armature should pull up when it is completed. If not, there is probably a disconnection in the machine circuit which may be due to :— *[margin: Faults in exploder.]*

> (a) Disconnection between ends of armature coil and commutator.
>
> (b) Dirty or loose connections in other parts of the circuit or imperfect contacts between brushes and commutator.

Make a visual examination for such defects and verify with the 2 ohm coil of the galvanometer and a cell.

The short circuit spring should be tested.

The contact should have no resistance when not broken by the handle.

A general weakness may be due to loss of residual magnetism, in which case a current must be passed through the machine from another source for a few minutes.

Other though less probable sources of failure are :—

> (c) Reversal of leads to brushes.
>
> (d) Windings of field magnets wrongly connected.

A spark should be seen when the contact at the bottom is broken.

There should be no resistance between the terminals except when the handle is pressed hard down, when the resistance should be about 9 ohms. 1 to 5 ohms on the armature and 2 ohms on each magnet coil.

It is important that the break in the short circuit at the bottom of the stroke should be very sharp; otherwise there is a loss of power. The contacts should also be separated sufficiently to prevent an arc being formed across them. To ensure this it may sometimes be advisable to remove the rubber pad under the short contact piece.

A certain amount of practice and natural dexterity is required to get the best results out of an exploder.

135. The firing battery should be tested by finding through what resistance it will fuze the standard wire. The total resistance of the circuit at fuzing point should not exceed this.

136. The test cell should be tested to make sure that:—

(a) It is not too weak for testing purposes.
(b) It is not too strong.

(a) can readily be ascertained by joining it up with the 1,000ω coil of the galvanometer. There should be a deflection of not less than 20°.

The simplest method of ascertaining (b) is to connect the test cell through a key to a fuze or detonator which must be placed in a safety box or other safe spot. Depress the key firmly for 4 seconds. If the fuze or detonator does not fire, the cell may safely be used for testing purposes.

137. If no test cell is available, then any Le Clanché type cell with 12 ohms resistance added may be used instead, the safety of the combination being tested as before.

138. Before making up the firing battery, each cell should, if time permits, be tested separately in order that defective cells may be rejected. It should be remembered that a defective cell may not only fail to produce its proper share of E.M.F. of the whole battery, but may cause it to give less current than it otherwise would.

The deflection of the 1,000ω coil of the galvanometer is a good indication of the E.M.F. of a cell and that on the 2ω coil of its internal resistance. In the latter case there should be a deflection of at least 60° if the cell is in good order.

A dry cell in good condition should fire a fuze and detonator on short circuit, and cells may be tested individually or collectively on this principle. If a number of cells are tested simultaneously in this manner by being joined in series, care must be taken to add to the circuit 2·6 ohms for every cell except the first.

Testing batteries.

139. The E.M.F. and internal resistance of any battery, if sufficiently powerful, *may* be found as follows:—

Beginning with a low resistance and making *short contacts* ascertain through what resistance (W) the battery will just fuze one standard wire.

Then similarly ascertain the resistance (W_1), through which the battery will just fuze two standard wires in divided.

The internal or liquid resistance (L) of the battery will be $W - 2W_1$, and the resistance per cell, assuming that the cells are identical, will be $\dfrac{L}{n}$ when n is the number of cells tested.

The E.M.F. of the battery will be, assuming the standard wire used to have been the service ·0014 inch diameter iridio-platinum wire, ·8 (*i.e.*, current required to fuze one wire) × (L + W + 2·6).

Le Clanché cells should not be tested by this method.

Testing firing key.

140. The firing key to be used with the battery should be actually tested to see that it really causes discontinuity when not depressed, and offers no resistance when depressed.

Sec. 8.   FIRING CHARGES BY ELECTRICITY.   63

141. When time permits, and the apparatus is available, all fuzes or detonators should be balanced by Wheatstone's bridge method, and their resistances marked on them. *Testing fuzes or detonators accurately.*

Fig. 1 shows the method of using the 100 ohms resistance coils as a Wheatstone's bridge, and a service test cell and the 10 coil of the 3-coil galvanometer would generally be used in conjunction with it. Any suitable apparatus, however, may be used, if the precaution is observed of not allowing more than 1/20 ampère to pass through the fuze or detonator.

To balance a fuze or detonator by this method, take out the two 10ω plugs in the bridge and put in all the other plugs, depress the key and observe the direction of the throw of the needle. This gives the direction when resistance is too low. Now unplug sufficient resistance to give a throw to the needle in the opposite direction. This resistance is too high. The correct resistance should be taken as a mean between resistances which give indications on the galvanometer as being just too high and just too low.

Fuzes or detonators varying 10 per cent. from the correct resistance should be rejected. Thus land service fuzes and detonators will only be used if between ·95 and 1·15 ohms.

142. If there is not sufficient time to balance each fuze or detonator tested accurately, the continuity of each should be tested with the 2-coil and a test cell. About the same deflection should be obtained whether the fuze or detonator be in or out of circuit. *Rough continuity test of fuzes of detonators.*

Note.— Fuzes or detonators thus tested must be connected up in series.

143. Fuzes or detonators to be used for very important work should be tested for over-sensitiveness; they should not fire in four seconds with a current of ·32 ampère. *Test for over-sensitiveness.*

144. A few fuzes or detonators from each box should be fired with ·45 ampère; if they fail to fire in four seconds with this current the whole box should be rejected. *Test for under-sensitiveness.*

N.B.—The above tests for over and under-sensitiveness can only be effectively carried out when means are at hand to accurately determine the constants of the testing batteries.

145. Conducting wires should always be tested for continuity and sometimes for conductivity and insulation. *Testing conducting wires.*

The mere continuity of a piece of wire can of course be ascertained by simply placing it in circuit with a battery and galvanometer.

Its conductivity resistance can, however, be obtained with fair accuracy by Wheatstone's bridge method.

A rougher method is that indicated in para 142, and if a wire has satisfied this test, its resistance for purposes of calculation may be computed by using the table referred to in para. 101, which gives the resistances of the various service wires per 100 yards.

146. In all cases, however, covered wires should be subjected whilst being paid out to a careful (though perhaps necessarily *Examination of wires.*

rapid) visual examination, with a view to discovering sharp kinks, bare places with sometimes partial fractures of the conductor, and bad joints. Rough electrical testing often fails to show up such "faults." On the other hand, careful electrical testing will generally detect defects which are not visible to the eye. Doubtful-looking joints should always be cut out and remade.

Insulation.
147. The insulation resistance of a cable used for firing a charge should be at least 1,000 ohms. This can be tested with the test or any other cell on the 1,000 coil thus :—Take the deflection on the 1,000 coil with the cell on short circuit, then try what deflection the same cell will give through the insulation of the cable. (See Pl. 26, Figs. 1 and 2.) If it is not greater than half the previous deflection, the cable has an insulation resistance of at least 1,000 ohms, and may be considered good enough. This test may be taken with the cable in a tank of water, or laid out on the ground, but it is better not to wet the cable if it is to be used in a short time. If, however, the cable is to be used in water, it should be tested in water.

Localizing faults.
The position of a bad leak may be ascertained by connecting up as before, and passing the cable through the water about a foot at a time. A deflection on the galvanometer will mean that a leaky portion is passing through the water. (See Pl. 26, Fig 3.) If it is intended to attempt to remove faults in an insulated cable, should any be found on testing, the cable should *first* be carefully tested in the manner just described, foot by foot, and finally, should be tested immersed as a whole in water. If the cable is first immersed as a whole in water, the localization of the faults is much more troublesome.

Testing the earths.
148. In the rare cases in which it is possible to use earths to complete a wire fuze circuit, they should be tested for resistance by the aid of a firing machine or battery, as follows :—

First, see through what resistance the firing apparatus will fuze a standard wire on short circuit, say W, and then what resistance it will fuze a similar wire through, completing the circuit with the proposed earth, say W_1; then $W-W_1$, will be the resistance of the earths, and should be included in the calculations.

A clean metal plate 4 inches by $7\frac{1}{2}$ inches has in a salt river a resistance of about 1 ohm; but in ordinary earth it might have a resistance of 40 ohms or more.

Testing the complete mine circuit.
149. When the mines are in position the resistance of the complete circuit should be balanced to see that there are no defective joints, &c. This is done with the *test cell* by the method of Wheatstone's bridge, the connections for which are shown on the diagram, Pl. 19, Fig. 3.

See also para. 141 as to method of taking the reading.

Let Fig. 4 Pl. 26 represent a system of mines in which the calculated or separately measured resistances are as follows :—

Fuzes. $7 \times 1·05 = 7·35$ ohms.
Main leads between A & B $2 \times 2 = 4$ ohms.
Branch leads between B C & B D $2 \times 1 = 2$ ohms.
Leads between charges 1 ohm in all.
Total C.R. of circuit should be 14·35 ohms.

If the C.R. measured from A is found to be, say, 20 ohms or more, there is probably a bad joint somewhere.

If the C.R. is found to be infinite there is a disconnection somewhere.

If the C.R. is considerably less than 14 ohms there is leakage between the various parts of the circuit.

If a steady reading is difficult to obtain, there is probably a loose connection somewhere.

If a disconnection or a fault of very high resistance be sought, a test cell should be connected to the mains at A ; a deflection on the 10ω coil of a 3-coil galvanometer placed in circuit across the joints at B will indicate that the mains are right. (Pl. 26, Fig. 5.)

If no deflection can be obtained, the galvanometer must be connected across the mains at some point (say P) intermediate between A and B. A convenient method of doing this is by what is known as the "pricker test," which consists of attaching two needles by flexible leads to the galvanometer and making the cross connection by piercing the insulation with the needles so that their points make good contact with the conductors. *Pricker test.*

Any points at which the insulation of a cable is thus pierced should be carefully marked, and the defect in insulation thus produced removed at the earliest opportunity.

Absence of deflection will indicate that the fault (disconnection or very bad joint) is between the point of examination and the point A.

By repeating this process the fault will probably come to light by careful inspection of the leads when it has just been passed and a deflection obtained.

If it be then not visible a third lead must be run between P and A and connected in circuit with the test cell and galvanometer and with each main alternately to ascertain which main is the faulty one, the faulty piece can then be cut out and renewed.

If sufficient wire be available, time may be saved by running a new main from A to B connecting it as above mentioned alternately to either main, to settle which is the faulty one, and substituting the new main for that one.

A disconnection in the branch leads may be localised in a similar manner.

Should the fault be found to be in a mine or shaft and to be covered by tamping, the officer in charge must decide whether to (1) unload and repair, (2) cut out that mine and fire the rest or (3) load another charge on the inside of the tamping.

Short circuits, contacts and earth-faults.

150. To localise leakage between the wires the galvanometer and test cell should be placed in circuit at A, the wires must then be disconnected in turn at B, C, and D, keeping the disconnected ends insulated.

A deflection will indicate in which branch the short circuit exists.

When a short circuit takes place through the earth between two points of leakage it is called an earth fault. One such point of contact with the earth will not affect the system, but if both positive and negative leads are "earthy," the effect is the same as that of a short circuit.

An "earthy" or leaky wire is located by taking the wires singly and testing them in turn as follows:—

Connect the positive pole of a test cell to earth and connect the negative pole through the 1,000ω coil of the 3-coil galvanometer to one end of the conductor, keeping the other end insulated.

A deflection will indicate the existence of a leak in that conductor, and by disconnecting the wire at known points, the leaky section can be determined.

Summary of procedure in preparing charges for firing by electricity.

151. (i.) Having ascertained by the calculation, on the lines laid down in paras. 127 and 129–130, that the requisite number of fuzes or detonators can be fired, and what is the best arrangement of circuit for the purpose, the fuzes or detonators should be tested while the charges are being prepared.

The fuzes or detonators may have been tested previously; if not the testing should begin at once.

When they are to be connected in divided, and in all important demolitions, they should be balanced accurately by Wheatstone's bridge (see para. 141); but if they are all in series and the demolition is not of very great importance, or if the time and apparatus is not available, they may be tested for metallic continuity as laid down in para. 142.

When the demolition is of great importance, the over and under sensitiveness tests should be applied (para. 143); and in any case, a few fuzes or detonators from each box should be fired to see that they are in good order.

(ii.) The lengths of cable required for the main and intermediate leads having been ascertained, they may be cut off a long length, leaving sufficient for slack, or more probably pieces, of approximately the right length, will have to be selected from lengths already cut. If cut off a long length, which has been previously tested and inspected, no further test will be required, but if old pieces are used each should be roughly tested for continuity and insulation, and the pieces with the best insulation should be used in places where they will be buried. Bad (leaky) pieces should, if possible, only be used in one main: good pieces should be used in the other, and in branches and connections. A bad leak on one main will not affect the circuit provided that the rest of the circuit is well insulated.

(iii.) The priming charges should now be prepared, the fuzes or detonators being first jointed together and to the intermediate leads, as laid down in para. 115, and the bags lashed up and the leads stoppered as laid down in para. 123. By this time the charges should be ready for their primers, which should be placed in position, and the leads disposed so as not to get damaged, and lashed along the galleries, as laid down in para. 123. The leads may now be connected together, or the loading may first be completed at the discretion of the officer in charge; in any case the branch circuits should be tested before the tamping is commenced. The method of dealing with disconnections and short circuits is given in para. 149.

(iv.) The testing being satisfactory, the loading and tamping is then completed, and the final tests taken of each branch circuit, which should then be connected to the main leads, and the test of the whole taken.

(v.) All is now ready for firing. If an exploder is to be used it can be tested and put ready to hand. If a battery is to be used its preparation will depend on the time when the explosion is to take place. The final test before firing is to see that the battery is capable of performing the work required of it, *i.e.*, to fuze the proper number of wires in divided through the calculated resistance.

(v.) The firing will be carried out as laid down in paras. 128 or 131 having due regard to Safety Precautions, para. 125.

152. Firing fuzes or detonators by means of an exploder is certainly to be preferred to firing by means of a battery, always provided that the number of fuzes or detonators to be fired *simultaneously* is within the power of one exploder. *Exploders preferable to batteries.*

If more exploders than one are available it may often be quite feasible to divide a large demolition work into sections, each to be fired by a separate exploder, or it may even be practicable to shift the main leads of each section in succession on to one exploder and fire them separately.

153. On service it may be necessary to use strange batteries and fuzes or detonators. *Use of strange apparatus on service.*

The method of arriving at the internal resistance of a battery, if sufficiently powerful, is given in para. 139, and if the standard fuze wire be available the E.M.F. of any battery can also be ascertained by the method laid down in that paragraph. *Method of testing strange batteries.*

The electromotive forces of any two cells of low resistance can be approximately compared by comparing the deflections given by them on the 1,000 coil of the three-coil galvanometer.

The resistance of fuzes or detonators at the moment when just hot enough to start ignition may be got as follows :—Let W be the resistance through which a given number of cells will only just fire one of them, and W_1 that through which it will only just fire two connected in series. Then $x = W - W_1$ *Measurement of resistance of fuzes or detonators.*

Measurement of least firing current.

In order to find the least current that can fire a fuze or detonator—

First ascertain its resistance when just hot enough to start ignition and that of the battery to be employed L, then find through what resistance W a certain battery power will only just fire it; we have then—

$$x = \frac{E}{L + W + \rho}.$$

Here E must be known in order to write down the value of x in ampères.

If E be not known, we can still use the value got above for calculations in which the same description of battery is employed.

For instance, if three cells of a battery fuze the $0\cdot0014$ wire through 2 ohms, the internal resistance per cell being $0\cdot1$ ohm, how many cells, x, will be required to fuze the same wire through 10 ohms?

We have $\dfrac{3E}{3 \times 0\cdot1 + 2 + 2\cdot6} = \dfrac{xE}{x \times 0\cdot1 + 10 + 2\cdot6}.$

From which we get $x = 9$.

If samples of the wire used in strange fuzes or detonators are available, the resistance at point of fusion and the least current that can fuze the wire can be ascertained by similar methods to those just described.

Electro-contact System of Land Mines.

Electro-contact system of land mines.

154. Land mines for the defence of a position would probably be arranged in close proximity to obstacles such as wire entanglements, abatis, &c., at varying intervals, not less than 20 feet.

Each main will probably contain 8 lbs. of dynamite or gunpowder with a primer of about 4 oz. gun cotton, provided with one detonator, which will be fired by a powerful battery, in rear of the line of mines, when the circuit of that mine is closed.

Each main lead from the firing station will form a complete loop, as shown in Pl. 24, passing along the rear of the line of mines, about 18 feet from them; each mine will be connected to one main lead and to a circuit closer, the other lead of which will be connected to the other main lead. One form of circuit closer is acted on by the enemy tripping over a stretched wire attached to it, and another form closes the circuit when trodden on. The battery must be of the Le Clanché type, and should be placed in a safe and dry place. It should be capable of firing at least four of the mines connected to it simultaneously.

To provide sufficient current without injuring the battery, it will be necessary to group two or more sets of cells in parallel.

The main and branch leads may be any of the service cables, such as E_2, D_5, or E_1, that with the lowest resistance being best, provided the insulation is good.

The leads should be tested for continuity and insulation every morning, and any fault localized and made good, although the fact that one or both of the main leads is broken will not necessarily put any mine out of action.

The continuity test can be taken at any time without putting the system out of action, by disconnecting one end of either main lead and attaching it to a galvanometer, the other terminal of which is connected to the next cell of the firing battery.

Care must be taken to *reconnect the ends correctly* after this test; for if they are joined on the wrong way round to the poles of the battery the effect will be to short-circuit the battery.

There are no sealed pattern circuits closers in the service, but Pl. 21 illustrates one of each of the above types, which could be improvised if required. The "Pull" circuit closer is made of brass or gun metal, and consists essentially of a plunger A working in but insulated from a barrel B and normally maintained in the position shown in the figure by a spiral spring. C C are bushes made of some insulating material, such as hard wood or ebonite. The wires are attached to the screws S S and secured in such a manner that when the wires are stretched, the spring is compressed and the collar D makes contact with the end of the barrel, thus closing the circuit. In many cases it would probably be better if the wires forming the conductor for the electrical circuit were not used as the trip wires as well, in which case the latter might be of bare wire of light gauge.

The "Tread" circuit closer consists of a circular wood block hollowed out to receive a bottom contact piece A, a spiral spring S and a top contact piece B, which are all of copper, brass, or other suitable metal. The conductors are soldered to the bottom contact piece and the spiral spring respectively. The recess must be large enough to allow the spiral spring to rest on the bottom of it without any risk of touching the bottom contact, which it surrounds as shown. The whole is enclosed in a thin metal box, in the centre of the lid of which is fixed a disc D. Anyone treading on the box will compress the spring and close the two contacts.

Section 9.—BORING AND BLASTING.*

General principles.

155. Blasting is the operation of bringing down and detaching from its bed or position masses of material by means of explosives.

This is done to obtain the dislodged material for some purpose, as in mines, quarries, &c., or simply to remove the material as in various engineering works, such as railway and canal cuttings, road cuttings, &c.

The procedure is the same in either case, with the exception that in the former case it is necessary to pay attention to the condition of the material after blasting, as to size of pieces, &c., and in the latter case it is not necessary to do so.

Use of blasting in military engineering.

156. In military engineering blasting will seldom be used in order to obtain material, and, therefore, it will only be necessary to consider the ways of actually removing it.

Method of blasting.

157. Blasting is usually carried on by means of relatively small charges of explosive placed in holes of small diameter, called bore-holes, and is only suitable for employment in hard materials, such as rocks of all sorts, coal, masonry, &c.

Large concentrated charges are also used for large blasts, where an increased volume has to be brought down at once.

The most common occasions when blasting is necessary in military engineering is in the making of mountain roads and in demolishing masonry.

Necessity of calculation.

158. It will often happen that only a small amount of the work will have to be done, and will have to be done in haste, in which case the disposition of the charges and their amount will be arranged straight away by inspection on the spot, without further consideration; but where a large amount of work has to be done, the consideration of the arrangement of the boreholes and the charges is very important, as labour and explosive can be greatly economised thereby.

In the consideration of these points, for convenience it is assumed that the work is being carried out in rock.

159. In ordinary blasting operations the charge is placed in boreholes in the form of a cylinder, which has a length several times its diameter. This is known as an "*extended charge.*"

Position of Boreholes.

160. In roadmaking in mountainous countries blasting has frequently to be undertaken on the face of an almost vertical cliff. The road has then to be cut entirely out of the cliff, and a very careful examination of the stratification of the rock and the lie

---

* The formulæ and table for calculating charges, and much of the information has been taken from "Blasting," by Oscar Guttman, A.M.I.C.E., published by Charles Griffin & Co., Ltd., Exeter Street, Strand.

of the fissures must be made before the work of blasting is begun. If the stratification of the rock is such that the layers slope downward into the rock as shown in Pl. 28, Fig. 1, the rock above may be often permitted to overhang the road without danger provided sufficient headway is given; but as the work proceeds, the rock must be constantly and carefully examined to note the presence of fissures either natural or caused by the blasting.

If, on the other hand, the strata runs down out of the face of the cliff, as shown in Pl. 28, Fig. 2, it will certainly be necessary to cut the face of the cliff vertically, and if the rock is at all unstable it will be necessary to cut back to the face of the strata. In these cases it is necessary to start blasting from the top and to work gradually down to the level of the roadway, otherwise accidents from slips will most certainly occur.

161. Besides experience of the stratification and lie of the fissures of the rock, there are certain positions of bore-holes which are the best for certain cases. *Position of bore-holes.*

In all extended charges the direction of the maximum effect of the charge (with properly tamped bore-hole) is at right angles to the bore-hole from the centre of the charge.

Bore-holes should, therefore, be so placed that this force is employed to carry the "burden" or overcome the "line of resistance" in the required direction.

162. *The line of resistance (L.R.) is the longest distance from the charge at right angles to the bore-hole in the direction required to be carried.* *Line of resistance.*

163. The best effect from a bore-hole is obtained when there are at least two free sides (Fig. 4).

The blasts in an untouched face are termed "Breaking in shots," and are so placed as to quickly create a second free side. *Breaking in shots.*

In Pl. 28, Fig. 3, $a\ b$, $a_1\ b_1$, $a_2\ b_2$ are three equal bore-holes, at angles of 30°, 45°, 60° with the free surface.

Bore-hole ab will not be entirely utilized.

Bore-hole $a_2 b_2$ will only have a small crater.

Bore-hole $a_1 b_1$ will give the best result.

For breaking in shots the bore-hole should not make a greater angle than 45° with the free surface.

As breaking in shots can only have a comparatively short depth, but require a large charge owing to the great resistance of the rock on all sides, enough room is not always available for the charge below the proper depth of tamping. *Therefore the harder the rock, the smaller should be the angle between the bore-hole and the surface.* (This gives a greater proportionate length of bore-hole to L.R.)

164. *Other cases.*—When blasting rock with several free sides, the bore-holes should be as nearly parallel to the longest free side as possible, so as to obtain the deepest bore-hole, and thus be able to use the relatively smallest amount of explosive.

165. *Vertical face with a free top.*—(Pl. 29, Fig. 1.)
The bore-hole should be vertical, so that the rock broken has not also to be lifted. Here the L.R. is shown, and the probable crater aCb.

166. *Vertical face with a free top, undercut.*—(Pl. 29, Fig. 2.)
The bore-hole must be vertical and as far as convenient from the free base. The depth of bore-hole to be three-quarters the length of the face and *not behind* the line of the face at d.

The probable crater is aCb.

If the upper part of the undercutting is irregular (*see* Pl. 29, Fig. 3) then the longest line at right angles to the bore-hole in the direction of effect must be taken as L.R. for calculating (the probable crater being aCb), not Co or Cb.

The charge must overcome the largest resistance for the best effect. Should Cb be taken as the L.R., the face would not be thrown down entirely, but a small crater would be blown out as fCg.

In this case the bore-hole can be made shorter, because the charge corresponding to the L.R. finds less resistance in the direction of the bore-hole.

The effect of the undercut base being that shorter bore-holes and correspondingly smaller charges can be used, and one more free face is available.

167. *Vertical face undercut, but without a top face.*—(See Pl. 29, Fig. 4.)
Here the hole should be parallel to the undercut face, and not deeper than usually, $\frac{3}{4}$ or $\frac{4}{5}$ its depth, as aC; the probable crater is aCe.

If the bore-hole be inclined downwards as aC_2 it will have to be longer, and the effect of the charge towards f will be insufficient, the probable crater being eC^2f_1.

If the bore-hole be continued beyond the face f as aC_1, the line of resistance (L.R.) falls in the solid rock, and the charge taking the shortest way will throw out a disproportionately small crater in the corner $e_1C_1f_1$.

If the bore-hole incline upwards as aC_3, then it becomes a breaking in shot and has a small effect.

Successive shots.
168. When several bore-holes are bored for successive firing, the distance between them may be taken equal to the L.R.

Simultaneous shots.
169. When they are to be fired simultaneously, equal to $1\frac{1}{2}$ L.R.

Stratification and fissures of rock.
170. If the individual strata are thick, the bore-hole can be wholly in one stratum (Pl. 29, Fig. 5).

Thick Strata.—The lack of cohesion between the layers of strata make the joint nearly equivalent to a free surface, and a slightly smaller charge can be used.

171. *Inclined Strata.*—(Pl. 29, Fig. 6.)
If the strata are inclined, the bore-hole should be arranged so that the L.R. is parallel to them.

The charge being helped by gravity, has less work to do.

172. *Thin Strata.*—(Pl: 29, Fig. 7.)

When the strata are thin, the bore-hole should be driven parallel to the strata wholly in one.

A bore-hole should never be driven between two strata, nor should it cross several at right angles, as the gases produced by explosion would leak away along the junctions of the strata.

Boring Tools.

173. The ordinary implements for hand boring are as follows:— Tools.

Boring bars (Pl. 30, Fig. 1).—These are octagonal steel bars of various lengths with cutting heads, for cutting holes up to 3 inches diameter. Boring bars.

One man holds the bar in position and turns it round between each blow, while two men strike with hammers. The weight of the hammer used varies according to the size of the bar, a 14-lb. hammer being used for bars from $1\frac{3}{4}$ inches to 3 inches, and a 5-lb. to 7-lb. hammer for bars from $1\frac{1}{2}$ inches to 1 inch. Use.

Jumping bars or jumpers are octagonal steel bars with a swelling in the centre to increase the weight (Pl. 30, Fig. 2). They are used by being lifted up by hand and allowed to fall. They require skill in use, but are more efficient than boring bars. They are only suitable for drilling holes which are vertical, or nearly so. Jumping bars.

The cutting portion of both the above is termed a bit. In all service bars and jumpers the bit is chisel pointed. Bits require very careful tempering and sharpening. Bits.

The steel must not be burnt in tempering, but should be let down to a bright straw yellow; the bits require sharpening roughly once for every foot of granite bored. Tempering and sharpening bits.

The use of the other tools is explained in the descriptions of the method of boring a hole.

These tools are classified according to the *diameter of the hole that they make*, which is slightly larger than the breadth of the bits themselves.

174. The rate of work depends on the nature of the material to be bored, the size of the bore-hole, and its direction. Briefly, the harder the rock, the larger the bore-hole, and the greater the angle to the vertical (working downwards), the slower will be the rate of work. Rate of work.

The following tables give some average rates of work which have been collected, but when work has been proceeding for some little time at any place, rates of work can best be arrived at on the spot.

F

1-inch Bore-hole, Cast-steel Tools.

Rates of work for different materials.

Material.	Rate per hour.
Ironstone...	$7\frac{1}{4}$ inches.
Granite ...	16–24 ,,
Greywacke	20 ,,
Slate	24 ,,
Limestone or dolomite ...	28 ,,
Quartz (mild)	32 ,,

The above is for trained quarrymen. With soldiers less work would be expected to start with.

Limestone. In limestone (mountain) a 1-inch steel jumper has been found best, with a rate of work of about 1 foot per hour.

Brickwork. For brickwork the rate varies with the quality of the brickwork. In good brickwork, 3 feet in 80 minutes is fair. A 2-inch hole is the best, as the smaller sizes become clogged with dust.

Rates of work in granite for different sized tools. 175. The following table shows what can be expected for different sized holes, per working day of 10 hours in hard granite, with boring bars :—

Men.	Hole.	Amount.
3	3 inch	4 feet.
3	$2\frac{1}{2}$,,	6 ,,
3	2 ,,	8 ,,
3	$1\frac{3}{4}$,,	12 ,,
2	1 ,,	8 ,,

In very hard granite a $\frac{3}{4}''$ bar has been found best, giving a rate of 12 inches an hour.

Rates of work in different directions. 176. Work proceeds fastest in a vertical direction *downwards*; it is half as fast in a horizontal direction. Between these directions it decreases from the vertical to the horizontal uniformly. If the direction of the hole ascends, the speed decreases very rapidly.

Sizes of service tools. 177. Table A gives the *only* sizes in which the service boring tools are supplied, all the bits being chisel pointed.

(Pl. 30, Figs. 10, 11, 12, show a few forms of crown-bits which are used commercially and may sometimes be found.)

SEC. 9. BORING AND BLASTING.

TABLE A.

Name of Tools.	3-in. hole.		1½-inch hole.		1¼-inch hole.		Remarks.	Sizes of service boring tools.
	ft.	in.	ft.	in.	ft.	in.		
Boring Bars—								
Lengths	4	0	4	0	3	0	Chisel bit at one end only.	
	3	6	3	6	2	6		
	3	0	3	0	2	0		
	2	6	2	6	1	0		
Jumping Bars—								
Lengths	7	0	7	0	7	0	Chisel bits at both ends.	
	5	6	5	6	5	6		
Tamping Bars— (Copper ends)								
Lengths	7	0	7	0	6	6		
	4	0	4	0				
			3	0				
Worms, miners—								
Lengths	7	0	7	0	4	0		
	4	0	4	0	3	0		
			3	0				
Scoops or Scrapers—								
Lengths	6	6	6	6	6	6		
	3	0	4	0				

Priming Needles........	7 ft., 4 ft., 3 ft. long.
Boring Hammers	7 lbs. and 5 lbs. weight.
Loading Hammers	4 lbs. and 3 lbs. weight.
Sledge Hammers	14 lbs. weight.

Besides the ordinary hand tools there are a large number of machines used for drilling holes in rock worked by hand and power such as compressed air, water, &c.

There are a large number of these boring machines on the market. They would prove useful (*see* para. 33) where rock blasting on a large scale was being undertaken.

Method of Hand-boring.

178. The surface of the rock must be flattened at the point to be drilled, and the hole must be started carefully in the exact position and direction required. The blows should be gradually increased in strength until the hole is deep enough to guide the drill properly. After each blow the drill is slightly lifted and turned in order to produce a round hole—this is called *setting* the drill. The dust produced must frequently be removed from the bore-hole, so that the effect of the blow may not be lessened by cushioning. This is done by the *scraper* (Pl. 30, Fig. 4), the flattened end being used to scrape out the dust, and a rag or tow wrapped round the other end serves to dry the hole.

Water should be poured into the bore-hole, as this lessens the hindrance of dust to the drill.

Method of boring.

Setting.

F 2

Loading Bore-holes.

Loading bore-holes.

179. The holes having been bored, the bottoms are dried out if necessary with wisps of hay, and the powder is then carefully poured in, through a tube of tin or similar material, if available. If the whole be vertical or nearly so, the powder will run down to the bottom; but if not, it must be pushed down with a wooden rammer, or copper scraper. If the hole be horizontal, a scoop (Pl. 30, Fig. 4), open at the top is used, which when turned round at the end of the hole, leaves the powder there. If the hole inclined upwards, or if the rock be split or honeycombed, a cartridge is employed.

Powder charges.

If the charge is to be fired by a powder train, a copper needle is introduced with its point well into the powder, the other end extending to the outside of the hole.

When large numbers of blasts are to be made the powder can be made up beforehand into cartridges of convenient size wrapped in paper. For wet bore holes, where water percolates in through fissures, the hole should be lined with clay, or the cartridges should be dipped in a waterproofing mixture, a suitable one being of eight parts pitch, one part beeswax, and one part tallow; or cartridges (some with the fuze attached) can be dipped in melted paraffin wax, as it is cooling.

Tamping.

180. For any explosive there should be at *least* 8 inches of tamping above the charge. As a general rule for bore-holes up to 3 feet in depth, the charge should not occupy more than half the bore-hole for powder charges.

In tamping, a layer of about 2 inches of wadding, hay, turf, or sand is inserted, and carefully *pressed* home on to the charge. The tamping over the wad usually consists of small fragments of quarry stone (avoiding flints or other substances likely to strike fire), vegetable mould, broken bricks, sand or dried clay, rammed down with a *copper-tipped tamping bar* (Pl. 30, Fig. 5) one or two inches at a time, the needle being frequently turned to prevent its becoming fixed. The last one or two inches of the hole being tamped with moist clay, the needle is carefully withdrawn, with a turning motion, and the opening primed with loose grains of fine powder, or a series of straws filled with powder. In ascending bore-holes the tamping may consist of clay wrapped in pieces of paper. A small piece of touch-paper of sufficient length to burn 30 seconds is inserted at the top, which, when lighted, communicates the fire to the powder train. The touch-paper is made by simply soaking coarse brown paper in a strong solution of saltpetre or gunpowder, and then drying it.

Means of firing. Touch-paper and portfire.

181. A small piece of portfire (para. 89) placed on the priming and kneaded round with clay is better than touch-paper; 1 inch in length suffices, care being taken that the composition is not loose in the paper casing of the portfire.

182. A better method of firing charges is by means of **Safety fuze.** safety fuze, a length of which is inserted into the powder, the end being cut off about an inch outside the hole, but with not less than a total length of 1 foot; a little wadding is then *pressed* down over the powder with the tamping bar, and upon that the tamping material in the usual manner, no moist clay on the top being required. The end of the fuze should be at the centre of the charge.

(For details of fuze, *see* para. 79.)

For long bore-holes, safety and instantaneous fuze could be used.

183. A somewhat dangerous means of firing, often employed, **Devils.** is by means of a "devil," which is formed from a small quantity of gunpowder well wetted, and worked up by hand into a pyramidal shape, and then placed on top of the priming.

184. Where dynamite or blasting gelatine, which are much **High** more convenient than powder, are used, the loading is carried **explosives.** on as follows:—

As many cartridges as necessary are placed one by one in **Dynamite and** the bore-hole and pressed firmly down with a wooden rammer **blasting** so that the wrappings break, and the dynamite is forced into **gelatine.** close contact with the sides of the bore-hole. On the top of these a cartridge, prepared with detonator and fuze (as described in Sec. 10, para. 205, and on Pl. 31), is gently pushed down. A paper wad is placed above this, and the tamping carried out as for gunpowder.

It is most important that the cartridges should be loaded singly, and not tied up in parcels of two or three.

The amount of tamping for dynamite or blasting gelatine **Tamping.** should be at least one-third the depth of the bore-hole, for bore-holes up to 3 feet in depth. Where the tamping is long, sand can be used. With blasting gelatine or dynamite, well waterproofed water tamping can be used.

185. Generally a sufficiency of primers with the last one **Gun-cotton.** fitted with detonator and fuze, as described in Sec. 10, para. 204, are placed in the bore, the tamping being the same as for dynamite.

Splitting Stone.

186. Stone may be split, either by boring holes and firing **Splitting** charges as above described, or by the use of plugs and feathers **stone.** of iron, of the form shown in Pl. 30, Fig. 9.

Short holes are bored in the stone in the direction required, into which the feathers and then the plugs are inserted and driven home with a sledge hammer.

Plugs and feathers are also sometimes made of hard wood, and after being driven in have water poured on them, which causes them to swell, thereby splitting the stone.

Calculation of Charges.

Necessity for calculating charges.

187. It will only be necessary to calculate the charges where a considerable amount of blasting has to be done in the same material.

If the nature of the rock to be blasted varies from one blast to the other, calculations will be a waste of time, and the charges should be allowed by eye.

It will only be at first necessary to calculate the charges, as, after a certain number have been calculated and fired, sufficient experience will have been gained for the charges to be sufficiently accurately estimated by eye. Charges are best calculated per foot run of bore-hole (though the actual charge is at one end only), as in bringing down material the length of the bore-hole affects the result.

Length of bore-holes.

188. Bore-holes (not in mines) are usually placed to give effect in one direction only, parallel to the face in that direction. Suppose that the charge C (Pl. 29, Fig. 8) would throw out a crater $a\,b$, if the length of the bore-hole is doubled, then the charge C_1 would have to be increased in order to obtain a crater to affect the face right up to the top edge. If charges are calculated by the L.R. only (here the same for both cases), C and C_1 would be the same, and the crater of C_1 would not reach up to the top.

Formulæ for calculating charges.

Let C = total charge in ounces.
  c = charge per foot run of bore-hole in ounces.
  L.R. = line of resistance in feet.
  k = a coefficient for the soil and explosive.
  B = length of bore-hole in feet.

N.B.—L.R. must be taken as the longest distance from the charge to the free surface perpendicular to the bore-hole in the direction of desired effect.

Then

$$c = k\,(\text{L.R.})^2 \text{ and } k = \frac{c}{(\text{L.R.})^2} \quad\quad\quad (1)$$

$$c = \frac{C}{B} \quad\quad\quad\quad\quad\quad\quad\quad\quad\quad\quad\quad (2)$$

Knowing the coefficient k and the L.R. the following table gives the value of c for various values of k and L.R. for two free sides :—

Table of charges for two free sides.

K	0·05	0·06	0·07	0·08	0·09	0·100	0·125	0·150	0·175	0·200	0·250	0·300	0·350	0·400	0·450	0·500
L.R. in feet.	Charges (c) in ounces and drams per foot run of bore-hole. The small figures are drams.															
1¾	0^{3}	0^{3}	0^{4}	0^{4}	0^{5}	0^{5}	0^{6}	0^{7}	0^{9}	0^{10}	0^{12}	0^{15}	1^{1}	1^{4}	1^{6}	1^{9}
2	0^{3}	0^{4}	0^{5}	0^{5}	0^{6}	0^{7}	0^{8}	0^{10}	0^{11}	0^{13}	0^{15}	1^{3}	1^{6}	1^{10}	1^{13}	2
2¼	0^{4}	0^{5}	0^{6}	0^{7}	0^{7}	0^{8}	0^{10}	0^{12}	0^{14}	1	1^{4}	1^{8}	1^{12}	2	2^{4}	2^{8}
2½	0^{5}	0^{6}	0^{7}	0^{8}	0^{9}	0^{10}	0^{13}	0^{15}	1^{2}	1^{4}	1^{9}	1^{14}	2^{3}	2^{8}	2^{13}	3^{2}
2¾	0^{6}	0^{7}	0^{8}	0^{10}	0^{11}	0^{12}	0^{15}	1^{2}	1^{5}	1^{8}	1^{14}	2^{4}	2^{10}	3	3^{6}	3^{12}
3	0^{7}	0^{9}	0^{10}	0^{12}	0^{13}	0^{14}	1^{2}	1^{6}	1^{9}	1^{13}	2^{4}	2^{11}	3^{2}	3^{10}	4^{1}	4^{8}
3¼	0^{8}	0^{10}	0^{12}	0^{14}	0^{15}	1^{1}	1^{5}	1^{9}	1^{13}	2^{2}	2^{10}	3^{2}	3^{11}	4^{4}	4^{12}	5^{5}
3½	0^{10}	0^{12}	0^{14}	1	1^{2}	1^{4}	1^{9}	1^{13}	2^{2}	2^{7}	3^{1}	3^{11}	4^{4}	4^{14}	5^{5}	6^{2}
3¾	0^{11}	0^{13}	1	1^{2}	1^{4}	1^{7}	1^{12}	2^{2}	2^{7}	2^{13}	3^{8}	4^{2}	4^{14}	5^{10}	6^{5}	7^{1}
4	0^{13}	0^{15}	1^{2}	1^{3}	1^{7}	2^{10}	2	2^{6}	3^{13}	4^{8}	4	5^{13}	6^{10}	7^{6}	8^{3}	9
4¼	0^{15}	1^{1}	1^{4}	1^{7}	1^{10}	1^{13}	2^{4}	2^{11}	3^{8}	3^{10}	4^{8}	5^{6}	6^{5}	7^{4}	8^{3}	9
4½	1	1^{3}	1^{7}	1^{10}	1^{13}	2	2^{9}	3^{1}	3^{9}	4^{1}	5^{1}	6^{1}	7^{1}	8^{2}	9	10^{2}
4¾	1^{2}	1^{6}	1^{10}	1^{13}	2	2^{4}	2^{13}	3^{6}	3^{15}	4^{8}	5^{10}	6^{13}	7^{14}	9	10^{2}	11^{4}
5	1^{4}	1^{8}	1^{12}	2	2^{4}	2^{8}	3^{2}	3^{13}	4^{6}	5	6^{4}	7^{8}	8^{13}	10	11^{4}	12^{8}
5¼	1^{6}	1^{11}	1^{15}	2^{3}	2^{8}	2^{12}	3^{7}	4^{2}	4^{13}	5^{8}	6^{14}	8^{4}	9^{10}	11	12^{6}	13^{12}
5½	1^{8}	1^{13}	2^{3}	2^{7}	2^{12}	3	3^{13}	4^{9}	5^{5}	6^{1}	7^{9}	9^{1}	10^{10}	12^{2}	13^{10}	15^{2}
5¾	1^{10}	2	2^{5}	2^{11}	3	3^{5}	4^{2}	4^{15}	5^{13}	6^{10}	8^{4}	9^{14}	11^{9}	13^{4}	14^{14}	16^{9}
6	1^{13}	2^{3}	2^{6}	2^{14}	3^{4}	3^{10}	4^{8}	5^{6}	6^{5}	7^{3}	9	10^{13}	13^{13}	14^{6}	16^{3}	18

To use this table we must know L.R., which can be got by measurement, and *k*.

189. To find *k* for the local soil and explosive in a mass with two free sides, make a bore-hole not more than 6 feet in length, charge it approximately and observe the effect. If the charge is too strong or too weak, repeat the experiment with a modified charge until two or three shots have been made, if possible, at different depths, giving full effects for the charge. To find *k*

From these data calculate the weight of explosive used per foot run.

From formula (2), $c = \frac{C}{B}$.

Then calculate the value of *k* from formula (1),

$$k = \frac{c}{(\text{L.R.})_2}.$$

This gives once for all the value of *k* for that soil and explosive by which the charge of all future shots can be worked out.

Example.—Suppose that from three blasts the following data have been obtained:—

Charge.	Depth of bore-hole. B.	Burden. L.R.	Charge. C.	Charge per foot run. $c = \frac{C}{B}$.
1	3¼	2¾	3^{10}	1^{3}
2	2½	2¼	1^{14}	0^{12}
3	4¼	4¼	11^{1}	2^{11}

Calculate k from the formula $k = \dfrac{c}{(L.R.)^3}$.

Or, more simply, find the L.R. in the charging table, and in the same line the next nearest weight to the c arrived at, then the value of k will be found at the head of the corresponding vertical column.

In the above cases k comes out to ·150 for all three charges.

If a value of k arrived at is not in the table, it can be found by addition, for example, if

K ·170, L.R. 4¼.
For L.R. 4¼, and k ·090, c = 1 oz. 10 dr.
For L.R. 4¼, and k ·080, c = 1 oz. 7 dr.
_____
For L.R. 4¼, and k ·170, c = 3 oz. 1 dr.

As a general rule, the bore-hole should not be longer than L.R.

190. If there are more than two free faces, the charge can be reduced as follows:—

For 3 free sides, ¾ ⎫
  „ 4   „   ½ ⎬ of the charge given in the
  „ 5   „   ⅜ ⎪ table.
  „ 6   „   ¼ ⎭

It must be remembered that the fissuring action extends beyond the breaking action; also the width of the crater must be taken into account, especially where several shots are to act conjointly, in which case a stronger charge may be fired first, so as to loosen the rock and allow more free surfaces for the other charges.

The explosives likely to be used are gunpowder, dynamite, and blasting gelatine where procurable, and gun-cotton, the latter being only suitable in the shape of primers. (For details of explosives see Sec. 10.)

191. As weighing the charge is not always possible, the following details are useful:—

Weight of explosives and specific gravities.

One inch length of 1″ bore-hole will hold, when the charge is well compressed, 10 drams of blasting powder, or about 15 drams of dynamite or blasting gelatine.

A pint of loose blasting powder weighs about one pound. The specific gravity of compressed powder is, roughly, 1·7; of No. 1 dynamite or gelatine dynamite is about 1·6.

The following rule will sometimes be useful:—

In mountain limestone use 1 oz. powder per foot run of **bore-hole**.

Section 10.—EXPLOSIVES.

192. Although a vast number of explosives have been invented,* the number in actual use is comparatively small.

Explosives may be divided into two great classes, viz. :—

I. Low explosives (non-shattering).

II. High explosives (shattering).

Shattering explosives contains a high proportion of explosive chemical individuals. Such an explosive individual is a true chemical compound containing in itself the fuel (carbon, hydrogen) together with oxygen or of other chemical element also bound together in a condition of strain.

Guncotton, nitroglycerine and picric acid (lyddite) are characteristic shattering explosives. All this class are produced by the action of nitric acid on organic substances, *e.g.*, in the three types given, cellulose, glycerine and carbolic acid respectively. In these explosives contact with a flame either has no effect or produces a fire which may or may not lead to detonation according to the degree of confinement of the explosive. The gaseous products of a high explosive which has not been properly detonated are poisonous.

In most non-shattering explosives explosion proceeds comparatively slowly from layer to layer and flame is sufficient to start the phenomenon. A typical non-shattering explosive is black gunpowder consisting of charcoal and sulphur (fuels) and nitre which supplies the oxygen necessary to support combustion. Some non-shattering explosives, however, are mixtures of such ingredients as above, with the proportion of a powerful explosive of the shattering type, and are chacterised by a low rate of detonation, the phenomenon not being started by flame. Such explosives are the coal carbonites.

It is therefore impossible to distinguish between the two broad classes of explosives by any general consideration of chemical constitution or means of ignition.

---

* *See* "Dictionary of Explosives," by Major J. P. Cundill, R.A., published by R.E. Institute, Chatham.

Rapidity of explosion.

It is the varying rapidity of action of explosives of different kinds which really governs in the main their relative suitability to different purposes.

Many erroneous ideas as to their action exist, based on single experiments or insufficient data. When a certain amount of solid explosive is converted into gas, the effects which will be produced depend partly on the suddenness of that conversion and partly on the resistance of the surroundings. Thus when a charge of gunpowder is exploded in a gun the endeavour of the gas to expand equally in all directions is met by a greater resistance from the gun than from the projectile, with the result that the former is thrown back a very little, but the latter is propelled forward very much. Again, no body can be started from a state of rest into a state of motion without its tendency to remain at rest (inertia) being overcome; and in the case of a heavy body the stress must be brought on gradually, otherwise there will be a probability of breaking up the body to be moved by reason of the sudden blow. For this reason the gas has to be developed comparatively gradually, as in the case of slow-burning pebble powder used in big guns. If in the same case a high explosive developing its gas instantaneously be used, there is not time to overcome the inertia of the shell, and the result must be either the bursting of the gun from the sudden and inordinate strain, or the breaking up of the shell.

Again, take the case of a charge of gun-cotton placed against an iron rail and exploded. At once the charge is converted into gas occupying the same space as itself, and in an extremely high state of compression. This endeavours to expand in every direction with enormous force, and the resistance of the rail is as nothing in comparison to the inertia of the gas. Consequently the rail is destroyed. The gas has also acted in the other directions, but there are no *visible* results; these have occurred in the form of sudden concussion of the air, causing the loud report.

To produce these effects with a high explosive, the charge must be in actual close contact with the substance to be destroyed, and the effect is so local that the explosive must cover just as much service as it is intended to destroy. For instance, if a shell containing sufficient explosive lodges immediately over the iron or timber roof of a field casemate, and is in actual contact with it, it will on explosion break through the roof; but if even a small amount of earth intervenes between the shell and the roof of the casemate, this will suffice to distribute the pressure of the gas, and the effect will not be nearly so great.

The sudden blow of the high explosive rends to fragments, whereas the slower-burning mixtures develop their force more gradually, and rather resemble in their action a push rapidly increasing in force.

The rule therefore is:—when movement is required, use a lower or more gradually burning kind of explosive; if destructive local effect is desired, use a true high explosive.

193. The requirements of explosives for engineer purposes are—
Safety in use and transport;
Stability under climatic conditions;
Simplicity in use;

and, for the warfare of mines, the absence of poisonous fumes. For the last-named purpose, gunpowder is by far the least objectionable; and, for the three first named, gun-cotton is superior to other high explosives.

Gun-cotton will now be described, and afterwards a few other high explosives in common use.

Gun-cotton.

194. Gun-cotton for field service is supplied in the form of wet slabs and dry primers.

Slabs are intended to form the bulk of a charge. They are stored and carried in the field wetted with from 15 to 20 per cent. (by weight) of water and are packed in sealed tin cases within wooden boxes.

Primers are intended to detonate the charges of wet gun-cotton. They are small cylinders or truncated cones of dry gun-cotton covered with paraffin wax, etc., to keep them dry, and are packed in tin cylinders.

The following are the details of the present* pattern slab and primer for field service:—

SLAB.

Name.	Weight.	Length.	Breadth.	Thickness.	Remarks.
Guncotton, wet :— Slab, field, 15 oz. (Mark I).	15 oz.	6 ins.	3 ins.	1¼ ins.	With one perforation for primer, field, 1 oz., Mark I.

PRIMER.

Name.	Weight.	Diameter.	Height.	Remarks.
Guncotton, dry :— Primer, field, 1 oz. (Mark I).	1 oz.	1·35 ins. to 1·15 ins.	1·25 ins.	Conical. One perforation.

Gun-cotton is now accounted for by slabs and primers and not by weight.

*The following may still be found, being obsolescent :—

WET SLABS.

	Name.	Weight.	Length.	Breadth.	Thickness.	Remarks.
		lbs.	ins.	ins.	ins.	
For R.E.	S	$1\frac{2}{3}$	$6\frac{1}{4}$	$6\frac{1}{4}$	$1\frac{3}{8}$	Two sizes of square slabs each with two perforations, one to fit primer F, one to fit primer G.
	T	$1\frac{1}{2}$	$6\frac{1}{4}$	$6\frac{3}{8}$	$1\frac{1}{2}$	
		ozs.				Special for Cavalry Pioneers. Each primer has one perforation for primer F.
For Cavalry and M.I. Pioneers.	V	14	6	$3\frac{1}{16}$	$1\frac{3}{8}$	

DRY PRIMERS.

	Name.	Weight.	Diameter.	Height.	For what sized perforations.	Remarks.
		ozs.	ins.	ins.	ins.	
General Service.	F*	2	$1\frac{3}{4}$	$1\frac{3}{8}$	2	Cylindrical in shape with a hole down the centre to take the shank of a detonator. Five packed in a cylinder.
	H	1	$1\frac{1}{4}$	$1\frac{1}{4}$	$1\frac{1}{2}$	

Igniting dry gun-cotton. 195. Dry or moderately moist gun-cotton, if unconfined, will burn away (if ignited) without explosion, but with a fierce flame and evolution of red nitrous fumes. If the quantity of gun-cotton is very large, combustion may end in explosion.

To detonate dry gun-cotton, a detonator is required containing fulminate of mercury. The gases produced by the detonation of gun-cotton do not contain any nitrous gases, but a considerable quantity of carbonic oxide (a poisonous gas).

* This primer becomes "Primer, rocket, 2 oz." but is obsolescent for R.E. service.

196. In the wet state gun-cotton requires a very much larger amount of fulminate in order to detonate it than is necessary for dry gun-cotton, but wet gun-cotton is easily detonated by the detonation, with a service detonator, of a dry gun-cotton primer in close contact with the wet charge. The effect of detonating wet gun-cotton is even more considerable than that of dry. The larger primer is sufficient to explode any charge of wet gun-cotton if in proper contact. Where for any reason a primer cannot be fitted closely into the hole in the slab, it can be tied to the slab with string, with its flat side touching. *Method of detonating wet gun-cotton.*

Gun-cotton, either in the wet or dry state, practically does not deteriorate with age, if kept at moderate temperatures, and not exposed to sunlight.

(Cases have come under notice of gas having been generated in torpedo war-heads charged with wet gun-cotton as a result of fungoid growth on the gun-cotton.

Dry primers have on inspection been found to be slightly acid, but these occurrences are rare.)

197. In handling gun-cotton, care should be taken to avoid accumulation of dust or fluff. *Precautions to be taken when handling gun-cotton.*

Wet gun-cotton is not inflammable, and can be sawed and bored with perfect safety if the precautions given below are taken.

A tenon saw is the best to use. The cotton should be prevented from flaking by being gripped firmly between two boards close to the cut. Pl. 34, Fig. 8, shows an apparatus for this purpose which is used in the service, but which can be readily extemporised.

Never cut gun-cotton when it is dry. See that it is properly wet, and frequently wet the tool and cut surfaces when cutting. At the completion of the cutting of each slab, water should be sluiced over the place where, and the apparatus with which, it was cut. When cutting gun-cotton a sufficient supply of water must be kept at hand.

As the chips and dust formed from cutting begin to accumulate, they should be gathered up and damped or destroyed.

198. Gun-cotton to be re-used must not be overwetted. Should it be necessary to dry gun-cotton at any time, this is best effected by exposing it for a fortnight to the dry air of an ordinary room. Gun-cotton should not be exposed to the direct rays of the sun. The only sure method of testing the dryness of the cotton is by careful weighing. *Drying gun-cotton.*

Test of dryness.

A rough but good indication as to whether the primers or slabs of gun-cotton are dry is afforded by holding a small piece of cold, clean plate glass and placing against it for a moment one of the pieces of gun-cotton which has been warmed. If moisture is given off, a film of dew will be at once seen upon the glass round the edge of the gun-cotton.

(Gun-cotton is never absolutely dry; it is considered dry with under 2 per cent. of moisture.)

Gun-cotton in blast or auger holes.

199. Dry primers are best for use in bore holes in rock, masonry, or timber, as in such a position it is found difficult to ensure perfect detonation of wet gun-cotton. They must be put in position without pressure.

Comparison of gun-cotton and gunpowder.

200. The explosive force of gun-cotton may be taken at from two to two-and-a-half times that of the same weight of gunpowder in positions, whether in earth or masonry, where the charges are well tamped. When the charge is placed without tamping, it produces at least four times the effect of the same weight of untamped gunpowder.

Under water, and with the same charges, the ratio of the radius of destructive effect with gun-cotton and with gunpowder is as 11 to 7, nearly.

ROYAL ENGINEERS.

Articles.		Field Company.	Field Troop.	Remarks.
Detonators	Electric, No. 13..........No.	200	100	In cylinders containing 25.
	No. 8 ....No.	400	250	In cylinders containing 25.
Fuze, Safety, No. 9............Fathoms		224	96	
Gun-Cotton	Dry, primers, field, 1 oz.........No.	720	480	In airtight tin cylinders, 10 to a cylinder.
	Wet, slabs, field, 15 oz. ....No.	560	280	
Bags, guncotton, 25 lb., clamps ....No.		16	2	In tins.
Exploders, dynamo, electric, quantity......No.		4	2	Canvas waterproofed bags.
Insulated leads (D. 15) ....Yards		1760	660	1 supplied in each wooden case, which holds 10 detonator cylinders
Do. do. (D. 14) ....Yards		—	1000	
Rectifiers, guncotton, primers ....No.		—	—	
Solution, India-rubber, 3 oz. tubes ....No.		24	8	
Tape, I.R. ....Lbs.		4	3	

CAVALRY.

Articles.		Squadron.	Regiment.	
Detonators, No. 8, with 2 ft. of safety fuze attached ... ... No.		48	144	
Gun-cotton,	Dry primers, field, 1 oz. No.	80	240	From Equipment Regs., Part II., Sec. 2.
	Wet charges, field, 15 oz. No.	32	96	
Matches, Vesuvian ... ... boxes		12	36	
Fuze, instantaneous ... ... yards		100	300	
Fuze, safety, No. 9 ... fathoms		24	72	

With an Army in the field, Engineer explosives are marked with a red circle:—

201. Gun-cotton is to be preferred to gunpowder under the following circumstances :—

1. When the charge cannot be thoroughly tamped ; as, for instance, when time is an object.

2. When it is necessary that the space occupied by the charge should be as small as possible.

3. When there may be danger of a charge of gunpowder being fired prematurely.

4. When the charge is liable to be wetted, in which case special precautions must be taken to keep the primers dry.

Gunpowder is to be preferred to gun-cotton when the effect which it is desired to produce is general rather than local (*see* also para. 60).

Disadvantages. Gun-cotton is not so convenient as plastic explosives for blasting rock, as it must not be pressed down into irregular-shaped bore-holes, and is difficult to place in chambers which can only be filled through a small aperture.

Supply in the field. 202. The supply of gun-cotton and detonators, &c., carried by various units is given in the tables above.

These (pp. 87 and 88) give the amount of explosive stores carried by a field company and field troop, R.E., and by the cavalry in the field.

Varieties of gun-cotton. 203. Many varieties of gun-cotton explosives are used for purposes other than military ; they are usually combined with nitrates, such as those of potassium and barium. Schultze and E.C. sporting powders, for instance, are mixtures of nitro-lignin or nitro-cellulose (about 50 p.c.) with nitrates of potassium and barium (about 35 p.c.) and other substances.

Preparing Charges for Firing.

204. A charge of gun-cotton may be made up in a single mass *The charge.* (as when required for a mine, or for blowing in a gate) or in a continuous line (as for a stockade or wall, *see* para. 262). In either case the primer is inserted in a hole of one of the slabs, or bound with the flat end in contact with one of the slabs by wire or twine, twine being always employed when using electric detonators. (*See* Section 8.) This slab should be as near the centre of the charge as possible.

205. When electrical arrangements are not used "*Detonator,* *Detonator for* *No.* 8, *Mk.* III, *for safety fuze*" is employed (Pl. 14). It consists of *safety fuze.* a hollow brass tube about 4 inches long, to the end of which a smaller tube, which contains 35 grains of fulminate of mercury, is fixed. Above the fulminate is a wooden plug, through which passes a piece of quick-match. The hollow tube is protected from dirt or wet by a paper cap. Safety fuze is generally employed to fire this detonator, and should be connected with it in the following manner :—

1. Cut off the required length of fuze. The end to be inserted in the detonator should be cut clean across at right angles to the length of the fuze, care being taken that none of the gunpowder is shaken out.

2. Uncap the tube of the detonator.

3. Measure off on the fuze, on the outside of the tube, the distance the fuze will have to be inserted to reach the quickmatch and then, holding this point between the finger and thumb, insert the fuze, pressing it gently home with a twisting motion to the full extent. If the fuze should be too thick to go into the tube, unwrap a sufficient amount of the tape covering and then insert.

4. Bend the upper portion of the tube slightly so as to grip the fuze and prevent its being withdrawn, *taking great care not to press on the lower end which contains the fulminate.*

5. The denotator with fuze or wire attached is then carefully inserted until the whole of the tapered end is in the primer. *On no account must force be employed in this operation.* If the hole be *Use of* too small it must be enlarged by means of a *rectifier,* a small *rectifier.* instrument of boxwood, supplied for this purpose with each cylinder of detonators. If the hole be too large, a piece of thin paper must be carefully wound round the tube until it will just fit with gentle pressure.

206. A Mark IV* detonator has been sealed to replace the Mark III. This detonator is $2\frac{1}{2}$ inches long and is provided with shoulders (Fig. 2, Pl. 14). The fuze is inserted in the detonator as with the Mark III, but to make the detonator grip

---

* This has recently been replaced by Mark V, which has the same dimensions, but the body is copper and the quickmatch in the tube is erect.

the fuze, the end must be squeezed with a pair of pliers and not bent. The detonator must be inserted in the primer until the shoulders bear against the surface of the primer.

The detonator may be further secured by being bound with twine to the primer or slab. If fuze be employed for firing, care must be taken that no portion of it can come in contact with, or throws sparks on, the gun-cotton. This latter precaution may be best effected, in untamped charges, by covering the gun-cotton with green grass or other handy material.

Instantaneous fuze. Instantaneous fuze is also used with this detonator, and is fixed in the same manner, but the outer covering has first to be removed to enable it to be inserted into the detonator. With the new pattern, only the linen thread need be removed.

When instantaneous fuze is used, great care must be taken so to secure it, either by lashing or by placing stones, &c., on it, as to prevent any possibility of the detonator being pulled out of the primer by the violent jump which the fuze gives at the moment of ignition.

Tamping. 207. When gun-cotton is employed for demolishing walls, arches, &c., if the line of least resistance through the tamping is equal to that through the wall, arch, &c., very little is gained by increasing the thickness of the tamping beyond this.

Tonite. 208. Tonite—another high explosive—is formed by impregnating gun-cotton with one or more nitrates. It is supplied in cylinders 2″ in diameter of weights ¼lb., ½lb., and 1lb., and in 5lb. blocks measuring 5 inches cube. The cylinders can be purchased in tins specially fitted with a screwed plug and rubber washer for use under water. It is detonated with a large size commercial cap, supplied by the manufacturers of the explosive.

Nitro-Glycerine.

Nitro-glycerine. 209. Nitro-glycerine is produced by the action of nitric and sulphuric acids on glycerine, and is a heavy liquid of oily appearance, of specific gravity about 1·6, varying from colourless when quite pure to a yellow or brownish yellow. It is of a very sweet taste, and without odour, and is an active poison. Mere handling of it will in most persons induce sickness and headache. It explodes when heated to about 360° F. or from shock, but in small quantities it ignites and burns with some difficulty by the mere contact of flame.

When perfectly exploded (by detonation) the resulting products are carbonic acid, nitrogen, water, and free oxygen. Imperfect combustion leads to the production of the poisonous carbonic oxide and nitrogen oxides ; hence, in the latter case, the fumes are much more dangerous than in the former.

The liquid freezes at about 40° F. as a rule, though some samples freeze much less readily than others. It contracts $\frac{1}{12}$ of its volume in freezing, when its specific gravity is 1·735. Once frozen it remains so even when exposed for some time to a temperature sensibly above its freezing point. When frozen it is very much less sensitive to a blow or to detonation than when liquid, and a detonator that will readily explode liquid nitro-glycerine will simply scatter it when frozen. This holds good with most of the nitro-glycerine explosives, though there are some curious exceptions (*see* " Blasting Gelatine ").

To render nitro-glycerine available for practical purposes it is made up into a solid form by mixing it with other substances, producing dynamite, blasting gelatine, &c.

Dynamite.

210. This is the generic name for a vast number of nitro-glycerine explosives, which may be divided into two great classes, viz. :— Dynamite.

1. Dynamites with an inert base acting merely as an absorbent for the liquid nitro-glycerine.
2. Dynamites with an active, that is to say, an explosive or combustible, base. Two great classes.

The second class contains admixtures of charcoal, gunpowder, or other nitrate or chlorate mixtures, or gun-cotton or other nitro-compounds.

"Dynamite No. 1 " is a sample of the first class and " Blasting Gelatine " of the second.

211. Before describing some of these it will be well to mention the tests for nitro-glycerine in an explosive.

The following are rough tests :—

1. If a liquid is oozing out or can be squeezed out from the substance, put the drop on a piece of blotting paper. If it is nitro-glycerine it will make a greasy stain, not disappearing or drying away ; if struck with a hammer on iron, a loud report will be heard ; if lighted and burnt, it will give a crackling sound and a greenish flame ; if gradually heated by a flame underneath, it will give a sharp report. Tests for nitro-glycerine.

2. Put a portion of the substance into a test tube and shake it up with methy-alcohol (wood spirit), first ascertaining that the spirit poured into water causes no turbidity or milky appearance. Filter the contents of the tube into another tube and add pure water to the latter. If nitro-glycerine is present, a milky appearance will be produced, and the heavy liquid will eventually settle at the bottom of the tube.

A much more delicate test is to use aniline and concentrated sulphuric acid as reagents. In the presence of nitro-glycerine a purple colour is produced which changes to green on the addition of water.

92 EXPLOSIVES. PART IV.

Conditions of stability.

212. Nitro-glycerine explosives, unless carefully made from pure ingredients, are apt to decompose spontaneously. Any indication of acid fumes or any tinge of green in them, should be followed by their prompt destruction with suitable precautions.

Detonation of nitro-compounds.

213. The best and handiest method of detonation known for all nitro-compounds now in use is to employ the service No. 8 detonator (para. 205), or a stout metallic (usually copper) cap or detonator, containing a charge of fulminate of mercury, with or without the addition of chlorate of potash. (Fig. 3, Pl. 14.)

The amount of the charge necessary to ensure detonation varies with the nature of the explosive to be detonated. The method of using the caps will be described later (para. 217). They are not used in the service.

When several charges are to be fired simultaneously electrical detonators should be used if possible.

Dynamite No. 1.

Composition and properties.

214. This is the ordinary dynamite of commerce as used in this country. It is a mixture of 75 parts by weight of nitro-glycerine with 25 parts of a porous infusorial earth called *Kieselguhr*, which consists mainly of silica, and is found in Germany, Scotland, and elsewhere. Dynamite varies in colour from buff to reddish brown. It is plastic in its nature, and is usually made up into small cartridges wrapped in parchment.

The direct contact of water disintegrates it, separating the nitro-glycerine, and hence great caution is requisite in using it in wet places. When it gets dry, pieces are easily broken off, which may become a source of danger.

Power.
Frozen dynamite.

Its power is somewhat less than that of gun-cotton.

It freezes at about 40°, and remains frozen at higher temperatures. When frozen it is much less sensitive to explosion by a blow or detonation. A rifle bullet fired into unfrozen dynamite readily explodes it, but will not do so when it is frozen. The reverse is the case with blasting gelatine.

When frozen, dynamite is more susceptible to explosion by simple ignition. For instance, so small an amount as 1 lb. has been exploded by ignition when frozen, while very considerably larger quantities of the unfrozen material will burn away without explosion. When partially thawed, dynamite is more sensitive to friction than at any other time. Dynamite is more sensitive to a blow than any of the other nitro-glycerine explosives.

Thawing.

215. Until thawed, dynamite is practically useless as a blasting agent. The thawing requires great care, for if dynamite or other nitro-glycerine preparations are gradually warmed up to a temperature approaching their explosive point (about 360° Fahr.) they become extremely sensitive to the least shock or blow, and once that point is reached they do not simply ignite, but explode with great violence.

Sec. 10. EXPLOSIVES. 93

They should never be warmed on or before stoves and fireplaces, nor exposed to the direct rays of a tropical sun; but thawed in an empty water-tight tin can, which should be placed in a vessel of hot water (heated separately to a temperature that can be borne by the naked wrist, *i.e.* about 130°); or a proper "warming pan," made for the purpose, should be used (Pl. 31, Fig. 1), which cannot be placed on the fire without destroying it. *Proper method of thawing frozen dynamite.*

216. Though it is impossible to get complete detonation with frozen dynamite, some effect can be obtained. During the Thibet Expedition 1903–04 extensive roadmaking operations were in progress at a temperature about zero Fahrenheit. About a couple of hundred pounds of dynamite were expended in the day and it was found quite impossible with only one or two warming pans to soften more than about one-tenth of this quantity. The frozen dynamite was therefore used as the blasting agent, with one thawed cartridge as a primer to explode the whole charge. In the boreholes, a couple of frozen cartridges were first inserted and a thawed cartridge with detonator on top (Pl. 31, Fig. 7). The frozen cartridges cannot be pressed down to fill the holes and it was found that two frozen and one thawed cartridge, so placed, had about the same effect as two thawed cartridges properly pressed in and tamped.

217. The service detonators will readily explode dynamite, but the ordinary commercial copper cap used in civil life contains less fulminate, and is therefore cheaper. It is used in the following manner (Pl. 31) :— *Method of detonation.*

1st. Cut a fûze clean and insert it into the detonator till it reaches the fulminate. The *upper* part of the cap is then squeezed with a pair of nippers (Fig. 3). The squeezing should not be neglected, as it not only secures the position of the fuze, but also serves to develop the power of the fulminate.

For use under water great care should be taken to have the upper end of the detonator made water-tight (with grease, tar, &c.) where it joins the fuze, to prevent the fulminate from getting damp.

2nd. A cartridge is opened at one end, and the detonator, with the fuze already attached to it, pushed in so as to leave about one-third of the copper tube exposed outside the explosive. The detonator is then securely tied in that position (Fig. 4). If the detonator is pushed too far into the cartridge the fuze may set fire to the latter before the explosion of the detonator, and loss of power and unpleasant (not to say dangerous) fumes may be the consequence.

3rd. For use in mining—One or more cartridges (as required) are inserted into the bore-hole (Fig. 5) and each squeezed separately with a wooden rammer so as to completely fill the bore-hole. Iron should never be used in squeezing home cartridges, nor unnecessary force at any time.

It is very dangerous to insert more than one cartridge at a time into the bore-hole.

4th. Over the charge, the cartridge, with detonator and fuze affixed, is inserted, but not squeezed, and loose sand or water (except with dynamite) is poured in as tamping. The charge is then ready for firing (Fig. 6).

Dynamite No. 2.

218. Dynamite No. 2 is milder and slower than No. 1, and was introduced to compete with gunpowder when the great power and local shattering effect of No. 1 was undesirable, for instance in coal mines and slate and granite quarries. It is sold in similar packets to No. 1, but has a black colour. It consists of 18 parts of nitro-glycerine mixed with 82 of a sort of rough gunpowder composed of 72 parts of saltpetre, 10 of charcoal, and 1 of purified paraffin (or ozokerit).

It is but little used, if at all, in England.

Blasting Gelatine.

Composition. 219. Blasting gelatine stands highest in the scale of power among the nitro-glycerine explosives.

It essentially consists of a mixture of nitro-glycerine and nitro-cotton, and contains 93 to 95 per cent. of the former.

It has been before mentioned that gun-cotton does not contain a sufficiency of oxygen for perfect combustion, and that in the explosion of nitro-glycerine there is an excess of oxygen. By combining suitable proportions of the two substances, therefore, the result is one of the most powerful explosives known.

Appearances. Blasting gelatine is a gelatinous mass, looking something like new honey in colour, and varying in consistency from a tough leathery material to a soft one like ordinary stiff jelly. It is, roughly speaking, 50 per cent. stronger than dynamite.

Power. Broadly speaking, the thinner the jelly the more sensitive it is to detonation, but on the other hand, a thin gelatine is more liable to liquefaction and possibly also to exudation, and thus to cause danger in storage and transport.

It freezes like dynamite at about 40°, but is on the whole less liable to freeze. It is also very sensible to friction when partially thawed. In the frozen state it is *more* sensitive to explosion by a blow such as that given by a rifle bullet than when unfrozen, being in this respect the opposite of dynamite.

It has the great advantage over dynamite of being practically unaffected by water unless exposed to its action for long periods, and so can, if desirable, be used under water like gun-cotton, and should be stored in water.

Blasting gelatine is cleaner to use than dynamite; and it is much less liable to crumble when handled.

It requires the greatest care in manufacture, otherwise it is apt to seriously deteriorate and even to decompose altogether in store.

220. Specially strong detonators, such as the Service No. 8, are required to explode blasting gelatine, or ordinary detonators with a primer of dynamite or gun-cotton. It requires confinement to develop its power of transmitting detonation, for a train of it cannot be exploded in the open (unlike dynamite) except by means of a very powerful initial detonator. *Detonation.*

The addition of a small percentage of camphor or other substances soluble in glycerine and rich in carbon and hydrogen (as benzene or nitro-benzene) renders it very insensible to explosion by shock or blow, and hence more difficult to detonate.

221. Blasting gelatine is made up in similar cartridges to dynamite, and is treated in the same way as regards thawing and preparation for explosion. *How made up.*

Gelatine Dynamite.

222. Gelatine dynamite (specific gravity 1·6) occupies a place midway between blasting gelatine and dynamite. It consists of a thin blasting gelatine, mixed with other substances. The varieties practically in use contain nitro-glycerine, nitro-cotton, nitrate of potash (saltpetre), and wood meal. They contain 80 to 60 per cent. of nitro-glycerine, the last named being called "gelignite," and its other ingredients being 8 per cent. of collodion cotton, 7 per cent. of wood meal, and 25 per cent. of nitre. *Composition.*

They resemble blasting gelatine very closely in appearance, and it requires practice to distinguish them apart. *Appearance.*

Gelignite, whether frozen or soft, appears to be about equally sensitive to a blow, and in either case to be more sensitive than soft blasting gelatine, and less so than frozen blasting gelatine.

Gelatine dynamite is made up in the same way as dynamite, and is similarly prepared for explosion. It is not so suitable for violent demolitions as blasting gelatine, being slower in its action.

Nitro-benzene Explosives.

223. The action of nitric acid on benzene (a brilliant colourless liquid obtained from coal tar) produces a heavy, yellow, oily liquid, with a characteristic odour of bitter almonds, called nitro-benzene. *Composition.*

All explosives in which this is an ingredient are at once distinguishable by their odour. It is an active poison, and great care should be taken not to handle nitro-benzene explosives which are not protected by a cartridge case more than is absolutely necessary. On no account after much handling should food be touched with unwashed hands. Persons who are obliged to deal much with the bare explosive should drink milk.

224. The best known explosives of this class are roburite, bellite, and securite, which are, however, more used on the Continent (Austria, Sweden) than in this country.

They are very difficult to ignite by ordinary flame, and require for their proper explosion very strong detonators.

In appearance they resemble moist sugar, and are made up in waterproof cartridges, having the characteristic smell of nitro-benzene.

Roburite.

225. *Roburite* essentially consists of a mixture of nitrate of ammonium with chlorinated di-nitro-benzene. It is a brownish-yellow powder, and volatilises without explosion or ignition when slowly heated, and burns slowly in the open, at all events in small quantities, but with great difficulty. . A red-hot poker may be inserted into it and it will merely frizzle away. The objection to roburite, as well as securite and bellite, &c., is that they readily absorb moisture, and are useless as explosives unless dry.

One of the objections to this and other explosives made up in rigid cylindrical envelopes is that, for such military purposes as demolishing stockades or rails, it is difficult, on account of the shape of the envelope, to secure that close contact with the object to be destroyed which is necessary for obtaining successful results.

Securite.

226. *Securite* is composed of about 26 parts of di-nitro-benzene and 74 per cent. nitrate of ammonium. It is a yellow powder with nitro-benzine odour.

Bellite.

227. *Bellite* is a similar explosive to the two last, and has much the same characteristics. It is composed of 4 parts nitrate of ammonium and 1 part of nitro-benzene. It is of Swedish origin.

Picric Acid Explosives.

Picric acid.

228. Explosives made from picric acid have found much favour of late, as bursting charges of shells.

Picric acid is prepared by the action of strong nitric acid on phenol (carbolic acid). It is a crystalline substance of a brilliant yellow colour, and is, as its name implies, intensely bitter to the taste. It ignites with difficulty, but when rapidly heated to above its melting point it burns with a very smoky flame and very pungent odour. It is largely used as a dye, but has not usually been considered as an explosive, nor indeed, does it behave like one under ordinary circumstances, though under special conditions it is capable of developing very considerable explosive properties.

It may be burnt away in an unconfined state in considerable quantity without explosion, but the mere contact of certain metallic salts or oxides with picric acid develops powerful explosives, which are capable of acting as detonators to an indefinite amount of the acid, wet or dry, which is within reach of their detonating influence.

229. Picric acid in powder detonates only with difficulty; but when melted and solidified (specific gravity about $1\cdot 6$), it can be detonated by using a primer of gun-cotton, picric powder (a mixture of nitre and ammonium picrate), or other high explosive. *Explosion of picric acid.*

230. The power of the latter form appears to be almost equal to that of blasting gelatine, but when in the powder it is not so dense and its power is less. *Power.*

Cordite.

230A. Cordite for demolitions may be obtained from gun cartridges. Cordite consists of nitro-glycerine and gun-cotton incorporated and gelatinized by the aid of a solvent, a small proportion of a mineral hydro-carbon being introduced. *Cordite.*

For demolition purposes cordite is uncertain in its action and should only be used when no better explosive is available. The small sizes are fairly reliable.

It is fired similarly to gun-cotton; a primer of gun-cotton or other high explosive must always be used.

A cordite charge should always be bound up tightly and fixed firmly against the object of demolition. It should in most cases be tamped, but this is not necessary when used against metallic structures, *e.g.*, rails and girders. No portion of a cordite charge should be more than 12 inches from a primer, since the rate of communicating demolition is slow.

An untamped charge must be well protected from possible sparks from the fuze, since cordite ignites very easily.

Where good contact can be obtained, the power of cordite may be taken as equal to gun-cotton, otherwise a cordite charge should be increased by about 25 per cent.

Other Explosives.

231. For further information on explosives, *see* "Dictionary of Explosives," by Major J. P. Cundill, R.A., from which much of the above information has been obtained.

Fulminates.

232. Fulminates are violent explosives, too dangerous to be used in bulk. They are employed to ignite or detonate other explosives, in copper caps, &c. That most commonly used is *fulminate of mercury*, which explodes with slight friction or percussion, or when heated to about 360° Fahr. When thoroughly wet it is inexplosive. It is used for the service detonators. *Fulminates.*

Section 11.—DEMOLITIONS WITH GUNPOWDER.

Use of gunpowder.

233. In deliberate demolitions the saving of time is no great object, and consequently we are able to study economy of the explosive agent; but in hasty demolitions the saving of time is of all importance, so that tamping and other aids to bringing out the full force of the explosion have often to be given up, or only roughly applied, and consequently a much larger charge in proportion is required than in the former case. For deliberate demolitions gunpowder is, as a rule, employed in preference to gun-cotton or any other detonating agent; it lifts a large mass of the opposing body instead of tearing through it, and it is also much cheaper. For hasty demolitions either gunpowder or gun-cotton is employed, the latter being preferable where time and portability are matters of very great importance. When gun-cotton

Tamping.

is employed there is less need for tamping than with powder. With the former it is sufficient to produce the maximum effect if the L.L.R. through the tamping is equal to that through the wall, arch, &c. (*see* para. 207), whereas with powder it should be

Moderate and violent demolitions.

at least from 1½ to 2 times that thickness. In deliberate demolitions it is often necessary not only simply to destroy, but also to scatter the "débris" to a distance. If simple destruction is intended it is called a *moderate* demolition; if the materials are to be scattered to a distance, a *violent* demolition. For charges *see* paras. 240 and 248.

Deliberate Demolition of Walls, Buildings, and Revetments by Gunpowder.

Revetment walls.

234. It is especially necessary to study economy in destroying revetments, because the aggregate quantity of powder required to demolish those of even a small fort might be considerable. As there is generally sufficient time to work deliberately, a partial failure is not of serious consequence.

To place the charges in position behind an escarp or counterscarp wall:—

1. Galleries may be driven through the revetment (Pl. 32, Fig. 1).
2. Shafts may be sunk at the foot of the revetment, and galleries driven under the foundations, if rock or water do not interfere.
3. In the case of a counterscarp wall, shafts may be sunk in the earth behind the revetment, or inclined galleries driven from a besieger's lodgment. (Pl. 32, Fig. 2.)

Each shaft or gallery may be made to serve for two mines, branches being carried right and left along the back of the revetment (*see* plan of Pl. 32, Fig. 2); or a separate shaft or gallery may be made for each mine. The latter involves more labour but saves time.

235. In practice it is desirable that the distance upwards to the surface of the ground should be at least 1½ times the horizontal distance to the face of the wall. If there are no counterforts the charges should be placed at 2-lined intervals in rear of the general line of masonry. <small>General rules for selecting positions of charges, &c.</small>

Where counterforts exist, the risk of finding a portion of them standing after the explosion has generally been the cause of their being selected as the point of attack: and the interval between the charges has been so arranged as to allow of a charge being placed in rear of or inside every counterfort, or at least every second one. This entails an alteration of the charges, by increasing or diminishing them in direct proportion to their actual interval. As regards level, it seems desirable that the charges should be placed about three feet above the bottom of the ditch. For charges see para. 248.

236. Counter-arched revetments may be demolished, either by numerous small charges lodged in or against the several walls of which they are composed, or by fewer and larger charges placed in the centre of each vaulted chamber (Pl. 32, Fig. 3). In the latter case the doors, loopholes, and all other outlets must be securely blocked up. For charges see para. 248. <small>Counter-arched revetments.</small>

237. In buildings having very thick walls, such as powder magazines, casemates, ancient towers and castles, &c., small galleries may be cut into the centre of the wall, and chambers formed in a recess on one side in the usual manner. But, if the masonry is much harder than the soil upon which it is built, it may be more convenient to sink shafts and lodge charges under the centre of the foundation. <small>Buildings having very thick walls.</small>

If the ground is not on the same level inside and outside, this irregularity must be corrected, or the position of the charges must be so adjusted that the resistance on both sides shall be equal.

The resistance of ordinary masonry may be roughly taken as equal to 1½ times that of a similar thickness of earth.

When the demolition of walls, carrying a heavy arch or mass of masonry, is to be effected, the calculated charges must be increased, in order to obviate the chance of simply lifting the mass upwards and allowing it to settle down again in a comparatively sound state. Usually an addition of one-fourth will suffice. A case of this kind occurred in the demolition of the Exhibition building of 1862.

A tamping of common earth, nearly double the line of least resistance of the masonry, will suffice for the strongest wall; but if the branches cannot conveniently be extended far enough to obtain so much tamping, more powder must be used.

238. In buildings having walls of moderate thickness (3 to 4 feet) it is difficult to make branches, because a man requires 2 feet to work in. In such cases, therefore, if there be <small>Buildings having walls of moderate thickness.</small>

earth at hand, a series of charges should be laid all along the outside of the wall. A trench may be dug 8 or 10 feet from the wall, and the earth thrown up over the charges as tamping. Pl. 33, Fig. 5 represents this arrangement; c is a charge place outside the wall of a building; ca is the line of least resistance; cb and cd the thickness of earth applied, which ought to be at least one and a half ca; de is the trench whence the earth is obtained. If the charges be sunk a little way into the wall, say about one-third of its thickness, so much the better, as this will lessen the line of least resistance, and thereby diminish the quantity of trench work required for the tamping, and the amount of powder to be expended.

The best position for such mines would certainly be inside, but generally the space is too limited to obtain a sufficient quantity of earth there, even if wooden floors, &c., did not, as they usually do, oppose an obstacle to use of this method. Area walls, pavements, arches, &c., may sometimes render it equally difficult to obtain earth for the tamping outside, for it would seldom be worth while to carry it from any considerable distance.

These methods, when practicable, are the simplest, as they may be executed by infantry, but it may not always be convenient to obtain earth, and there may further be a scarcity of powder, when recourse should be had to blasting (Section 9).

Boring for demolition of buildings.

239. Buildings can be demolished more economically by charges placed in the centre of the walls than by those laid along the sides and covered with earth. Charges of gunpowder of one-third L.L.R. placed in the centre of a wall at two-lined intervals, will produce complete but moderate demolition; but this only applies when each charge is in a compact form, which cannot be the case when borers are used of less diameter in inches than the wall's thickness in feet. The charges that should be used according to the size of the hole are given in para. 188.

It must be remembered that a boring bar or jumper always makes a hole of rather greater diameter than the size of its own bit. In boring into a wall, the holes should always be made at an angle of 45° downwards. When a depth has been attained equal to $1\frac{1}{10}$ L.L.R. the middle of the wall will have been reached. The hole must then be lengthened so much as to contain one-half of the proposed charge, so as to make the centre of the charge coincide with the centre of the wall. It will then be ready for loading and tamping.

Whenever the saving of gunpowder is an object, it may be worth while to cut away the lower part of the walls, leaving piers sufficient to support the upper part, at clear intervals of from 6 to 12 feet, according to circumstances, and then to blow up the piers, the holes having been prepared in them in the first instance.

In a building well bonded together by a strong roof, floors, or substantial cross walls, it might be advantageous to use unequal charges, so as to shatter some parts more than others.

Holes of the following description may be used :—

Single, driven at an angle of 45° downwards, and bored alternately from opposite sides of the wall.

V *holes* when two holes driven from the opposite sides of a wall at angles of 45° meet at the point of the **V**.

X *holes* when two holes driven from opposite sides of the wall at angles of 45° cut each other at the centre of the **X**.

Table of charges for walls.

240. The following table gives the charges of powder, placed at two-lined intervals in holes of various diameters, necessary for the complete, but moderate, demolition of walls. The L.L.R. is always taken in feet, and is equal to half the thickness of the wall :—

Case.	Diameter of hole in inches.	Charge of powder in lbs.	Depth to which each hole is to be bored in feet.	Description of hole.	Length of each hole occupied by powder in feet.	Remark. The Charges should be fired simultaneously.
1	2 L.L.R.	$\frac{1}{2}$ L.L.R.^{3}	$1\frac{1}{3}$ L.L.R.	Single	$\frac{3}{4}$ L.L.R.	This is the best size of hole.
2	$1\frac{1}{3}$ L.L.R.	$\frac{4}{15}$ L.L.R.^{3}	$1\frac{1}{2}$ L.L.R.	Single	$\frac{2}{3}$ L.L.R.	Single holes should be bored alternately from opposite sides of the wall.
3	L.L.R.	$\frac{1}{3}$ L.L.R.^{3}	$2\frac{1}{3}$ L.L.R.	Single	$1\frac{1}{3}$ L.L.R.	(as above)
4	L.L.R.	$\frac{1}{3}$ L.L.R.^{3}	$1\frac{4}{15}$ L.L.R.	V	$\frac{1}{2}$ L.L.R.	Half the charge, or $\frac{1}{6}$ L.L.R.^{3} to be in each hole forming the V; the holes should overlap slightly.
5	$\frac{2}{3}$ L.L.R.	$\frac{1}{3}$ L.L.R.^{3}	2 L.L.R.	X	$1\frac{1}{2}$ L.L.R.	Half the charge, or $\frac{1}{6}$ L.L.R.^{3} to be in each of the two holes forming the X

A charge of $\frac{1}{3}$ L.L.R.^{3} in a **V** hole of a diameter in inches of $\frac{2}{3}$ L.L.R. has effected demolition, when a similar charge in a single hole of greater length, but of the same diameter, failed.

If the holes have to be made less than $\frac{2}{3}$ L.L.R. in diameter, which is bad, **V** or **X** holes can be used with diminished intervals ; or from the same side of the wall two parallel holes can be bored close to each other, and the partition between them cut away thus : ●●. If the diameter of the holes in inches be equal to L.L.R., two holes cut into one may be considered equal to a single hole of $1\frac{1}{3}$ L.L.R. diameter, and may be treated as in Case 2.

If the diameter of the holes in inches be equal to $\frac{2}{3}$ L.L.R., two holes cut into one may be considered equal to a single hole of L.L.R. diameter, and may be treated as in Cases 3 and 4.

It has been found that charges fired in two undersized holes parallel and close to one another, produce a very violent effect, even when not cut into one.

Deliberate Demolition of Bridges by Gunpowder.

Objects to be obtained in the demolition of bridges.

241. The object to be obtained in the demolition of a bridge, as a military in contradistinction to an ordinary operation of such a nature, is to create in a comparatively short time the greatest obstacle in a line of communication.

It is unnecessary here to enter into a detailed description of any of the numerous circumstances under which it may become necessary to destroy bridges in the course of military operations. Under most circumstances, however, the time for preparation would be limited, it would rarely exceed three days, and in some cases less than three hours would be available. In addition to this it would probably be necessary to make every preparation without interrupting the traffic, frequently very great, over the bridge till the very last moment, and the arrangements should be such that the charges may be fired together, so that the whole structure may be destroyed in a moment when the proper time has arrived.

Sometimes bridges are ordered to be prepared for demolition, many days or even months previous to the order for destroying them being given, and occasionally, owing to alteration of circumstances, they have to be made good again. Finally the demolition must be complete, because there would probably be no time to remedy any partial failure, which might have a very disastrous effect by leaving a bridge in such a condition as to be available, with little or no repair, for the passage of an enemy's infantry, if not cavalry and artillery.

It is evident, therefore, that the conditions differ essentially from the mere deliberate demolition of a bridge, where the operations may be extended over weeks or even months, as in the removal of the old bridge over the Medway at Rochester. In the latter case also it is generally important that fragments should not be thrown far, a matter of no consequence in a military demolition.

Deliberate military demolition of bridges.

242. The best mode of destroying a bridge of a single arch, or with short thick piers, is to attack the haunch, or better still both haunches. In a bridge with high piers, mines should be placed as close as possible to the bases of the piers, as the fall of one pier will bring down two arches. A series of charges seems preferable to a single charge, however large or theoretically well calculated, for any slight imperfection in the masonry might permit action in that direction, under which circumstances a breach as shown in Pl. 33, Fig. 1, might be made without actually bringing down the pier. With a number of charges the chances of a failure of this nature are reduced to a minimum.

The charges should be at 2-lined intervals and fired simultaneously.

When the piers are broad and thick, it would be uncertain, and therefore dangerous, as a military operation, to attempt to destroy the bridge by simply blowing them up. In the bridge at Magenta, which the Austrians attempted to destroy on the advance of the French during the Italian campaign of 1859, the piers were short and thick, probably strongly built, and the arches were of granite. The charges were placed in two piers, and their only effect was to raise the structure for a moment, to shatter and loosen it considerably and to allow it to subside again in a dilapidated, but still in a serviceable state, upon its original supports. It certainly proved itself sufficiently safe to enable the French to pass over at a point where the Austrians were unprepared to oppose them, which circumstance contributed in no small degree to the success of the former on that occasion. Hence to destroy such a bridge, it is better to attack the arches than the piers. The object to be attained is to drive out a wedge, or series of voussoirs in a line, completely across the structure, or to cause flexure in the arch, which, carried beyond a certain point, also produces demolition. To do this, it would be necessary either to place a single charge in the centre, or a series of charges in a line across the arch.

The arch of a bridge, owing to its form, offers a greater resistance to the explosion of a charge than a flat wall of the same section. Hence if a charge were placed at the same distance from the arch, and from the side wall, the latter would offer the least resistance, and might be destroyed while the arch was left standing.

In order to obviate this, the distance ca (Pl. 33, Fig. 4) should be increased as compared with cb, and as a general rule, it may be assumed that if $ca = 2cb$, or $= 2$ L.L.R. it will be sufficient for practical purposes. The distance from the surface of the roadway, in which direction also it is probable the tamping would be placed, should be such as to ensure the charge acting chiefly through the arch, and not upwards, where the resistance would probably be less, owing to the nature of material used for filling in the arches and for the roadway. It is therefore desirable that ce (Pl. 33, Fig. 3) should never be less than $2cb$, or 2 L.L.R., and it is better if it be $3cb$, or 3 L.L.R. The tamping also should be at least 3 L.L.R.

If the arch is to be destroyed with a single charge, the L.L.R. (cb), measured through it, should be equal to one-fourth of the breadth of the bridge. Except with a very narrow bridge, it would be better to place two or more smaller charges across the haunch of the arch, than to place a single large one in the centre: first, because it would require less powder; and secondly, because there would be less chance of blowing a hole through the centre, and leaving the two sides comparatively intact.

When two or more charges are arranged across the arch, they should not be distant from each other more than 2 L.L.R. The L.L.R. should be regulated by the depth of the voussoirs, and should not as a general rule be less than $1\frac{1}{2}$ nor more than 5 feet. If less, the number of charges would have to be increased, with the risk of partial failure; while, if greater, the charges would be very large, with the chance of unequal action.

Schaw's rule.
243. From experiments at Corfu the following formula was deduced by Captain H. Schaw, R.E., for determining the charge of powder required for the demolition of a strongly built arch, when placed over the haunch at a depth below the roadway equal to twice the distance measured through the arch, and well tamped:—

$$C = \tfrac{2}{3} \text{L.L.R.}^3 \times B.$$

where C = total charge of powder in lbs. required, to be placed at a haunch either in a single mass, or in a line of charges across the arch; L.L.R. = the line of least resistance in feet measured through the arch; and B the breadth of the bridge in feet.

General remarks on the demolition of bridges.
244. In order to reach the positions for the charges in a wide bridge, a shaft may be sunk in the centre, traffic being still carried on at the sides, precautions being taken to keep the wheels, &c., from coming too near the shafts. In a narrow bridge over which traffic has to be conducted, the mines must be reached through the side walls, or other convenient means, the roofs of the galleries being propped up when necessary.

If mining a pier be a work of great difficulty, one overcharged mine may be better than several common mines; not otherwise.

It is often advisable to prepare a bridge for hasty demolition as described in paras. 250 and 252, as well as for deliberate demolition, in case there be not sufficient time to complete the preparations for the latter.

Examples in Peninsular War.
245. In the Peninsular War the bridges were in general of stone, with semi-circular arches 20 to 40 feet span. When the charges were to remain for some time before being exploded, the mines were loaded with every necessary precaution, the powder placed in boxes, the hose laid in wooden troughs, and, when required to remain any time underground, the boxes and troughs were well pitched and covered with straw, tarpaulin, &c. The hose was brought to the surface of the road up the shaft, which was then stolidly and compactly filled in with the material which had been taken out, and, if thought necessary, some of the stones of the parapet were laid over the mouth of the shaft to increase the resistance. If a corps or division of the army was to pass over after it was prepared for destruction, the hose was brought within a foot of the surface of the roadway, and then carried in a groove, cut on purpose, to the side of the parapet, the groove being filled in so that the road remained clear for the passage of troops or artillery, without the chance of the hose being disturbed. Precautions were taken to drain the roadway in case of rain, in order to preserve the train from getting injured by wet. When pressed for time the barrels

were placed in the chamber or the powder was tied up in a piece of tarpaulin, or in sand bags: the hose was sometimes laid without a wooden trough, but with care that it should not be choked during the tamping. The use of electricity or of instantaneous fuze now simplifies and renders far more certain such operations.

246. When a bridge is formed of large iron girders supported on masonry piers, the most complete mode of demolition is to destroy the piers. The girders in falling will generally be so buckled as to prevent their being used again. The introduction of gun-cotton gives special facilities for the destruction of the girders themselves. *See* para. 274. Demolition of iron girder bridges, &c.

Small iron girders can sometimes be levered off their bearings, and broken by being made to fall on rails, masonry, &c.

Wrought-iron girder bridges may be destroyed by means of large fires of sleepers, &c., lighted against the girders, which, if made red hot, will sink by their own weight.

247. Suspension bridges can be destroyed by uncovering and loosening one anchorage, or by blowing up one of the supporting piers of the cable at a point some distance below the saddle; but the quickest method is to cut through the chains by gun-cotton, as was done by the German Engineers near Rouen in 1871. *See* para. 277.

248. The following table gives the charges of gunpowder to be used for the complete demolition, moderate and violent, of revetments and bridges. Those for walls are given in para. 287. Charges for deliberate demolition.

DELIBERATE DEMOLITIONS WITH GUNPOWDER.

Charge of Gunpowder, in lbs.	Object to be demolished.	Position of the Charges, Intervals, &c.	REMARKS.
$\frac{1}{10}$ L.L.R.³	Revetments without counterforts	At the back of the revetments, at two-lined intervals.	*Whenever the distance between the charges is made more or less than 2 L.L.R., the charges must be varied in the proportion $\frac{\text{Actual interval}}{2\text{ L.L.R.}^4}$. To increase the interval is often convenient and economical, as it reduces the number of shafts and galleries, but unless the masonry be exceptionally good, the interval should not exceed 2 L.L.R., or portions of the masonry may be left standing. The best positions for charges for the demolition of revetments are about 3 feet above the level of the external ground. The charges, their intervals, and L.L.R. need not all be equal. Charges of 2⅜ L.L.R.³ at two-lined intervals, demolish the intermediate parts, and shatter the counterforts without bringing them down. Charges of ⅓ L.L.R.³ at 1½-lined intervals produce violent demolition.
$\frac{1}{8}$ L.L.R.³	Revetments with counterforts	In the centre of each counterfort; greater intervals than two-lined not recommended.	Two lines of mines may be used, but one is more common. If the distance between the counterforts be unusually great in proportion to the thickness of the revetment, one or two mines should be placed between them at the back of the revetment. It is not expedient that the L.L.R. should be less than the thickness of the revetment near its base, nor much greater. The L.L.R. is measured from centre of the charge to the face of the revetment. The demolition with ⅛ L.L.R.³ will be very moderate.
$\frac{1}{5}$ L.L.R.³	Counterarched revetments	In the centre of each chamber	
$\frac{1}{10}$ L.L.R.³	Compact solid mass of masonry, with circular, polygonal, or square base.	In the centre of the mass of masonry or brickwork.	
$\frac{1}{10}$ L.L.R.³	Line of masonry or brickwork	In the centre of the wall, at two-lined intervals.	● See above.
$\frac{4}{10}$ L.L.R.³	Line of masonry founded on earth, with an equal pressure of earth on both sides.	Under the centre of the foundation, at two-lined intervals.	● See above.

SEC. 11.   DEMOLITIONS WITH GUNPOWDER.   107

Charge of Gunpowder, in lbs.	Object to be demolished.	Positions of the Charges, Intervals, &c.	REMARKS.
$\frac{1}{5}$ to $\frac{6}{10}$ L.L.R.³	Line of masonry founded on woodwork, with an equal pressure of earth on both sides.	Under the centre, at two-lined intervals.	*See above.
$\frac{1}{5}$ L.L.R.³	High bridge piers of 20 or more feet.	In the centre of the pier, as close as possible to the base, at two-lined intervals.	
$\frac{4}{10}$ L.L.R.³	High bridge pier founded on earth with an equal pressure of earth on both sides.	Under the centre of the foundation, at two-lined intervals.	
$\frac{1}{5}$ to $\frac{6}{10}$ L.L.R.³	High bridge pier founded on woodwork with an equal pressure of earth on both sides.	Under the centre of the foundation, at two-lined intervals.	A little more powder should be used if the woodwork be very strong.
$\frac{1}{5}$ L.L.R.³	Short thick bridge pier	In the centre of the pier, at two-lined intervals.	
$\frac{4}{10}$ L.L.R.³	Short thick bridge pier founded on earth, with an equal pressure of earth on both sides.	Under the centre of the foundation, at two-lined intervals.	Double the charge for a violent demolition.
$\frac{1}{5}$ to $\frac{6}{10}$ L.L.R.³	Short thick pier founded on woodwork, with an equal pressure of earth on both sides.	Under the centre of the foundation, at two-lined intervals.	
$\frac{3}{4}$ L.L.R.² × B.	Arch of bridge; B being the breadth of the bridge in feet.	Behind the haunch of the arch, the distance to the surface of the roadway being twice that to the soffit of the arch.	In this last rule (Captain Schaw's, R.E.), the charge given is the total required for the demolition of the bridge, placed either in a single mass or in a line of charges. If a single charge is used, L.L.R. should = $\frac{1}{4}$ B; if several charges, they should not be at greater distance than 2 L.L.R.

NOTE.—Attack a building by the same rules as revetments (except when bore-holes are used), laying the charges along the side and covering them with rammed earth twice the thickness of the wall; the charges will have better effect if placed inside the building. If bore-holes are used, the rules in paras. 239 and 240 should be applied. When charges of powder are just calculated to produce complete but not violent demolition it is of little importance whether they are fired simultaneously or successively; when few in numbers they may be fired in pairs.

It may be assumed in using gunpowder that the resistance of an arch is considerably greater that that of a straight wall of equal thickness (perhaps twice as great).

Tunnels.

249. Either the crown of the arch or the side walls of a tunnel may be attacked. The crown may be reached by shafts from above, if the depth of earth is not too great, or by mines driven through the masonry or brickwork from below, rough scaffolding having been erected to enable them to be commenced at suitable points.

The easiest parts to attack are the side walls, but the most serious injury would be done near the crown, especially in those cases where the tunnel is through loose material.

When a mine is driven through the brickwork one or two branches should be driven at right angles to it, so that the charges may be lodged behind the uninjured parts. A sufficient number of charges should be employed to bring down several yards in length of the tunnel, and the powder used should be largely in excess of the calculated quantity, the object being not merely to destroy the retaining wall, but to loosen and bring down as much as possible of the earth or rock above. For this reason it would be best, if time allowed, to lodge the charges at some little distance from the brickwork or masonry, and to calculate them as overcharged mines (para. 63), reckoning the resistance of the wall as equivalent to that of earth two or three times its thickness, as the brickwork is usually built more or less in an elliptical form so as to increase its strength all round. Or the charge (gunpowder) may be taken as $\frac{1}{5} T^3$ lb., where T equals total distance from charge to tunnel. If possible, the part selected for demolition should be some distance from either end of the tunnel, as it will then be more difficult to repair. Injury may also be done by blowing in ventilating shafts.

When the tunnel passes through wet soil it might be very seriously injured by blowing up the invert, and so allowing the subsoil to be pressed up through the floor. This would greatly assist the total destruction of the fabric.

Hasty Demolitions with Gunpowder.

Hasty demolition of masonry bridges.

250. When in the case of the demolition of bridges, **time will not admit** of an attack on the haunches or piers, operations must be confined to those portions where there is the least covering over the arch, viz., the vicinity of the keystone. A charge of 500 lbs. of powder placed in a trench 18 inches deep, over the keystone of a semi-circular arch of 26 feet span, 4½ feet thick, has broken it in. Over the keystone itself, as at *a* in Pl. 33, Fig. 6, is no doubt the place where the arch could be reached with the least amount of excavation, but in most cases it would be quite practicable to dig two trenches across at points *b* and *c*, by the employment of two working parties simultaneously, and by firing charges in the latter positions a greater breach would probably be effected ; for example, if a breach, *de*, were formed by a single line of charges across the bridge at *a*, a breach, *fg*, would probably result from the effect of two lines at *b* and *c*. The

charge of powder to be employed may be calculated from the rules given in para. 248.

251. Captain Schaw, R.E., deduced from the experiment made in the demolitions at Corfu, the following rule:— *Schaw's rule.*

$$C = \tfrac{3}{4}\, L.L.R.^2 \times B,$$

where C = total charge of powder in lbs. required to be placed in each trench either in a single mass or in a line of charges across the arch; L.L.R. = the line of least resistance in feet, measured through the arch; and B = the breadth in feet. The charge was placed in a shallow trench cut clean to the keystones. The excavated rubbish was heaped over the powder.

In all demolitions of this nature, it is of importance that the charges should be fired simultaneously.

Some arches have a certain amount of concrete over the haunches. To dig through this may take more time than is available. In such a case it is necessary, either to include the concrete in the thickness of the arch, or to attack the underside of the crown. If there is any concrete over the crown, this should be included in the thickness of the arch.

252. Another mode of hasty demolition seems feasible, especially when the arch is a very thin one, viz., to suspend the charge below the crown of the arch, in a trough, in such a manner as to extend completely across the bridge. (See D., Pl. 33, Fig. 3.) By this arrangement the arch would be attacked at its weakest point, and in a favourable direction, and there would be no interruption to traffic. In such an operation the same quantity of powder or gun-cotton should be used as would be required for the hasty demolition of an arch when the charge is placed above it.* *Charge under the arch.*

253. In all hasty demolitions powder must be used freely in excess of the calculated charges. Though this may produce a large expenditure as regards the single operation to be performed, it will be small as compared with the general consumption necessarily incurred during a campaign, and, further, the difference between partial failure and complete success would often be productive of serious results.

At Duenas, in 1812, on the retreat from Burgos, when the rear guard was closely pressed by the enemy, the bridge was of solid masonry from the arch to the roadway. The miners had only time to strip off some of the pavement, lodge two barrels of powder in the hole, and cover them as hastily as possible with the small quantity of materials at hand; when fired the

---

* When gunpowder is used this method is far from certain, two decided failures having occurred in bridge demolition at Chatham and at Corfu; but if gun-cotton be used *and the contact of the charge with the under side of the arch be secured* there can be but little doubt of the desired result being gained. Proper contact can be obtained rapidly only when it is possible to strut the charge from underneath. When this cannot be done, and trussing is necessary, it should be noted that this will take one or two hours at least, and is a difficult piece of work.

effect was to break down the entire breadth of the arch, making a gap of 15 feet.

In the lines of Torres Vedras a bridge was destroyed in a similar manner, by merely placing the powder on the crown of the arch, without any tamping whatever. This latter is the most precarious and dangerous method of using powder, and ought never to be resorted to except in a case of absolute necessity.

Wooden bridges.

254. Wood is extensively used in America in the construction of bridges, and during the war of 1861–1865 the Confederates had a corps regularly equipped for destroying bridges by burning. The men were mounted, and carried with them small kegs of kerosine oil, which was poured over the woodwork, and the latter then set on fire. This mode of operation was attended with considerable success, but it was not of course so instantaneous in its effects as a demolition by gunpowder or other explosives.

For destroying wooden bridges instantaneously gun-cotton should be used (*see* paras. 263, &c.), but when it is not at hand, the simplest way is to bore auger holes about 2 inches in diameter in the timber at right angles to each other, place in each a tin cylinder, the ends of which are connected with a strong bolt and nut, containing a charge of gunpowder, and fire them simultaneously. Some experiments have been tried with these at Chatham, and the results seem to show that if the bridge be not thereby actually brought down, it may be so thoroughly shaken as be too dangerous to be used.

Stockades, barriers.

255. In blowing down a stockade or barrier, the powder is placed in a tarred sand-bag or two, or a leather bag made for the purpose. (*See* para. 68.) A single untarred sand-bag should on no account be used, as any fire dropping on it from the fuze is liable to cause an explosion. Against a gate or barrier, the best place for the charge is opposite the lock, bolts, or hinges, where it should be either secured by a prop, or suspended from a nail or gimlet. Against a stockade, the gunpowder should be laid on the ground at the foot, and the effect of the explosion will be much increased if the bag containing the powder be surrounded with five filled sand-bags, as shown at B, Pl. 34, Fig. 5. The powder-bag being laid on the ground with the fuze outwards, a sand-bag is placed on the top, one at each side, and two in front, so as to allow the fuze to project between them. A charge of 40 lbs. covered with sand-bags, or 60 lbs. uncovered, will make a breach 6 feet wide through a stockade formed of timbers 10 inches thick.

Fortress gate.

256. When a fort gate has to be breached, it would be unsafe to depend on a smaller charge than 200 lbs. of powder covered with sand-bags, as in all probability the gates would be strengthened by cross-bars and struts.

Placing powder-bags.

257. The placing of powder-bags is a critical operation, and it is therefore desirable as a security against failure from casualties, to attempt to place them at several points of the enclosure

attacked. The bags containing powder should be clearly distinguished from the tamping bags by material or colour so as to prevent mistakes in placing the charge. If the same kind of bags is used for both, those containing powder should be conspicuously marked by paint or otherwise.

There should be several spare men in the assaulting party to take up stores dropped by wounded men. Every man of the party should carry means of firing the charge and know how to apply them. Assaulting party.

258. The siege manœuvres of 1907 at Chatham gave some data of the destruction of a concrete counterscarp wall. Counterscarp revetment.

Five charges were fired with the object of destroying the counterscarp wall and so filling up the ditch as to render an assault practicable. The charges were at 20 feet intervals placed 18 feet below the surface and 10 feet from the counterscarp wall. The wall was of concrete 1 foot thick, the soil hard chalk. The counterscarp wall was breached for a length of 110 feet and a practical approach formed to the parapet by means of the débris hurled into the ditch. The charges used were, five each of 225 lbs. gunpowder.

259. The following table gives the charges of gunpowder to be employed for the hasty demolition of bridges, bomb-proofs, stockades, &c. :— Charges for hasty demolition.

Hasty Demolitions with Gunpowder.

Charge of gunpowder, in lbs.	Object to be demolished.	Position of the charges, intervals, &c.	Remarks.
$\frac{5}{9}$ L.L.L.² × B.	Arch of bridge; B being the breadth of the bridge.	In a trench over the crown of the arch, and cut down to the key-stone.	This is the total charge. The gap made in the arch would be greater if two trenches were made across the arch, and each trench loaded with the charge here given.
3 L.L.R.³	Arch of bridge	In a trench over the crown of the arch.	This is the amount for each charge, the charges being placed at two-lined intervals.
2½ to 3 L.L.R.³	Wall	Against the wall at two-lined intervals.	These modes are precarious. If time permits, the arch or wall should be cut into, and the charges covered with stones or rubbish. The gap made would be greater if two trenches were cut, and each treated similarly. In demolition of walls the gap to be made should be not less than the height of the wall, to ensure complete demolition.
$\frac{1}{6}$ L.L.R.³	Square bomb-proof casemates	In the centre of the building	An increase of charge of from one-half to one-third may make the difference between the partial injury and complete demolition, or between moderate and violent demolition.
$\frac{1}{4}$ L.L.R.³	Bomb-proof casemates of two squares.	In the centre of each square	If a range of casemates, attack that at the end, and then every alternate casemate.
$\frac{1}{3}$ L.L.R.³	Bomb-proof casemates of three squares.	In the centre of each square	All the openings should be blocked up; if the case-mates be open to the rear, more powder must be used.
1 barrel (100 lbs.)	Galleries or countermines	In the centre of the gallery at 10-feet intervals.	Both ends of the gallery should be tamped. These charges would probably convert a gallery 15 feet total depth below the surface into an open trench.
40 to 100 lbs.	Barrier-gate or stockade	Against the centre of the gate or stockade, or on the ground at the foot.	The charges should be placed in sand-bags or leather powder bags. The effect is much increased if five sand-bags filled with earth be placed round the charge. 40 lbs. of powder thus tamped will have about the same effect as 60 lbs. untamped.
200 lbs.	Fort gate	On the ground, covered with sand-bags.	

* These L.L.L.B. are measured from the centre of the powder on the floor to the nearest external surface of the building.

Section 12.—DEMOLITIONS WITH GUN-COTTON.

260. In arranging charges it must be remembered that the service slabs weigh 15oz. They can of course be sawn into pieces, but the process is somewhat tedious. As a general rule these slabs should be used whole. Making up and placing charge.

The charge, as calculated in the following paragraphs, may be made up in one mass and placed against the object to be demolished, or, in the case of a single round timber of small size, it may be hung round it in the form of a necklace. In the former case it is essential that it should extend across the whole breadth of timber to be cut. In both cases all portions of the charge must be in close contact with one another and with the timber. The concentrated charge gives the most certain result, but the necklace gives the cleaner cut. A necklace is, however, liable to failure through imperfect detonation on account of the difficulty of securing perfect contact between the discs. There is also often some difficulty in securing close contact with the timber.

See paras. 204 to 208 for the way to prepare the charge for firing. Preparing charge for firing.

261. The necklace may be made and fixed by threading discs on a string or wire and driving a few nails into the timber on which it may rest. The two ends of the string are then tied tightly together and the detonator inserted in the last disc. To avoid the risk of premature ignition by sparks from, or contact with, the fuze, it is advisable to cover the necklace with fresh grass, &c. Necklace, fixing of.

262. When the charge is of slabs against one side of the timber a good method is to cut a piece of board of the length of breach to be made, bore a hole in it with a 2-inch auger, tie the slabs on to one side, put a primer in the hole in close contact with one of the slabs, and place the slabs against the timber. The board reduces the risk of premature ignition by sparks and also enables the charge to be carried and placed conveniently. Further security against sparks may be given by scattering earth or fresh grass along the top of the charge. A few sharp pointed pickets should be driven in at the back of the board to keep it in position, or, if convenient, it may be fixed by nails. Concentrated charge, fixing of.

263. For demolition of hard-wood trees, or timbers, without boring into them, the charge $= 3 \, BT^{2*}$ where B is breadth and T is thickness, in feet, of the timber to be cut through. Demolition of timber.

---

* This formula has been arrived at as the result of numerous experiments against very hard teak timbers. In many cases a smaller quantity would be sufficient and $\frac{5}{2} BT^2$ might be used where a risk of partial failure might be incurred without imprudence.

For soft wood (larch, fir, &c.) the charge is $\frac{3}{8}$ BT^2.

Rectangular timbers.

264. With rectangular timbers the charge should be placed against the longer side of the timber (which is B) so as to have the least thickness to cut through. Thus for a hard wood timber $18'' \times 12''$ the charge $= \frac{3}{4} \times 1\frac{1}{2} \times (1)^2 = 4\frac{1}{2}$ lbs.

Pl. 37, Figs. 2 and 3 show methods of placing charges to cut wooden piles under water.

Fig. 2 shows the charge bound to a pole or spar which is jambed up against the pile at the place to be cut.

Fig. 3 shows the charge fastened to a loose iron ring which is allowed to slide down the pile. The explosive on the up stream side where there is any stream.

Timber stockades.

265. Against timber stockades the formula is practically applicable whether there is a banquette or not, but as it would usually be impossible to know the exact strength of the stockade, and as failure might be disastrous, the calculation should be made for the greatest thickness of timber believed to exist; and a liberal allowance (say 50 per cent.) should be made to allow for the chance of extra resistance being given by struts, &c., and also in case of good contact between the charge and timber not being obtainable on account of the timbers being round or of varying sizes. B will of course be the length of breach required.* The gun-cotton for demolishing a stockade for convenience in carrying may be sewn on to a plank with string or spun yarn as shown in Pl. 34, Figs. 1 and 2, the gun-cotton being placed next the stockade.

Earth and plank or sleeper stockades.

Stockades or breastworks of earth 2 to 3 feet thick rammed between planks or railway sleepers on edge may be demolished by 4 lbs. per foot run, but sufficient débris often remains to give cover to men lying or kneeling behind the breach.

Rail stockades.

Stockades of heavy rails touching each other require 7 lbs. per foot run of breach.

Palisades.

266. The charge for palisading is calculated by the general rule given in para. 263, B being the breadth of breach to be effected, and T the thickness of the palisades. If time admits, the space between the charge and the sides of the palisades should be packed with sods, &c., to secure more perfect contact. The charge is somewhat excessive, but the spaces between the palisades cause waste of power.

Charges in auger holes.

267. The most economical method for the destruction of trees, or single timbers, is to place the charge in an auger hole. Primers alone should be used, *and they must all be dry.* The charge required is $\frac{2}{3}$ T^2; T being the thickness of timber in feet. If the timber is not perfectly symmetrical T is the smaller axis. The hole is bored perpendicularly into the timber with a $1\frac{1}{2}$-inch auger. It should be of such a length that the centre of the

---

* *See* para. 257 as to assaulting party.

charge is in the centre of the timber. If the length of the charge is not greater than the diameter of the timber a single hole should be used, bored right through the timber if necessary. If the length is greater, two or three holes may be used (Pl. 37, Fig. 1), meeting in the centre, or two holes bored parallel almost touching (Pl. 37, Fig 5).

268. The amount of gun-cotton required for destroying brickwork or masonry of any kind will be very greatly affected by the manner in which the charge is placed. — Brickwork or masonry.

In dealing with revetments, much will depend on the disposition of the counterforts, if any, and the quality of the cement or mortar and brick or stone. — Revetments.

The most economical method of using gun-cotton is to place it in a continuous charge along the whole length of the back of the breach to be made, and in a groove cut to receive it. The groove should be continued into the sides of the counterforts as shown in Pl. 35, Fig. 2. This procedure needs time for driving the gallery and cutting the groove, but with a revetment without counterforts it should be used, when time permits, to ensure a good effect. With hard masonry the groove would not be feasible. In using a continuous charge in this manner behind a wall, the quantity may be determined by the formula $C = \frac{1}{4} BT^2$, where C = the charge in lbs., B = length in feet of the breach to be made, and T is the thickness of the wall in feet. — Continuous charges.

Where there are counterforts, the best method of disposing the charge will depend upon their position and dimensions, and the Engineer officer will have to use his judgment. If the counterforts are deep, it will probably be necessary to place charges behind them, as in Pl. 35, Fig. 1; and in this case it *may* not be necessary to place additional charges behind the wall between the counterforts. The charges behind the counterforts should then be placed and calculated for in the same manner as gunpowder (*vide* Sec. XI); remembering that, as in this instance the gunpowder would be acting under the most advantageous circumstances, as compared with gun-cotton, less than the full superiority of gun-cotton should be allowed for. — Counterforts.

269. The weight of gun-cotton to be used as compared with the weight of gunpowder, must depend on the circumstances of each case. Probably half would suffice, but there are no actual data available.

270. For demolition of gates, 50 lbs. of gun-cotton made up and placed against the gate will suffice to blow in a gate however strong. — Gates.

271. To cut iron plates the charge must extend along the whole breadth of the material to be cut (but *see* para. 274 for demolition of girders). — Iron plates. Position of charge.

For wrought-iron, charge in lbs. = $\frac{3}{5} Bt^2$ ... ...
For cast-iron, charge in lbs. = $\frac{3}{4} Bt^2$ ... ...
B = breadth to be cut in feet, t = thickness in inches. — Amount of charge.

Thin plates.

Laminated plates should be treated as solid. In the case of very thin plates, it will sometimes be found that the charge as given by the above formula will not be sufficient to allow of *whole slabs to be placed across the distance to be cut, "B." It is essential that the charge should extend across the whole distance B, and to enable this to be done the slabs can be halved,* but this should not be done unless economy in explosives must be studied. It is better to use whole slabs and increase the charge.

When divided slabs are used great care must be taken that the contact between each piece is good.

Iron girder bridges.

272. The quickest and most economical way of destroying girder bridges with gun-cotton, is to cut the girders themselves.

Main girders.

All girder bridges have at least two main girders crossing the span, which carry the cross girders and roadway. The main girders alone need be attacked.

The part of space to be cut. Continuous girders.

Where there is a continuous girder across several spans, the shore spans should be cut near a pier at XX (Pl. 36, Fig. 1). If the spans are large it will usually be sufficient to cut one span.

Separate girders.

Where the girders are not continuous right across the bridge, at least one span should be completely destroyed, preferably the longest. To destroy one span the girder should be cut—

(a) near one point of support, if the girder is of uniform section throughout, as is usually the case with small bridges, when the girders consist of R.I. beams (XX, Pl. 36, Fig. 2).

(b) at a point just before the first thickening plate on the flanges, when the girder is not of uniform section throughout, as is always the case with large bridges. This reduces the amount of explosive used, as "t" is less here than it is at the centre (XX, Pl. 36, Fig. 3).

Method of cutting girders.

273. There are so many different forms of girders in use, that it is impossible to lay down rules for their destruction which shall be applicable to all. The engineer must be prepared to use his own judgment. (*See* paragraph 280A.)

All girders are made up of a top and bottom "*flange*" or "boom," connected by a "web," the web consisting of continuous plates or of open cross bracing of varying design.

In demolishing girders there will always be the difficulty of obtaining proper contact between the charge and the metal owing to the almost invariable presence of rivet heads. The best method of meeting this difficulty is to fill up the spaces between the rivet heads with clay and include the depth of this layer in the thickness to be cut.

---

* This refers to the obsolescent slabs (para. 194). The present service slab should, as a rule, be used whole.

One of the forms of girder most frequently met with is the plate girder. Except in the case of rolled steel girders, the flanges usually consist of a number of plates rivetted together. They are joined to the web by means of angle irons. These increase the strength considerably. The web itself is usually a single plate.

274. A series of experiments with built up plate girders of this type have recently been carried out at Chatham. Their object was :—

(a). To determine the charge required for complete demolition.

(b). To ascertain the best position and method of placing that charge.

(a). As regards the former, it was found that the flanges should be considered as steel plates of a width as measured, and of a thickness as obtained by a measurement of the flange where it joins the web, plus the height of one rivet head; the above would include the thickness of the angle iron when used. The web, again assuming angle irons to be present, was treated as consisting of three separate portions ; the reinforced portion at the top (plate and angle irons), a central portion, and the reinforced portion at the bottom.

The thicknesses of the top and bottom portions were obtained for calculation purposes by adding to the thickness of the single plate, forming the main web, the maximum thicknesses of the two reinforcing angle irons, together with the height of one rivet head. The breadth was taken, as measured, from the angle of the angle iron to the bottom edge of the same.

The central, unreinforced portion, was considered as a single plate, the breadth being the distance between the bottom edge of the top angle iron and the top edge of the bottom angle iron.

Charges for the above series of steel plates were then calculated by the usual formula, their sum giving the total amount of explosives required for the demolition.

(b). After exhaustive experiments the following was found to be the most satisfactory method of placing the charge. When the top flange and angle irons are of equal section with the bottom flange and angle irons, the total amount of explosive, as calculated, should be divided into two equal parts and placed in the diagonally opposite angles of the girder formed by the junction of the web with the top and bottom flanges. The spaces between the rivet heads should be packed with clay, in order to provide a uniform surface for the charge to rest on. It must be kept in position by strutting it against the opposite flange. The two charges must be fired simultaneously. Pl. 38, illustrates the above.

When the top and bottom members of the girder differ in section, the charge should be divided up in the amounts as found by calculation for top and bottom, the charge for the central portion of the web being halved between them.

Pl. 39 shows the construction of various girders in use and likely to be met with.

275. Open web girders differ greatly in their structure. It is therefore impossible to give a general statement which shall include all cases. They may be demolished in the manner above described for plate girders, or it may be necessary to attack the web as well as the flanges. Pl. 36, Figs. 4, &c., gives several examples of open web girders showing where the charges (C.C.) may be placed.

In all girders the lower or tension flange is the most important part, and the web the least.

To ensure complete demolition of a girder, it should be cut through both flanges and the web.

It is true that the flanges are the essential parts of the girder, and if they are cut, it is impossible that the girder should carry the loads for which it was originally designed. At the same time, there is always a large factor of safety in such structures, and it is possible that the web might keep the girder from collapsing. In such a case the enemy might be able to repair the girder with less trouble than replacing it would cause; or it might be of use to him even in its weakened state for the passage of light loads.

Cutting the web alone is not an efficient means of demolition. To be effective it would have to be done throughout several adjacent panels, and this would probably cost as much explosive and be more troublesome than cutting the flanges. Here, again, however, it is impossible to lay down a general rule. When the panels are wide, and the struts and ties few and large, it may be better to attack them. Again, some bridges, owing to faulty construction, have not a large factor of safety, and might not be proof against any attack on the web.

Cast-iron arches. 276. Cast-iron arches should be cut in two places on the slant as shown in Pl. 36, Fig. 8, to allow of a piece falling right out without jamming. As the web is usually comparatively very thick in cast-iron arch girders, it should be cut as well as the flanges.

Suspension bridges. 277. The cables of suspension bridges should be cut. Each cable should be cut in one place at least, if possible in two places. The best place for the charge is near the centre of the span as at A Pl. 37, Fig. 4.

In the case of large permanent suspension bridges the cables will probably be made up of links, and they also should be cut in the centre, where they are thinnest.

Such cables can be cut by the ordinary rules for cutting iron: with wire cables, care must be taken to get contact between the charge and the cable.

SEC. 12. DEMOLITIONS WITH GUN-COTTON.

Complete destruction of the wire cable of a suspension bridge is difficult. By experiment the best method is to cut the charge in half and place it as shown in Pl. 37, Fig. 6. For a 6″ cable 1½ lb. of gun-cotton is sufficient. The formula $\frac{C^2}{24}$ appears reliable. C = circumference in inches.

278. For demolition of detached brick walls over 2 feet thick the charge in pounds = $\frac{1}{2}BT^2$ if untamped, or $\frac{1}{4}BT^2$ if tamped, where B is length in feet of the breach to be made, and T is the thickness of wall in feet. The charge is lodged at the foot of the wall in close contact. — Detached walls.

If the wall is less than 2 feet thick, a charge calculated by the above formula will only cut a hole, and if it is necessary to effect a practicable breach the charge should be 2 lbs. per foot run of breach.

In all cases the length of breach (and therefore the length of charge) should be at least equal to the height of wall which it is necessary to being down in order to effect the required demolition.

279. Demolition of brick piers of bridges: Charge in lbs. = $\frac{3}{4}BT^2$, placed against the pier in close contact, the slabs to be in a continuous line along the whole length to be breached. B is the breadth, and T the thickness of pier, in feet. — Piers of bridges.

When arches are attacked, either at the crown or haunches, each charge in lbs. = $\frac{3}{4}BT^2$ if untamped, or $\frac{3}{8}BT^2$ if tamped. B is the breadth, and T the thickness of arch, in feet.* — Arches.

280. For field and siege guns it will suffice to detonate two slabs on the chase (outside) near the muzzle. Tamping is not necessary, but it increases the damage. — Destroying guns.

Heavy wrought-iron guns can be rendered totally unserviceable by placing a 4-lb. charge at the bottom of the bore and tamping it by filling up the bore with water or sand.

Heavy cast-iron guns can be burst by detonating 1 lb. gun-cotton in the bore tamped with sand or water.

For B.L. guns the following procedure should be followed.

(1.) A shell having been loaded in the ordinary way, the gun-cotton charge necessary for the destruction of the gun should be packed in behind it so as to be in close contact with the shell and with the sides of the chamber. After the insertion of the primer, sods, earth, paper, or other material that may be at hand should be used to keep the gun-cotton in position. — Field and siege guns.

(2.) The breech block should then be swung to as far as possible, just allowing room for the safety fuze or electric leads for igniting the charge.

(3.) The charges required for guns from 3-inch to 6-inch calibre are given by the following rule :—

"For a 3-inch gun use 2 lbs., and double the charge for every inch increase in calibre, e.g., for a 4-inch gun use 4 lbs., and for a 5-inch, 8 lbs."

---

* *See* para. 251 as to concrete filling above haunches of arches.

Two slabs of gun-cotton placed on the chase near the muzzle should also be used in concurrence with the above.

280A. In carrying out the destruction of metallic substances (guns, girders, rails, &c.), it should be remembered that fragments are liable to be blown 1,000 yards away from the spot where the demolition is being carried out.

Buildings. 281. The demolition of small farm-houses and cottages can be best effected by means of charges placed in the interior of the building. The charges should be tied to boards and placed in the angles of walls. For a small brick cottage a charge of 10 lbs. per room on the ground floor would be generally sufficient, for larger buildings or cottages of stone, a charge of 20 lbs. per room on the ground floor will generally be effective. If all openings, *i.e.* doors, windows and chimneys, can be closed, the effects of the explosion will be greatly increased.

These charges may prove excessive in the case of buildings built with sun-dried bricks and mud mortar. The experience gained during the South African War shows that with the badly built small farm-houses which there abound, a charge of about 4 lbs. per room was sufficient, provided that the closing of all openings was possible.

Towers of stone and mud. 282. Towers such as those in the North West frontier of India, may be hollow or with a solid base up to a height of about 15 feet. The walls are usually 3 to 4 feet thick. The towers are either circular or square in plan. For deliberate demolition (a) in the case of a hollow tower, a hole should be dug 2 or 3 feet deep in the centre of the floor for the charge. The latter should be well tamped. (b) in the case of a solid base tower, a hole should be made for at least 5 feet into the base from the outside. In certain cases there are layers of brushwood in the structure of the tower. Where these exist, the hole should be made under one of them. The charge should placed at the end of the hole and be well tamped.

For hasty demolition, all towers should be treated as if they were hollow and the charge placed inside.

The charges of gun-cotton required for deliberate demolition may be obtained by measuring the diameter or one side of the base in feet, adding 4 feet and allowing one pound for every foot in the total.

For rapid demolition a pound or two extra should be added to the charge as calculated above.

Mud huts. 283. At Metemmeh, on the Nile, in 1885, stongly built mud huts (of Nile clay, lime and chopped straw) consisting of one room, 15 feet to 18 feet square, with walls about 2 feet thick at bottom, were destroyed. It was found that a 2-lb. slab laid against the foot of the wall on the outside merely blew a hole through the wall without cracking or shaking it much; but less than double that charge placed inside the hut at a corner, well away from the door and other openings, brought the whole hut down in such small pieces as to be easily removed.

284. The following notes on the use of gun-cotton have been abstracted from a report of the Thibet Expedition, 1903-04 :— Thibet.

Deliberate demolition :—

A breach had to be made in the outer wall of Naini Monastery. Wall 35 feet high, 9 feet thick at base, 7 feet thick at top, built in very good clay.

Two 15lb. charges were placed, 10 feet apart in holes 4 feet deep and 3 feet up from base. The charges were carefully tamped.

Result :—A breach in wall 20 feet long.

Hasty demolition during attack :—

(I). At the storming of Palla, the wall was breached with a 45lb. charge of gun-cotton carried ready made up in a box. Wall 15 feet high, 3½ feet thick at base. Stones built in mud. Charge placed as close to the wall as possible and untamped.

Result :—Breach 8 ft.—10 ft. wide.

(II). The court-yard gate of Szechen Monastery. The gate was 8 feet square, of 3″ planks with gate posts 12″ square. It was backed inside with a heap of stones 3 feet high. A charge of 14 lbs. of gun-cotton, untamped, was exploded in the angle formed by the gatepost and gate. The whole was completely wrecked. Probably 12 lbs. would have been sufficient.

(III). For interior doors, a charge of 4 lbs. of gun-cotton untamped, and placed in the angle between the door and frame was sufficient to blow them in.

If the enemy are known to be inside, a charge of 8 lbs. may be used with advantage, as such a charge will stun the occupants; it has the disadvantage however of wrecking the house considerably.

285. The siege manœuvres of 1907 give some data of the effect of tonite on concrete walls. Four mine galleries had reached the counterscarp wall. Three galleries struck the wall at the counterscarp gallery, and the fourth the wall of the ditch. Siege manœuvres.

The following table gives the results :—

Charge.	L.L.R.	Nature of Soil.	Remarks.
30 lbs.	3ft. 6ins.	2ft. Concrete, 1ft. 6ins. Chalk.	Entrance to counterscarp gallery gained. Took about 1 hour to clear debris. Countermines of defence uninjured.
20 lbs.	2ft. 0ins.	Concrete.	
30 lbs.	2ft. 0ins.	Concrete.	
3 of 20 lbs. 1 of 30 lbs.		2ft. 0ins. Concrete.	Daylight visible from gallery, and passage to ditch cleared in a few minutes.

Thatched buildings.

286. Thatch and other inflammable materials may easily be fired by placing one or two dry discs of gun-cotton among them and igniting (not detonating) the discs. The fierce flame produced will at once set them on fire. A piece of paper (wrapped round the dry disc and lighted) will ignite it.

287. The following table gives a summary of the usual rules for calculating charges for hasty demolitions:—

Charges for Hasty Demolitions.

NOTE.—The charge is in lbs. B = length to be demolished in FEET.
T = thickness to be demolished in FEET.
t = thickness to be demolished in INCHES.
(in the case of iron plate only).
In the presence of the enemy increase the charges by 50 per cent.

GUN-COTTON (UNTAMPED).

Object attacked.	lbs.	Remarks.
Brick arch—haunch or crown	$\frac{1}{2}BT^2$	Continuous charges; the length of breach B not to be less than the height of the wall to be brought down.
Brick wall—up to 2 feet thick	2 per foot	
Brick wall—over 2 feet thick	$\frac{1}{2}BT^2$	
Brick pier	$\frac{2}{3}BT^2$	
Hard wood—stockade or single	$3BT^2$	In a single charge outside. For a round timber, charge = $3T^2$. ⎫
Hard wood—necklace	$3BT^2$	Trees up to 12 inches diameter. For a round timber, charge = $3T^2$. ⎬ Soft wood half this.
Hard wood—auger hole	$\frac{1}{2}T^2$	Where the timber is not round, T = smaller axis. ⎭
Stockade of earth between timber up to 3 feet 6 inches thick	4 per foot	⎫ Single charge.
Heavy rail stockade	7 per foot	⎬
Fort gate	50	⎭
Field or siege gun	$1\frac{1}{2}$	On chase near muzzle.
Heavier gun	4	At bottom of bore; water or sand tamping.
First class rail	$\frac{1}{2}$	Against the web near a chair.
Iron or steel plate	$\frac{1}{5}Bt^2$	t is in INCHES.
Wire cable	$\frac{C^2}{24}$	C being the circumference in inches.

GUNPOWDER (Tamped).

Object attacked.	lbs.	Remarks.
Brick arch—one haunch	$\frac{1}{8}BT^2$	Total amount divided into charges placed apart about twice the thickness of brickwork.
Brick arch—crown	$\frac{1}{4}BT^2$	
Brick wall	$\frac{1}{4}BT^2$	
Wood stockade—hard wood	40 to 100	One charge. Soft wood half this.
Stockade of earth between timber up to 3 feet 6 inches thick	60 to 80 per 5 feet	One charge.
Fort gate	200	One charge.
Tunnel	$\frac{3}{4}T^3$	T = total distance from surface of lining to charge.

Demolitions by other high explosives.

288. Other high explosives, such as dynamite and blasting gelatine, may be used (subject to the precautions mentioned in Sec. 10) in place of gun-cotton. The charges may be calculated with sufficient accuracy by the rules given for gun-cotton, although dynamite is rather less, and blasting gelatine decidedly more, powerful than gun-cotton. When the charge is to be placed in bore-holes a plastic explosive is most suitable, but otherwise gun-cotton is preferable for military work.

Section 13.—DEMOLITION OF RAILWAYS.

General principles.

289. Operations under this head are never to be carried out except upon definite instructions from the highest authority. It is to be borne in mind that railway works and equipment are costly, and take long to replace, and the possibility that they may be required after a longer or shorter interval by ourselves is one which must regulate the extent of the demolitions. When the possibility of reoccupation is so remote that time would practically be available to the enemy to construct the railway entirely anew, the demolition must be the most complete possible in the time available. Hence the demolitions fall into the following classes :—

1. Operations to deny to the enemy the use of the line between specified points for a specified time.
2. Deliberate operations for the entire destruction of the railway, its works, track, and equipment.
3. Hasty operations to effect maximum damage in the time available.

It follows that for 1 and 3, knowledge is necessary of the time requisite to the enemy to make good the damage to specific details. Hence when possible all demolition works should be preceded by a reconnaissance, not only of the section of railway to be attacked, but also of the adjacent lines from which material for repair may be procurable.

290. When effecting the hasty demolition of a railway, damage may be done to it in all or any of the following ways :—

Points and crossings, closers and special rails, blown up.

Breaking chairs by sledge hammers.

Destroying every rail for as many miles as time and quantity of explosive permits.

Explosion in water tanks or rivets in same knocked off with sledge hammer and leakage caused.

Leakages in water mains and water directed in the channel which will cause most damage.

Explosions in boilers of steam pumps, removal of portions of pumping machinery.

Breaking or removing telegraph, telephone or electric block instruments and all cells of electric batteries.

Breaking one telegraph pole, fixing rope to same and pulling with many men at right angles to line, cutting of wires and breaking of poles.

If only one wire exists remove altogether about 100 feet of it.

Putting on faults by connecting with wire telegraph line with the pole or bracket (if iron), or with the earth if the pole is wood.

Destruction of wood bridges by fire.

Breaking by explosive the girders of a bridge.

Destruction by explosive of piers or trestles of bridges.

291. **Blocking of tunnels.** If these run through material which necessitates the tunnel being well lined with brick or stone, this lining should be extensively attacked with explosive, so that the enemy will not only have to remove the debris which falls in but have to renew the lining. If the tunnels run through hard rock requiring little or no lining, then explosions in the tunnel, bringing down a certain amount of rock, will not cause much delay. In such a case the best plan is to arrange a collision in the tunnel between two trains loaded with heavy material, and, after the collision, to attack the axles of the locomotives and rolling-stock with explosive. The removal of this wreckage within the cramped space of a tunnel is then a difficult and lengthy proceeding.

292. Damage to engines or dynamos of locomotive workshops and to machinery within them.

Damage to locomotives by blowing in the fire-box. Removal of parts, such as connecting rods.

Burning trucks and coaches.

Burning buildings.

Derailing locomotives and rolling stock at important places, such as entrances to stations, in narrow cuttings, &c., or running them down an embankment or into a river, by removing a pair of fishplates, and slewing the track sideways.

293. In carrying out demolitions the principle to be observed is that it is far better to destroy all the available material of one description including spares, than to destroy something of everything. This principle applies to attacking the same part of similar objects, thus preventing, for example, a lesser number of girders, engines or trucks, from being made up from the dismantled parts of damaged ones.

If the quantity of explosive is limited it is best to attack any locomotives that may be found in a station. Next in order of importance is the water supply, as a damaged water supply may cause engines to burn their boilers out or, at any rate, put them out of action for some time by dropping their fusible plugs or causing them to draw their fires. It also dislocates traffic and causes blocks. *Damage to locomotives. Damage to water supply.*

With limited explosive, points and crossings should be attacked rather than the main line. The demolition which delays an enemy most (if time and explosive is available) is the destruction of several miles of rails by small explosions. *Damage to points and crossings.*

The removal of the damaged rails and top ballast and replacement by new rails is not likely to be carried out faster than at a mile a day, while the necessity of allotting rail transport, for bringing up a considerable quantity of rails when rolling-stock is probably fully requisitioned, will cause considerable inconvenience *Damage to main line.*

In attacking bridges the girders are the most important part. Piers can be improvised, but girders cannot. If the enemy has not got girders of the same length to replace the damaged ones, he is obliged to shorten the spans by making more piers, which, *Damage to bridges.*

in a deep stream, is a difficult matter, and, in any case, a work of some magnitude. Although the dropping of the span by breaking each main girder in the middle will cause delay the girder can be easily repaired, so that if explosive and time are available it should be attacked in several places, especially at the ends.

Damage to rolling-stock. Rolling-stock is usually scarce in time of war and difficult to replace quickly, consequently no opportunity should be lost of burning trucks, or damaging them by throwing them down embankments, subject to the proviso contained in para. 2.

Damage to buildings. Damage to buildings and platforms causes the enemy only minor inconvenience.

Permanent way without explosives 294. The first and simplest method when explosives are not used, is to remove portions of the line at intervals, specially curves, switches, &c., and carry them away.

The enemy will find considerable difficulty in fitting in rails of the right length in the demolished portions; but if this method is adopted on a double line, at least one line of rails must be entirely removed, and the other partially so, otherwise an adversary might renounce the advantages of a double line for a time, and employ the material from one line of way to complete the partially destroyed one. Very rapid destruction to a line laid with double-headed rails in cast-iron chairs can be effected by knocking out the oak keys and breaking off the *outer* lip of the chair with the side blow of a sledge hammer. Experiment with first-class permanent way shows that four men can destroy nearly one mile per hour in this way. The fish bolt should be left untouched, as all the nuts will have to be unscrewed or knocked off before the rails can be separated and fitted into new chairs.

A second method, used where many men are available, and where the time is short, and the plant not required elsewhere, is to attack the line at several points at once, tear up the permanent way and render it useless on the spot. A system used with great success in the American war of 1864, is to unfish at each end of a long length of line, and leave all the intermediate fastenings intact, and to lift the whole track on one side and turn it bodily over, down an embankment if possible.

The longer the length the harder to replace without complete separation of the parts. English experiments show two men per yard ample for the heaviest permanent way, of whom one man per two yards should work a crowbar or lever to aid the lift. There is *no need to remove the ballast.* Another American method was to divide the destroying party into squads of 10 men each, and to equip each with two U-shaped irons (Pl. 31, Fig. 2), two axes, and two ropes, each 6 yards long. On arrival at the place for work, each squad provides itself with two levers, B, and two wedges, C. The irons were then fixed as shown in Fig. 2. By bearing down first on one lever then on the other a few times, the rail is twisted, one end only having been previously disconnected. Twelve rails were told to each squad, and each rail required five minutes' work, so that in one hour the men destroyed 12 lengths of rail.

A third method, known as demolition with simultaneous transport, is used where men are scarce, but the time is long. This is by far the best method of the three, but it is necessarily a slow operation, especially on the single line, where the trucks can only be loaded at the head of the line in process of demolition.

295. The most rapid method of injuring the permanent way is by the use of explosives. The rails should be cut in the middle as they will then be the least satisfactory to relay, and the repairing party will probably have to remove the fishplates before they can handle the rails for cutting. (See paragraph 280A.) The most effective obstruction will be on the outer rail of a curve if possible on a high bank or bridge.

The modern hard steel rail is more easily broken than the old mild steel or iron rail.

A "bull-nosed" rail (Pl. 34, Fig. 7) is more easily destroyed than a "Vignoles" or flat bottomed rail of the same weight per yard.

For destroying a heavy bull-nosed rail such as may be found on any first-class railway, and 60lb. Vignoles, *i.e.*, flat-bottomed rails as used on many colonial railways, a charge of 6 ozs. of gun-cotton is sufficient. For heavier Vignoles rails, a charge of 12 ozs. should be used. When time permits the charge should be trimmed to rest close against the web of the rail as shown in Pl. 34, Fig. 6. The charge should be pressed into close contact with the web of the rail, on the same side as the wooden key in rails fixed with chairs and close to the chair. If time is short the untrimmed charge should be placed resting on the bottom flange close to the web and leaning against the top flange. The amounts given above are suitable for untrimmed charges. Dynamite and blasting gelatine are very suitable for this class of demolition owing to the ease with which the charge can be fitted to the shape of the rail.

A great length of railway may be destroyed at a very rapid rate by making use of trollies loaded with slabs of gun-cotton, prepared lengths of safety fuze inserted into detonators, and provided with a quick-match priming at the other end, port-fires and slips of lead or copper wire for binding the slab against the rail.

A party of eight men can be employed, of whom two push the trolly; two sit on the trolly, fix the detonators into the slabs, prepare binding slips, and hand out the prepared charges to two men, who place them against the rail. The remaining two men follow at 400 yards distance with port-fires, and fire the charges as they pass.

In this way, with a little preliminary drill, the rails can be destroyed as fast as the trolly can be pushed by the two men, that is to say, at almost four miles per hour.

If only gunpowder be available, the charge should be placed below the rail under a sleeper next to a rail joint. The fishplates should be removed. A charge of at least 20 lbs. should be used, and even then the damage is not likely to be very great.

Removal of permanent way with simultaneous transport.

296. Several important series of experiments have been carried out in Austria and England to determine the quickest method of bodily removing the actual permanent way, for stacking or re-use elsewhere.

The English experiments carried out on the Cromford and High Peak Railway (L.N.W. Railway) under the superintendence of Mr. H. Footner, M.I.C.E., permanent way engineer, in 1894 (about 10 miles of railway being removed) being the more recent, the conclusions derived from them are given in detail. The English permanent way consisted or 72 lb. double-headed rails 21, 24, and 30 feet long, laid in cast-iron chairs weighing about 40 lbs. each. A single sleeper with two chairs affixed, weighed 160 lbs. The conclusions are practically independent of the length and weight of plant within the usual standard limits.

Train arrangements.

297. The work has usually to be done from one point only, towards which empty trains must be backed from the nearest cross-over road or siding. Speed of trains, whether backing empty or going away loaded, should not exceed 15 miles per hour between the nearest turn-out and the rail-head. Any mishap here would delay the work very greatly. Should a cross-over road on a double line, or a siding on a single line, not exist within five miles of rail head, one should be temporarily laid. A gang of 50 men can lay 100 yards of temporary siding and connections in one hour. This will accommodate a train of 12 wagons, with one brake van next the engine to carry tools, &c. This train will carry about 250 yards of single line, and is found to be the most convenient length. A goods wagon (English type) will carry 40 chaired sleepers or 6 tons of rails. The train should be in charge of a reliable guard, accustomed to permanent way work.

Double line—removing one line only.

298. This line should be prepared in advance by four men with sledge hammers, knocking off three out of four fish-bolts at each joint, and removing all keys except three per rail, viz., on each side of joints and at centre of rail.

They can prepare 500 yards per hour without stopping traffic, which can pass safely at low speeds over the line in this state. It is erroneous to suppose that the rate of removal is governed by the time necessary to remove fish plates, which time is negligible when the bolts are knocked off. When necessary to unscrew and preserve the bolts, three minutes per pair of plates is sufficient, but any number of men can work simultaneously when spanners are plentiful. The material is loaded direct into the wagons standing opposite the place from which it is taken, the remaining bolts being knocked off at the

SEC. 13.   DEMOLITION OF RAILWAYS.   129

last moment. Party for loading up each wagon, one rail length
= 7, 8, or 10 yards.

> In each wagon, packing ... ... 2 men.
> Loading into each wagon ... ... 12 ,,
> Removing remaining bolts, collecting
>   fish plates, and unbedding sleepers 4 ,,

Total party for one train 12 × 16 = 192 men. Tools: two
sledge hammers, two picks, two crowbars. To load a rail
requires 12 men, or generally 1½ men per yard; a chaired sleeper
six men. Removal proceeds at the rate of one train length in
10 minutes or 500 yards per hour.

While the train is away, the road can be prepared, sleepers
unbedded, &c., in advance. On a double line it should be
possible to reduce this interval to a minimum.

299. For this two trains of standard length, as above, will   Removal of
work simultaneously.   both lines.

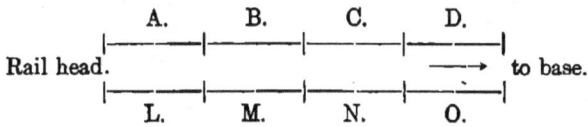

Double line.

Dividing the line into imaginary train lengths as above, one
train will stand at A, while the material of L is loaded into it as
above described. The train then proceeds to C, and the material
of A is loaded into train at M. The average length of carry will
be 80 yards, and each rail length will require two journeys for
the rails, and one half as many sleeper journeys as there are
sleepers, since each rail gang of 12 makes two sleeper gangs at 6.
For 24-ft. rails that will be eight sleepers, or a total of six
separate journeys, say 12 minutes time. Hence a train length
can be loaded in 20 minutes. Working with two trains a double
line should be removed at 350 yards per hour.

300. For single line removal there are two methods, that of Single line
direct carrying and loading into the train, and that of loading on removal.
to trollies and pushing forward to such a distance that the loading Direct
up by a separate gang does not interfere with the continuous loading.
work at the rail head.

For direct loading the tail of the train should be at two rail
lengths from rail head. A longer distance loses time in carrying,
and a shorter distance causes confusion through the space being
contracted. The train will move forward two rail lengths as the
material in rear is loaded up. The rail wagons should be in
rear, as the rails are most difficult to carry quickly. Gang for
this system—

Preparing road in advance	... ...	2 men.
Removing remaining keys and bolts	...	2 „
Unbedding sleepers; turning rails	...	4 „
Loading rails in gangs of 12 (two)	...	24 „
Loading sleepers in gangs of 6 (ten)	...	60 „
Packing 4 wagons at once, 2 in each	...	8 „
		100 „

Tools as for double line removal.

It is not found possible to use a greater number of men owing to confusion in working in the limited space between the train and the fence or cutting of a single line, and if more men are available the surplus is best used in giving frequent relief at rail head. The results by this system after a short drill showed one rail length per four minutes, or say one train load, 250 yards, in two hours. The rate was practically independent of length of rails, and is thus greater with long rails. The average length of carry is one rail length plus half the length of the train. When the train is away the time is best utilised in carrying forward material to such a distance as by calculation should be reached in the time at which the empty train is due.

Removal with lorries.

301. These should always be used when available. On English railways a platelayer's lorry will be found about every two miles. Four or five are required, placed first at intervals of one rail length beside the line clear of the rails. Six men are told off per lorry to push and unload them, but not to load them. The line is prepared by men in advance as already described. The rail head gang is as follows:—

Loading lorries	... ...	...
Bolts and keys	... ...	...
Unbedding sleepers, turning rails	...	...
		30
Lorry gangs, 5 or 6 men	...	30
Train loading gang—		
For 2 rail wagons, 2 gangs of 12	...	24
packing ...	...	4
For sleeper loading, 5 gangs of 6	...	30
packing	...	10
		128
Add for relief	...	12
Total for system	... ...	140

Tools as for direct system.

The work is very quick and quite continuous; hence it is desirable to give the rail head gang a stand off for 10 minutes every 20 minutes.

SEC. 13.   DEMOLITION OF RAILWAYS.   131

Each rail length complete is loaded by the 24 men on to one lorry, which is pushed forward and unloaded beside the line at 200—300 yards distance, the rails in two stacks and the sleepers in 10 stacks, to come opposite to the respective wagons of the train. When about 120 yards of material is deposited, the train backs and is loaded. The rail head work goes on during the loading, the lorries being pushed up to the tail of the train to clear the rail head. Six spare lorries are wanted for use at this time while the first six are waiting for the train to be loaded up. Thus with 12 lorries in all the rail head work can be made continuous. Empty lorries returning to rail head must be derailed to allow full loads to pass. A loaded lorry can be safely pushed over line from which all bolts, fishplates, and keys have been removed. The mean of several days' continuous practice gives one minute per rail length as a working time. This gives 600 yards per hour removed or, say, one train load per half hour. Experiments further proved that by reverse of this system the same material could be unloaded and relaid on prepared formation level at the rate of two minutes per rail length.

From the above experiment the time and labour can be calculated for stacking at any required interval. If for burning, the material may be stacked at 50 yards intervals, rails on top. This can be done at the same rate as for removal by the lorry system and thrice as fast as removal by direct loading, say 600 yards, or 300 yards per hour respectively with the same parties. The time, however, depends on the labour available, since any number of men can be used at one time in different gangs. *Stacking for destruction or storage.*

302. Secs. XI and XII have shown how the engineering works on a railway may be destroyed by means of explosives. It is, however, important to know that where slips are made in cuttings and gaps in embankments they should be made far from the ends, that the enemy may have a maximum distance to move the earth ; and that several gaps in one embankment, or several slips in one cutting, are a greater obstacle than one in each of several embankments or cuttings, since the enemy will be unable to use his trucks where they are most needed. The time required to repair a damaged bridge will be greatly increased if a train is wrecked among the débris. This especially applies to a small bridge where the clearing of the wreckage is often the longest part of the repair. *Engineering works.*

303. When all large bridges, stations and other vulnerable points on a railway are garrisoned, and access is obtained for a short time to an intermediate portion of the line, a greater effect may be obtained by the employment of mines ; for if successful, their material results may be more important than a single demolition would have been, and the moral effect of a few successful mines will seriously handicap traffic working. As the actual explosion will, at most, damage one vehicle, mines should be laid if possible where the unexpected derailment of a train will have most disastrous results—*e.g.*, on, or shortly before a *Mines.*

bridge or on a curve on a high embankment. It is not easy to improvise a mine; and any must be fully and carefully tested by actual experiment before use.

304. A device successfully used by the Boers during the South African War was as follows:—The stock and trigger-guard were removed from a rifle and the barrel was cut off short close to the breech. The rifle being cocked was placed beneath the rail, half way between two sleepers, with the trigger just touching the rail. The passage of a train bent the rail, pressed the trigger and fired the rifle. To fire a mine, a cartridge with bullet and powder charge removed, was placed in the rifle. A small piece of gun-cotton or dynamite was placed in the cartridge against the cap and instantaneous fuze inserted after it. The firing of the rifle ignited the dynamite and instantaneous fuze and the detonator in the mine was then fired.

Electrical devices for exploding mines are likely to be the most reliable, and circuit closers can be easily devised using the bending of the rail as in the preceding paragraph.

A railway fog signal with a piece of instantaneous fuze inserted through a hole and communicating with the charge is an excellent makeshift, but has the disadvantage that the fog signal must be fixed on top of the rail.

Section 14.—DEMOLITION OF TELEGRAPH LINES.

305. The amount of damage that can be done in a short time to a line of telegraph depends chiefly on the number of separate wires running parallel to each other on the same poles in the case of an aerial line, or the number of separate cables contained in the same set of pipes in a subterranean line. These two forms are by far the most likely to be encountered on service, although a subaqueous line may sometimes be found.

It is assumed that the line to be destroyed lies in country occupied by the enemy, to which access has been obtained for a short time by a raid; since if any part of the line lay in a part of a country from which the enemy had been expelled, it would be of course easy either to disconnect the wires and appropriate them, or, leaving the lines intact, to interpose instruments, and thereby read any message sent by the enemy.

306. The poles can be readily cut or blown down, care being taken that the wires and poles do not fall on the party; the easiest and safest poles to attack being those that have stays. *Destruction of aerial line.*

A rope should first be fixed to the top of the pole or thrown over the wires, in order to put a strain on tending to overthrow the pole.

The pole should then be partly cut through at about 4 feet from the ground. All hands should then commence to strain on the rope except one man, who should cut the stay through with a file or pliers. The men on the rope must be sufficiently far from the pole to be well clear of the wires when they fall.

The destructive effect will be increased by previously cutting partly through the adjacent poles on each side, and, if several adjacent poles are also stayed, cutting their stays at the same time.

Iron poles would be best attacked with gun-cotton.

Having brought down as much as possible of the line in this way, the wires should be cut at each end as far as can be reached, and twisted up so as to be rendered useless. The insulators should also be broken.

Any damage of this sort, however, can be quickly repaired by the enemy using cable; and even the complete restoration of poles and wires will not take very long to accomplish.

307. Probably an equal amount of delay could be occasioned with less trouble by skilfully placing what are known as "faults" on the line. *Faults.*

Faults consist of "disconnections," "leaks," and "contacts."

"Disconnections" are partial or complete breaks in the continuity of the conductor.

"Leaks" are partial or complete connections of the conductor to earth, a complete connection being known as "dead earth."

"Contacts" are formed by one wire touching another or being put in connection with it by some conductor. They are very troublesome faults, since they affect two lines, and cannot be overcome, as other partial faults can be, by increasing the battery power.

All artificial faults to be successful as causes of delay, however, require to be skilfully made, and, if possible, a skilled electrician should be employed. The easiest method is to twist a piece of wire round several of the telegraph wires so as to connect them together. They may also be connected with the earth wires which run down the poles. Another plan is to cut out a portion of the wire and to replace it by a piece of very low conducting power, but of approximately the same gauge, so as not to be readily detected by eye. Even where faults are made it is desirable to cut down portions of the line also. The faults may then escape detection at first, and a second examination of the line by the restoring party rendered necessary.

Damage done to an office.

308. If possession can be obtained of an office considerable damage can be done by breaking the batteries and instruments. Any papers with rules for the working of the line should be forwarded to the officer in charge of the field telegraph.

Records of messages should be sent at once to the nearest General Staff Officer.

Destruction of subterranean line.

309. A subterranean line is naturally more difficult to discover than an aerial one, and for this reason among others they are now extensively employed in countries liable to invasion. In England they are rarely met with except in large towns, where overhead wires are dangerous.

The existence of such a line being known or suspected, marks should be searched for at equal distances apart, indicating the position of test boxes.

These marks are usually about 100 yards apart, and generally consist of blocks of wood or stone numbered in succession. They would very probably, however, have been removed by the enemy.

If not to be found where the line is known to exist, a cross trench should be dug in easy soil at right angles to the probable direction of the line, about 3 feet deep, and in this way the pipes may be discovered. These can then be dug up as far as possible, and bent or otherwise destroyed if means are available, the wire being pulled out and cut to pieces.

If possible the trench should be carefully filled in and all traces removed.

310. Subaqueous lines are rarely employed except for crossing seas or considerable rivers, but in time of war they may be laid along the course of the rivers to connect towns on their banks, as was done at Paris in the Franco-German war.

Destruction of subaqueous line.

To destroy such a line it should be grappled for with a grapnel, and when caught, as large a piece as possible cut out of it; the piece should then be cut into smaller pieces and thrown into deep water.

APPENDIX I.

Tests for Explosives.

1. *Dynamite, Blasting Gelatine,* and *Gelatine Dynamite* should be tested as laid down in " Regulations for Army Ordnance Services," paragraphs 388-396.

2. *Test for Bellite, Securite, Roburite, and other Explosives containing Ammonium Nitrate.*—The danger with these explosives lies in their getting damp and failing to explode. A few cartridges should be detonated in the open to see that they are serviceable.

Test for Sensitiveness of Chlorate Explosives.—Place a small quantity of the explosive on a stone or wood floor, and give it a glancing blow with the end of a common broom stick held lance-wise. If the sample will explode easily on a stone floor it should not be used for charging boreholes, and if it will explode on a deal floor it should be used with care. This test is only applicable to explosives containing chlorates.

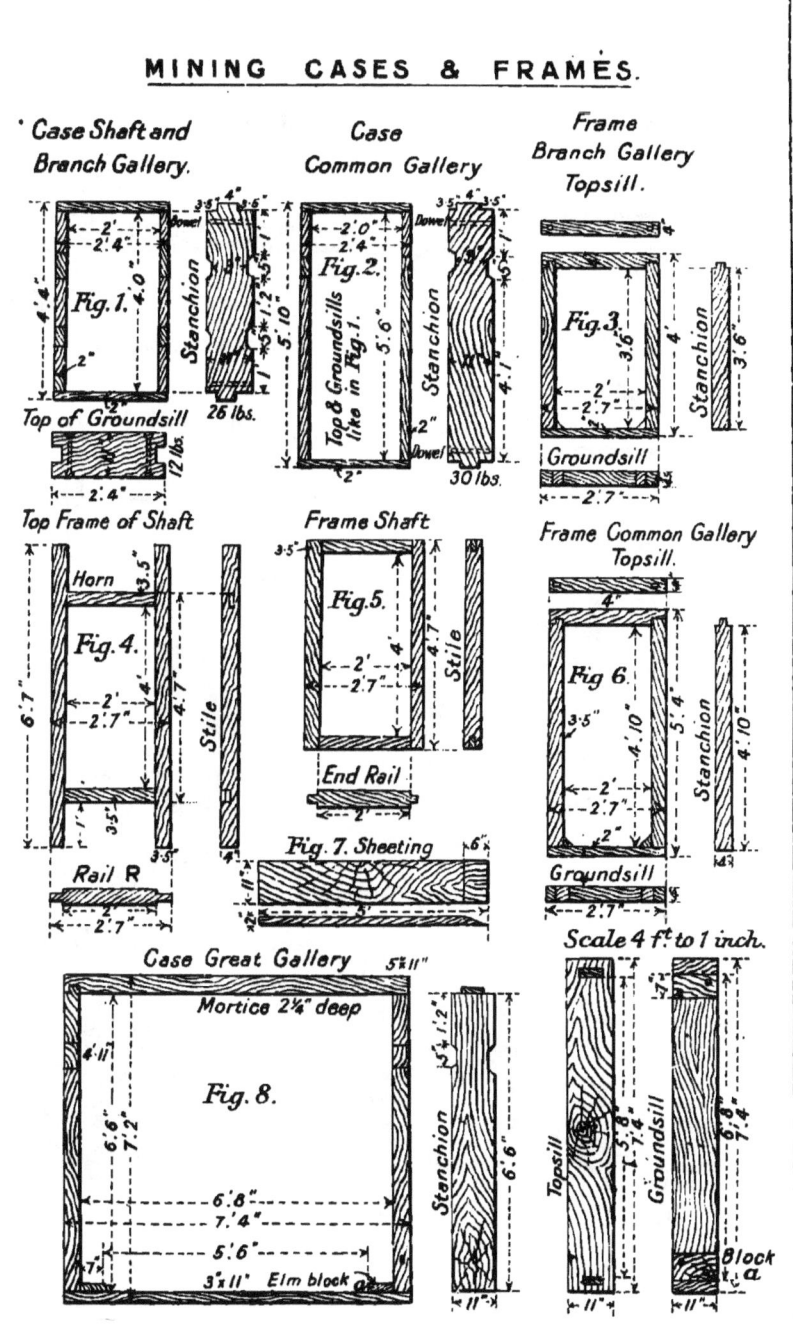

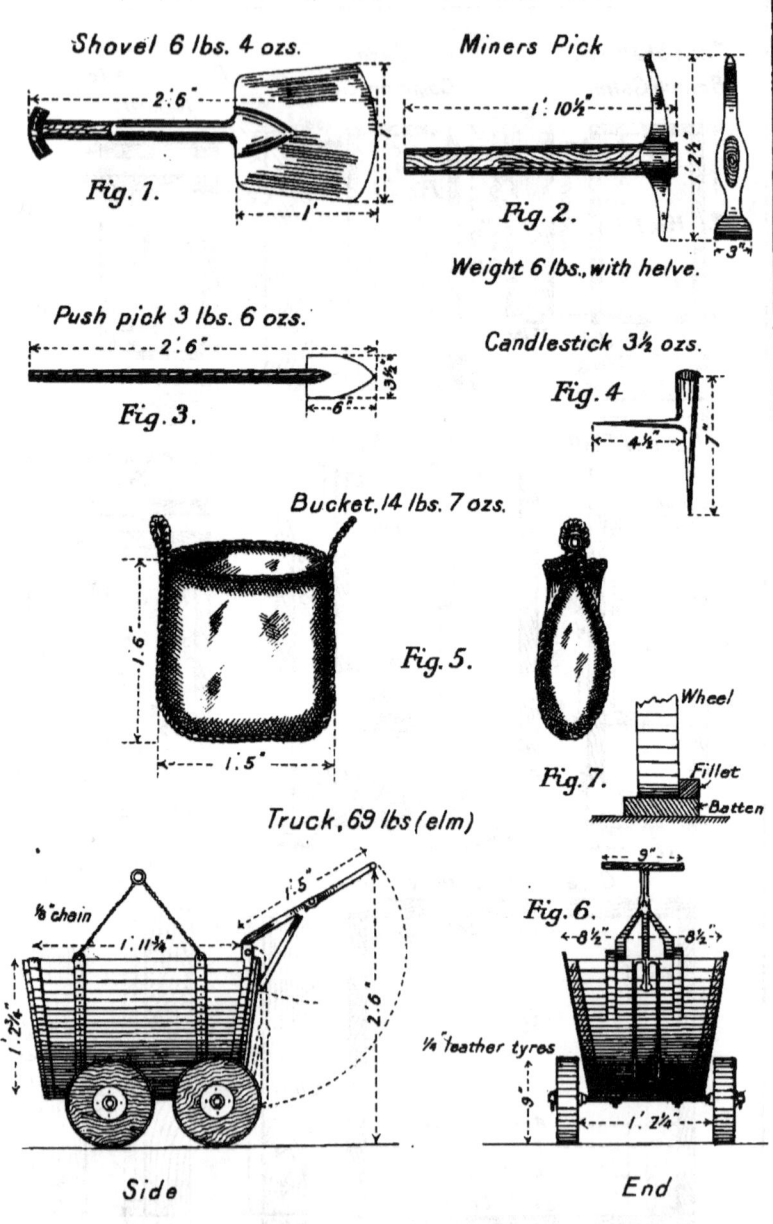

PLATE III.

SHAFTS & GALLERIES.

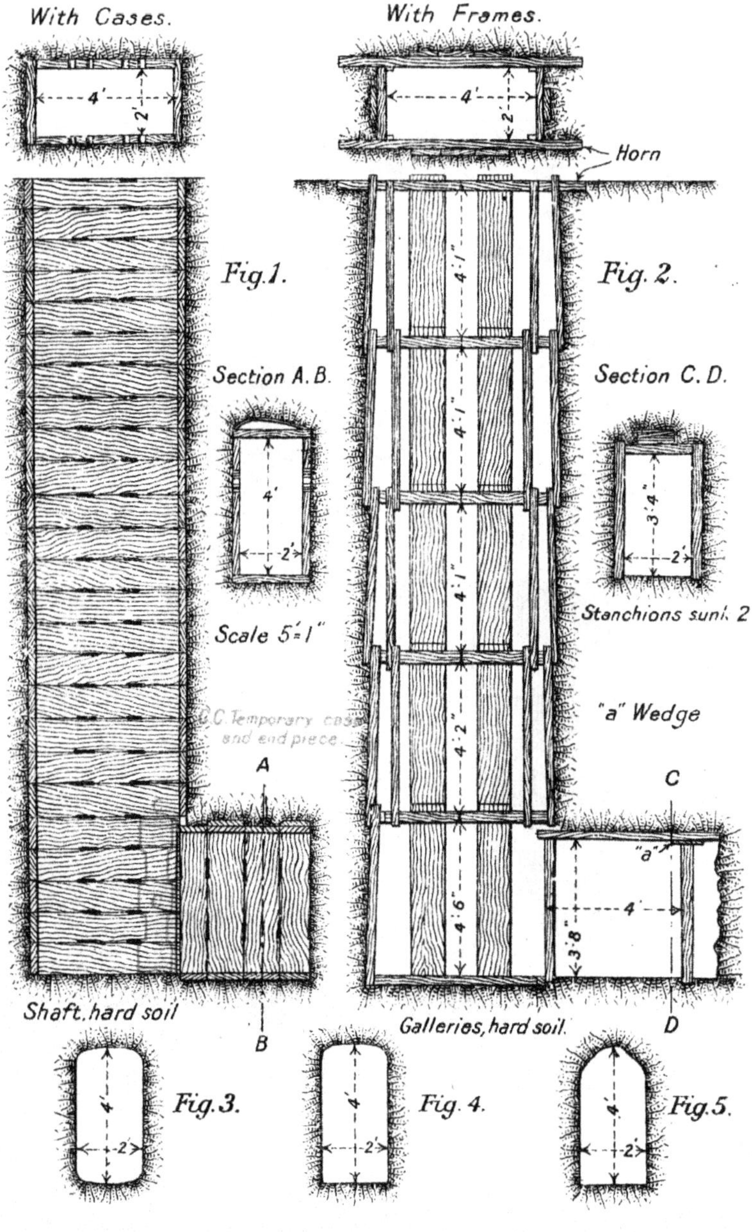

With Cases.

With Frames.

4' × 2'

4' × 2'

Horn

Fig. 1.

Fig. 2.

Section A.B.

Section C.D.

4' × 2'

4'·1"

3'·4" × 2'

Scale 5'=1"

4'·1"

Stanchions sunk 2'

4'·1"

"a" Wedge

C.C Temporary case and end piece.

4'·2"

A

C

"a"

4'·6"

3'·8" 4'

Shaft, hard soil.

Galleries, hard soil.

B

D

Fig. 3. 4' × 2'

Fig. 4. 4' × 2'

Fig. 5. 4' × 2'

5186.

Malby & Sons, Lith.

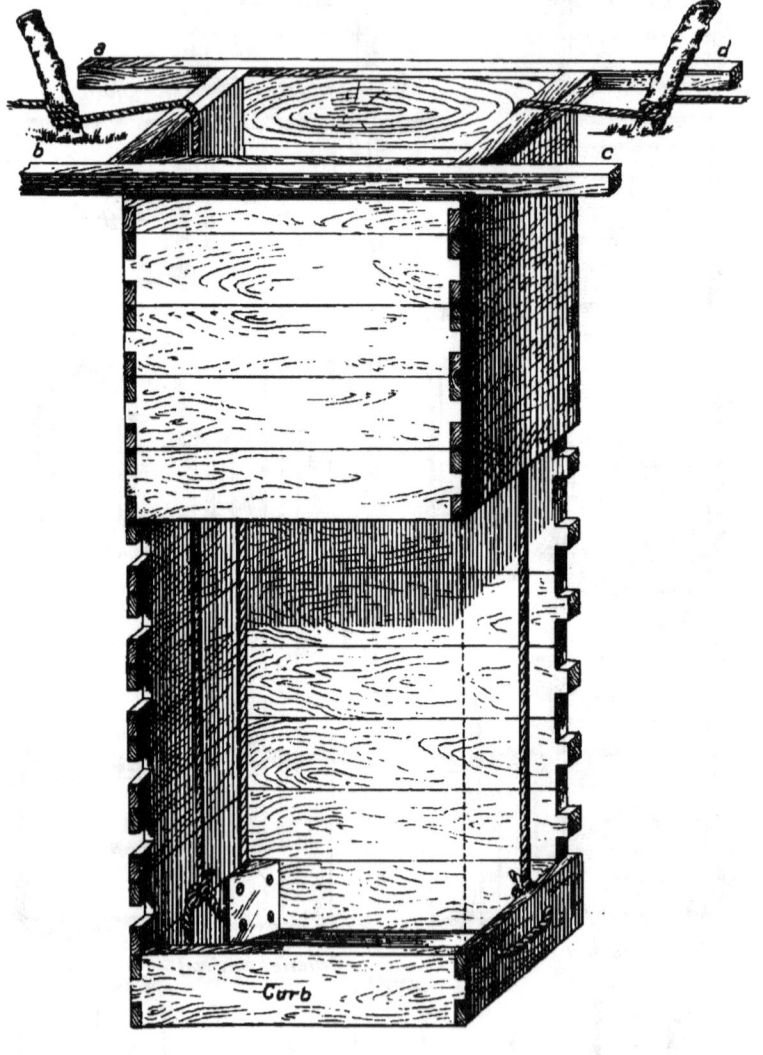

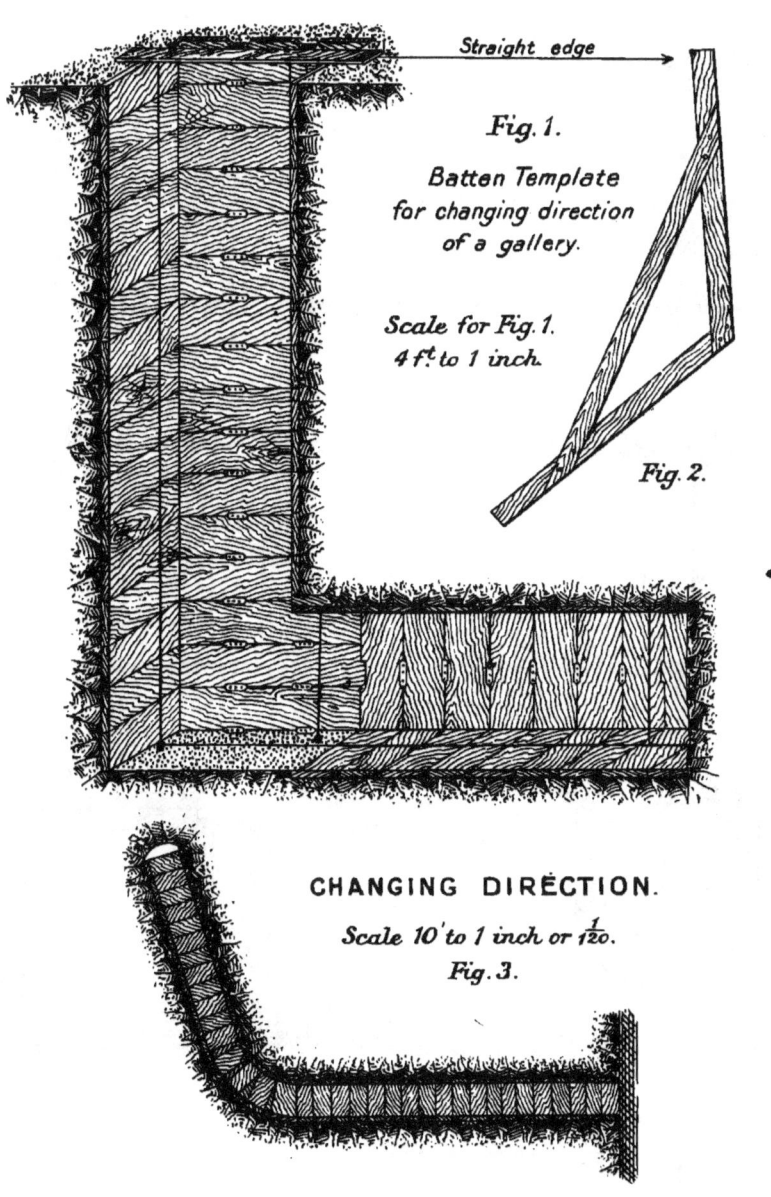

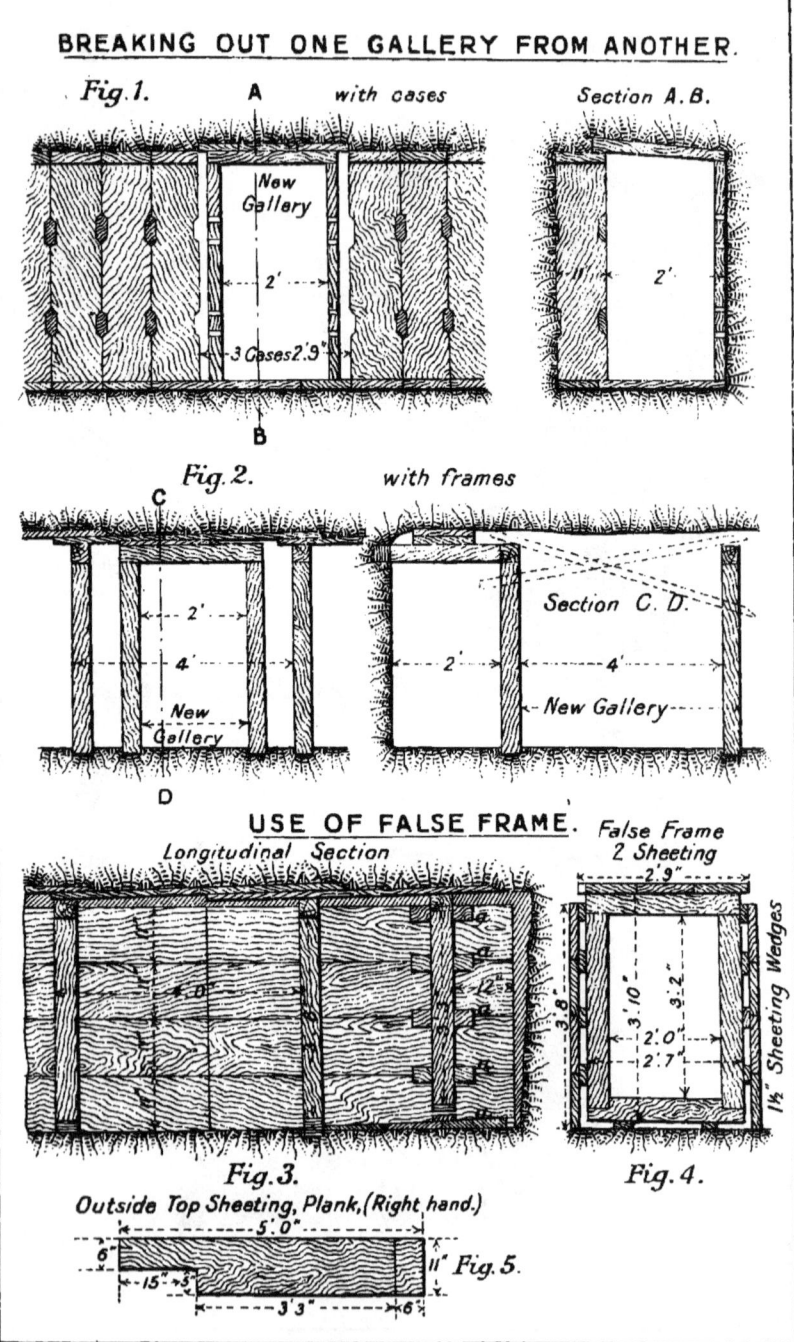

PLATE VII.

INCLINED GALLERIES &c.

With Frames and Sheeting.

Fig. 1.

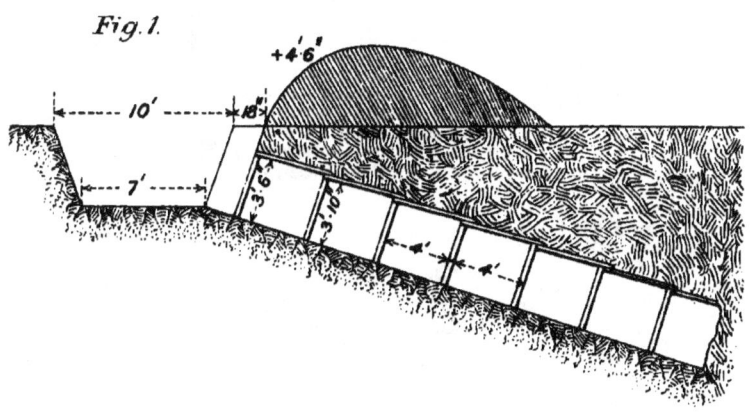

Fig. 2.

With Cases.

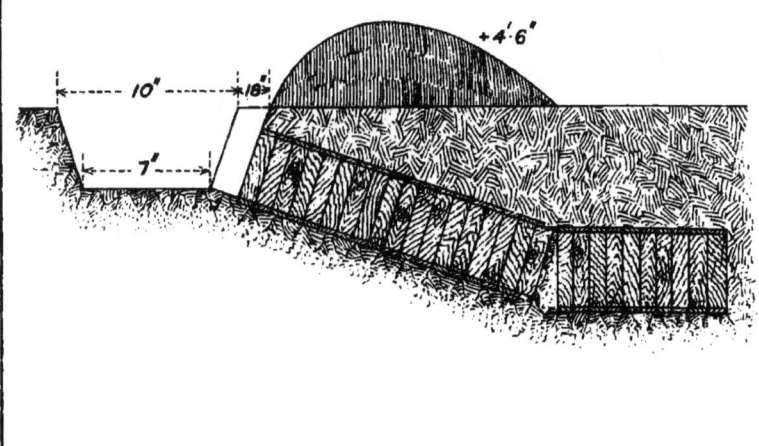

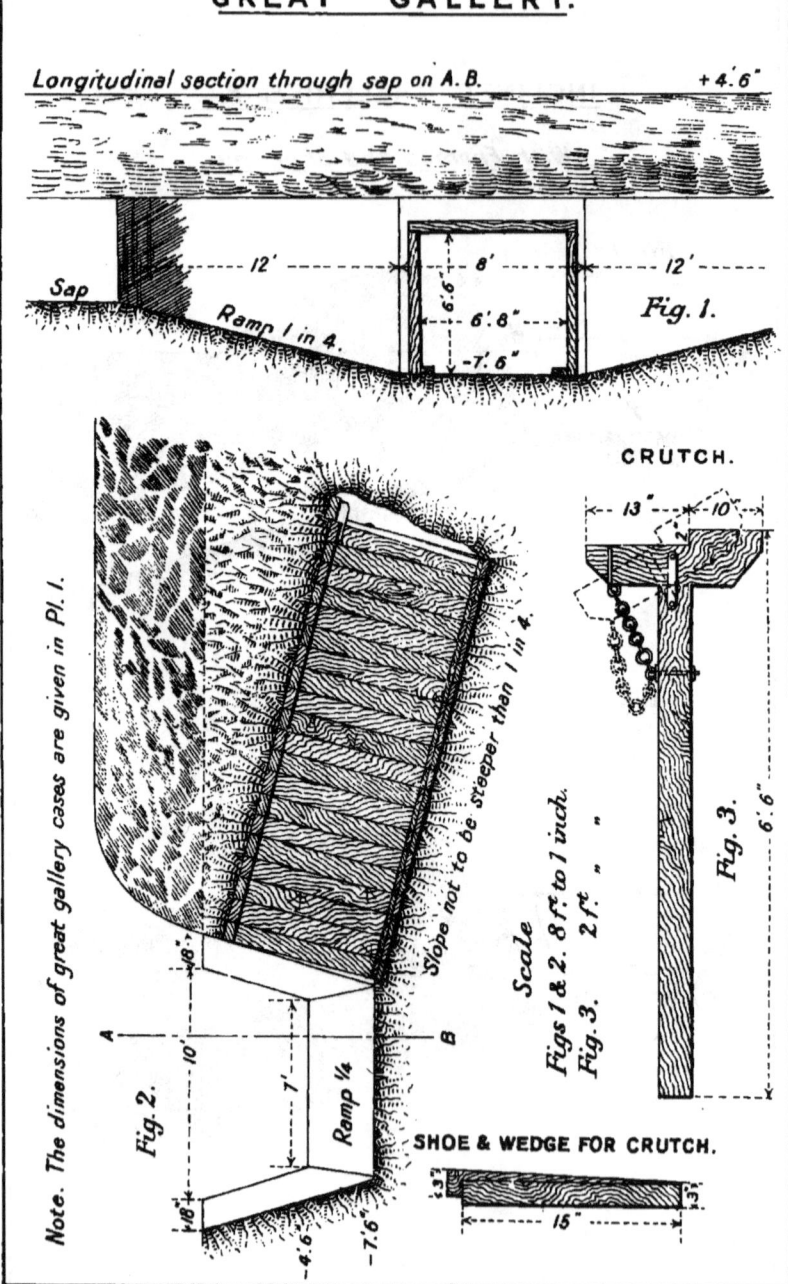

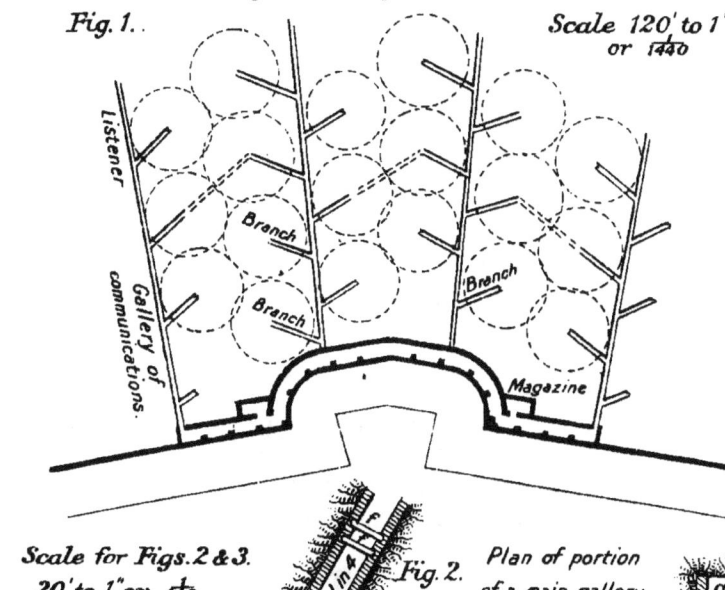
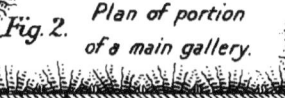

PLATE X.

VENTILATION OF MINES.

Fig. 1.   *Rotary Fan*

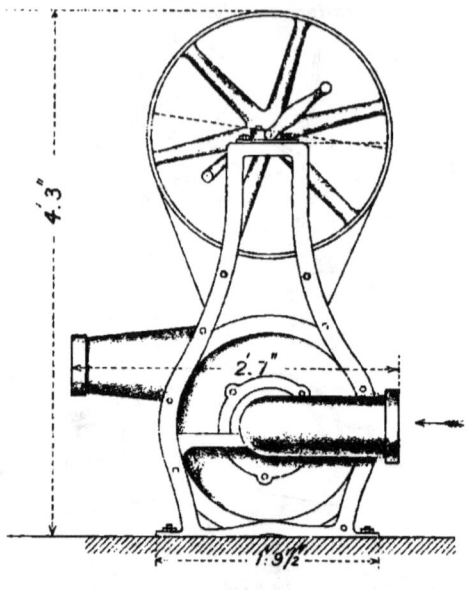

Fig. 2.

Section of Hose union

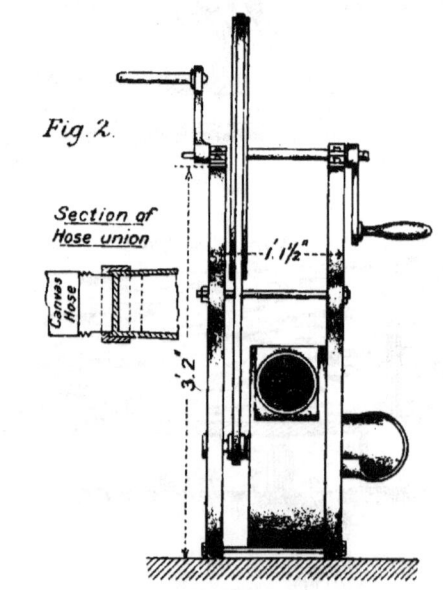

PLATE XI.

APPARATUS FOR BREATHING IN FOUL ATMOSPHERES.

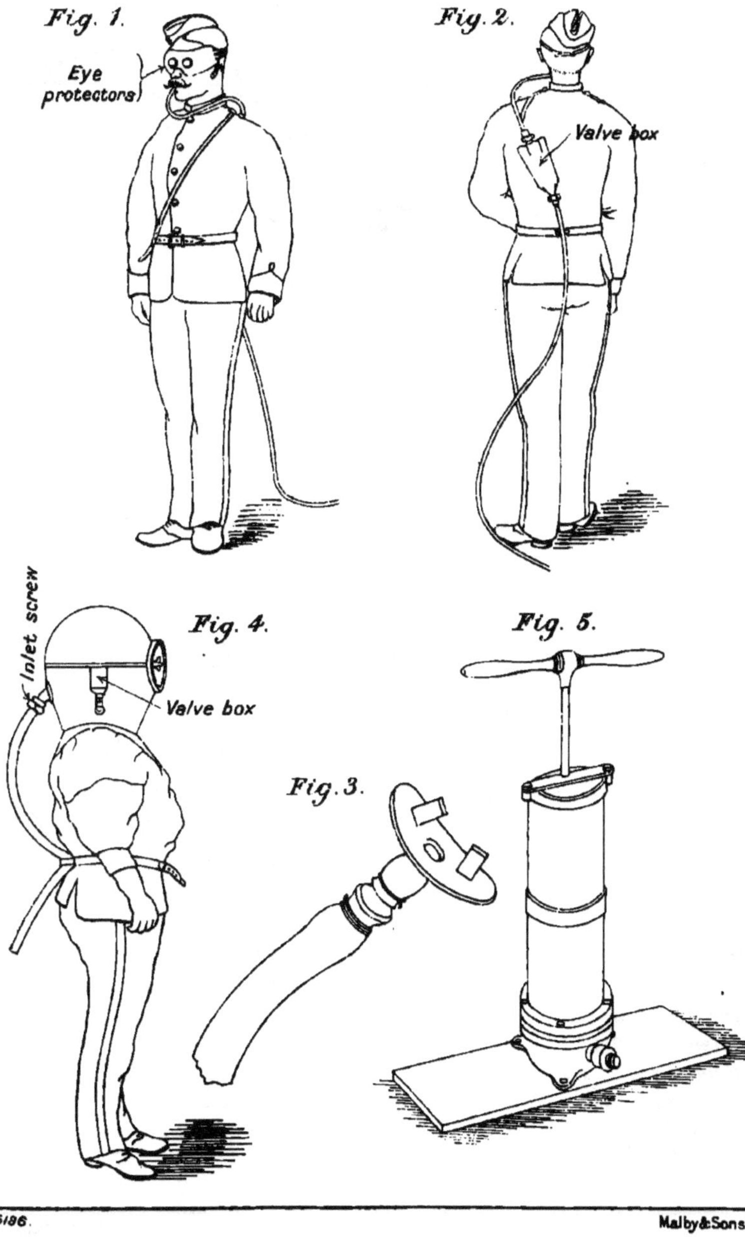

Fig. 1.
Eye protectors

Fig. 2.
Valve box

Fig. 4.
Inlet screw
Valve box

Fig. 3.

Fig. 5.

PLATE XII.

FIRING MINES.

Diagram of the action of a common Mine.

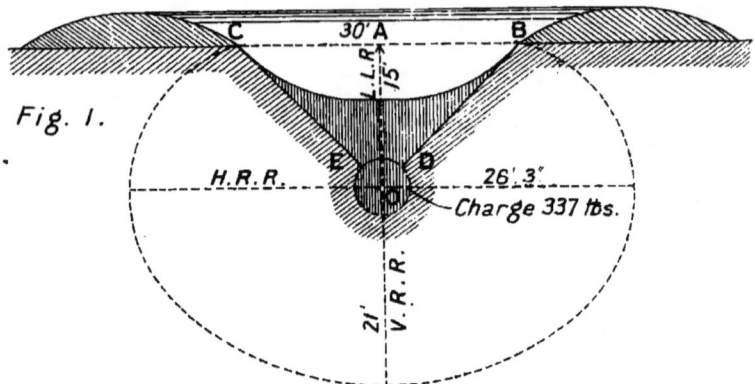

Fig. 1.

Diagram showing probable spheroids of rupture for overcharged Mines.

Fig 2.

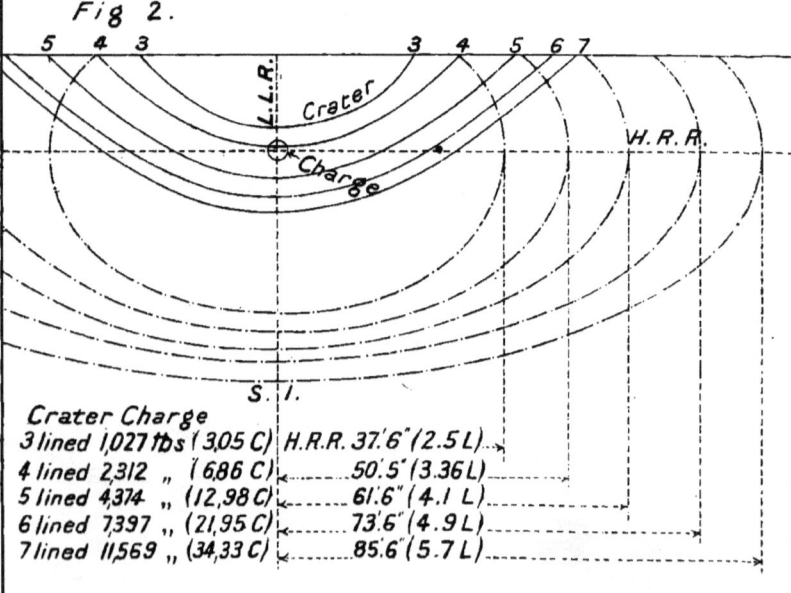

Crater Charge
3 lined 1,027 ℔s (3.05 C) H.R.R. 37′.6″ (2.5 L)
4 lined 2,312 „ (6.86 C) 50′.5″ (3.36 L)
5 lined 4,374 „ (12.98 C) 61′.6″ (4.1 L)
6 lined 7,397 „ (21.95 C) 73′.6″ (4.9 L)
7 lined 11,569 „ (34.33 C) 85′.6″ (5.7 L)

FUZES.

Fig. 1. Safety and instantaneous fuze cut on slant.

Fig. 2. Scarf Joint.

Fig. 3. Scarf joint between safety and instantaneous fuze.

Splint of wood

Fig. 4. Lighting end of safety fuze prepared with a piece of quickmatch.

Fig. 5.

Piece of flaked guncotton.

Fig. 6. Junction Box.

Fig. 7.

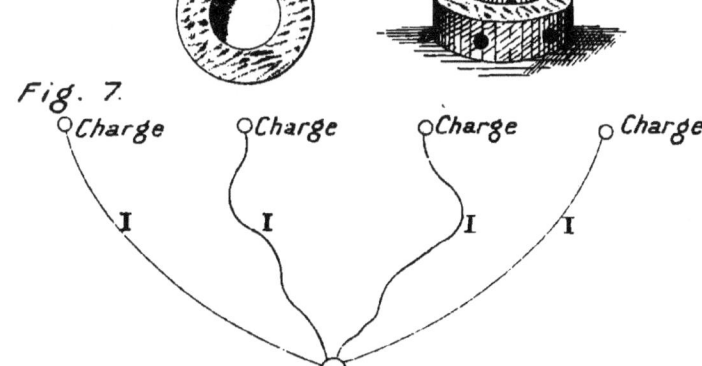

PLATE XIV.

FUZES AND DETONATORS.
FIELD SERVICE (FULL SIZE).

Fig. 1.   Nº 8. (Mark III) Detonator.

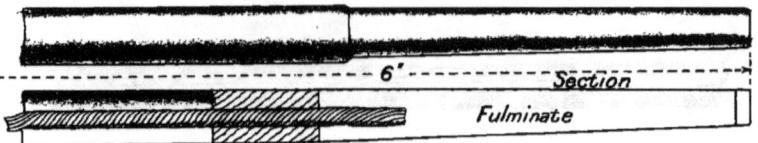

6"   Section
Fulminate

Fig. 2.   (Nº 8. Mark IV) Detonator

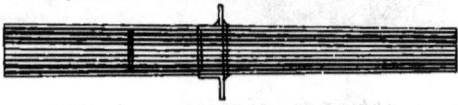

Section

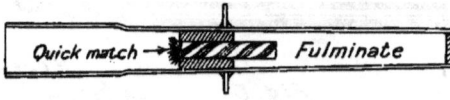

Quick match → Fulminate

Fig. 3.   Commercial Cap   Section

Fulminate

PLATE XV.

ELECTRIC FUZES AND DETONATORS

FULL SIZE

No 14 Fuze

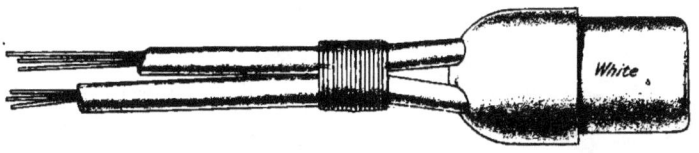

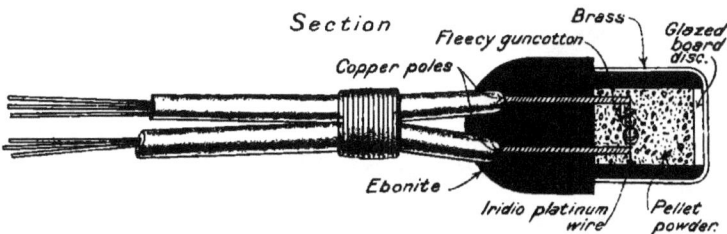

No 13 Detonator Mark III.

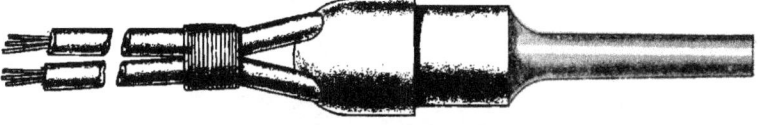

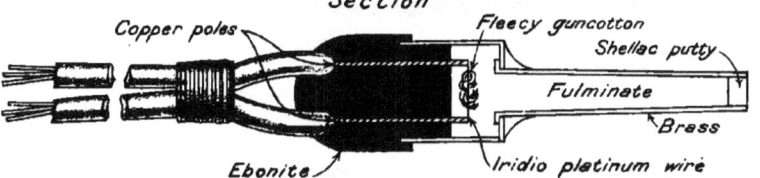

No 20 Detonator Mark II (Drill)

PLATE XVI.

ELECTRIC FUZES AND DETONATORS.
FULL SIZE
NAVAL SERVICE.

Nº 9 Detonator.

METHOD OF JOINTING FUZES.

Semi-circular nick in Safety Fuze.

Semi-circular nick in Instantaneous Fuze.

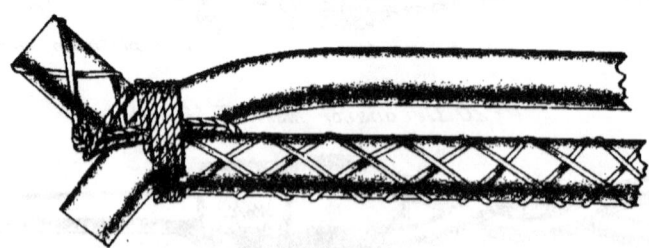

Nicked joint between Safety & Instantᵈ Fuze.

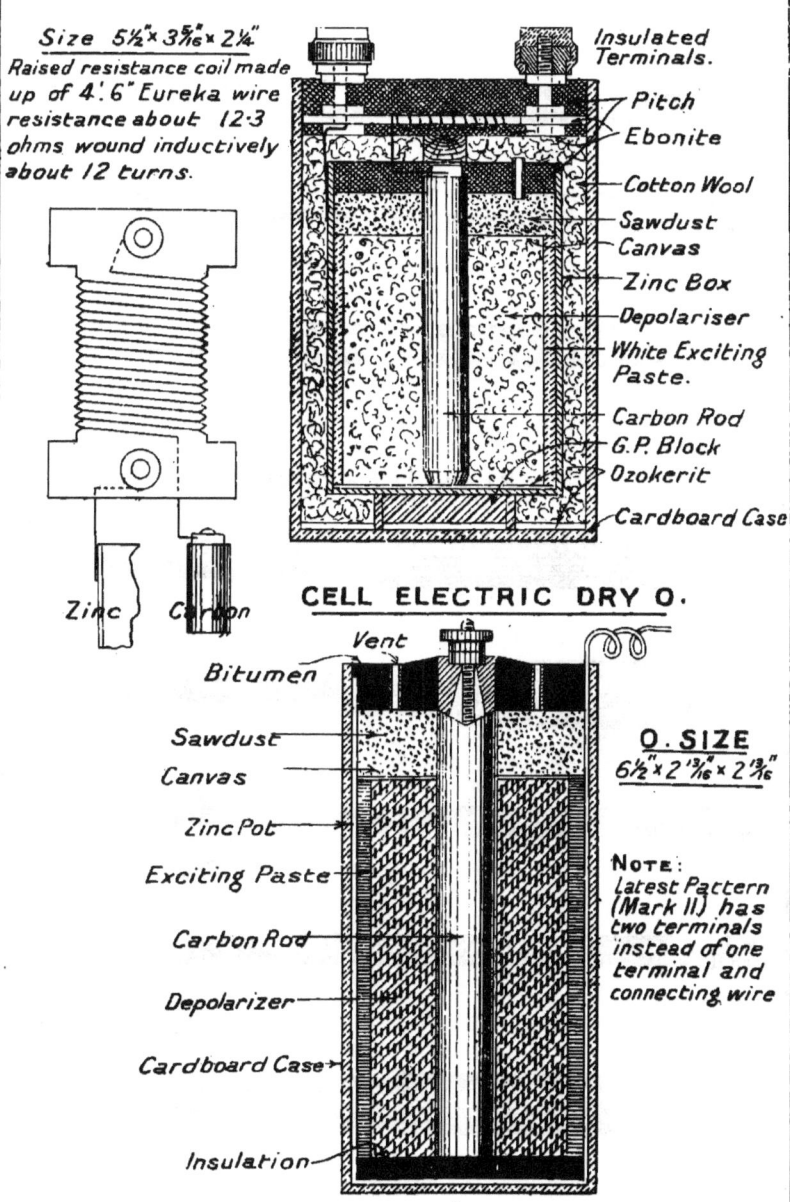

PLATE XVIII.

WIRES ELECTRIC.

S.11.
Mark I.

S.11.
Mark II.

S.3.
Mark I.

CABLES ELECTRIC.

E.2.
Mark I.

C.I.

D.5.
Mark IV.

E.I.
Mark II.

J.5.

Malby & Sons, Lith.

PLATE XIX.

KEY, CONTACT MARK IV.
Scale, 1/3.

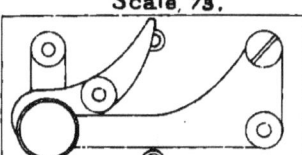

Fig. 1.   PLAN.

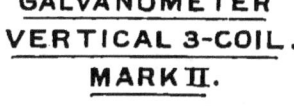

ELEVATION.

GALVANOMETER VERTICAL 3-COIL. MARK II.

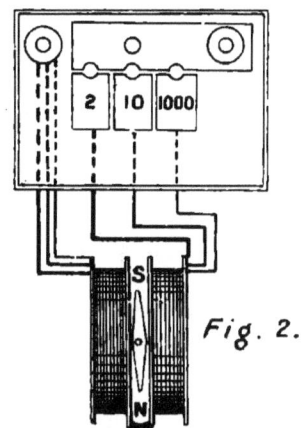

Fig. 2.

DIAGRAM OF CONNECTIONS.

COILS RESISTANCE 100 OHMS.
Connections for testing the Resistance of line, Fuzes &c.

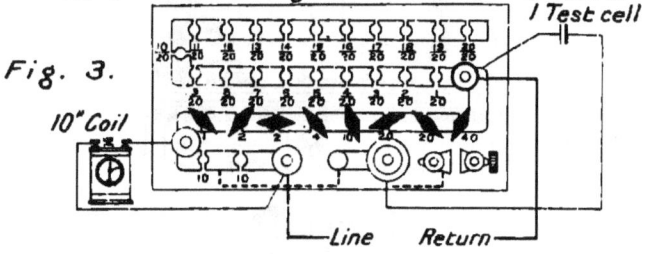

Fig. 3.

10" Coil

—Line   Return—

Scale, 2/3.

Connections for testing firing Battery or Exploder

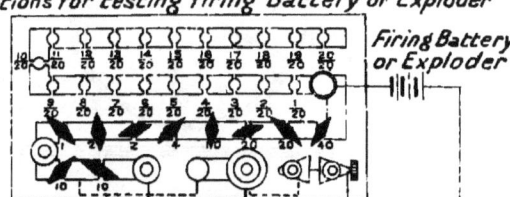

Fig. 4.

Firing Battery or Exploder

When Exploder is being tested the Key should be cut out by a short lead as shown here.

PLATE XX.

GALVANOMETER VERTICAL 3 - COIL.
MARK II.
SCALE, ½ FULL SIZE.

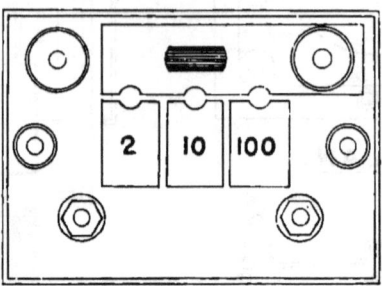

PLAN OF TOP

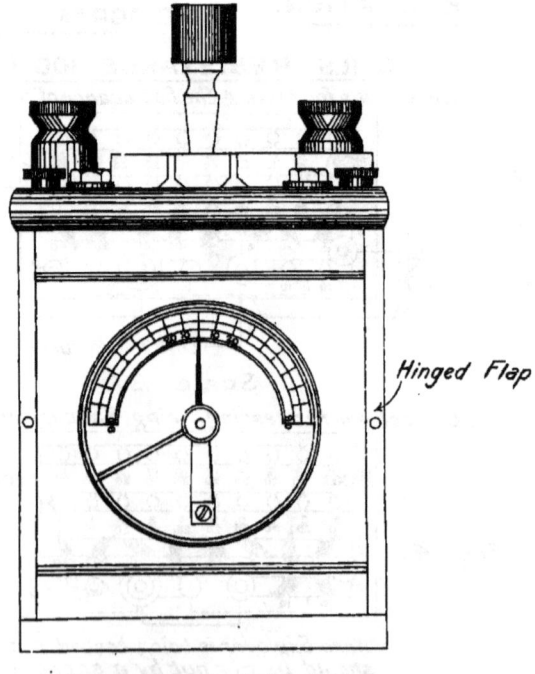

FRONT ELEVATION

PLATE XXI.

PULL CIRCUIT CLOSER
Full Size

PLAN

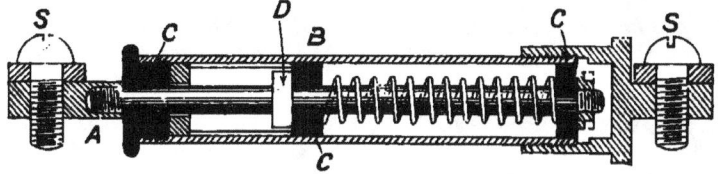

SECTION

TREAD CIRCUIT CLOSER
½ Full Size

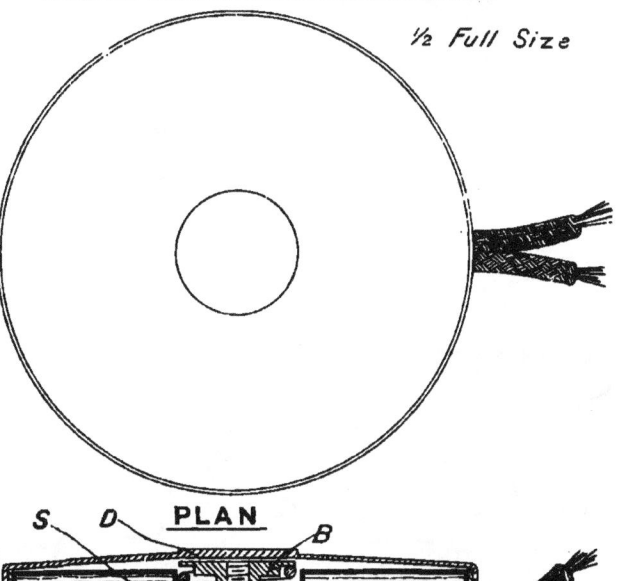

PLAN

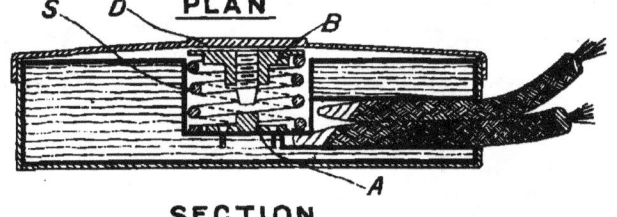

SECTION

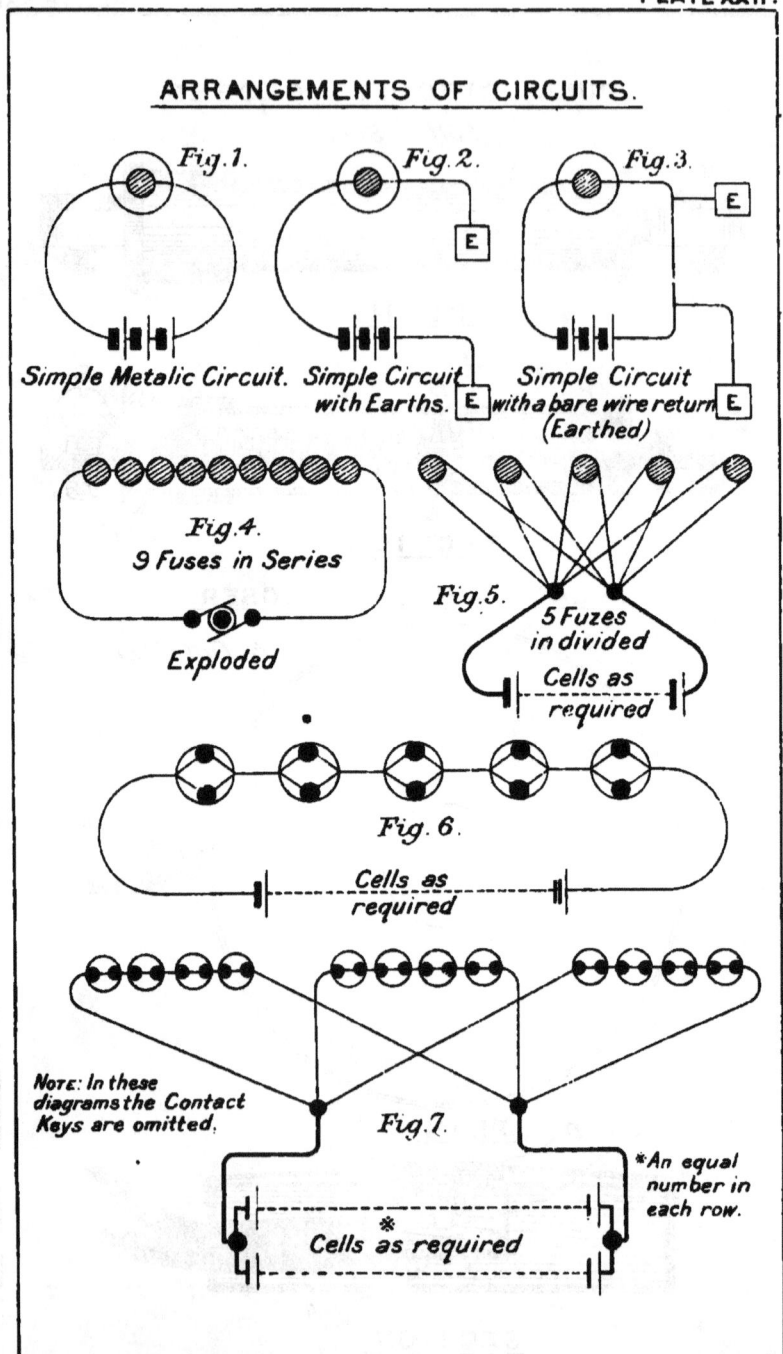

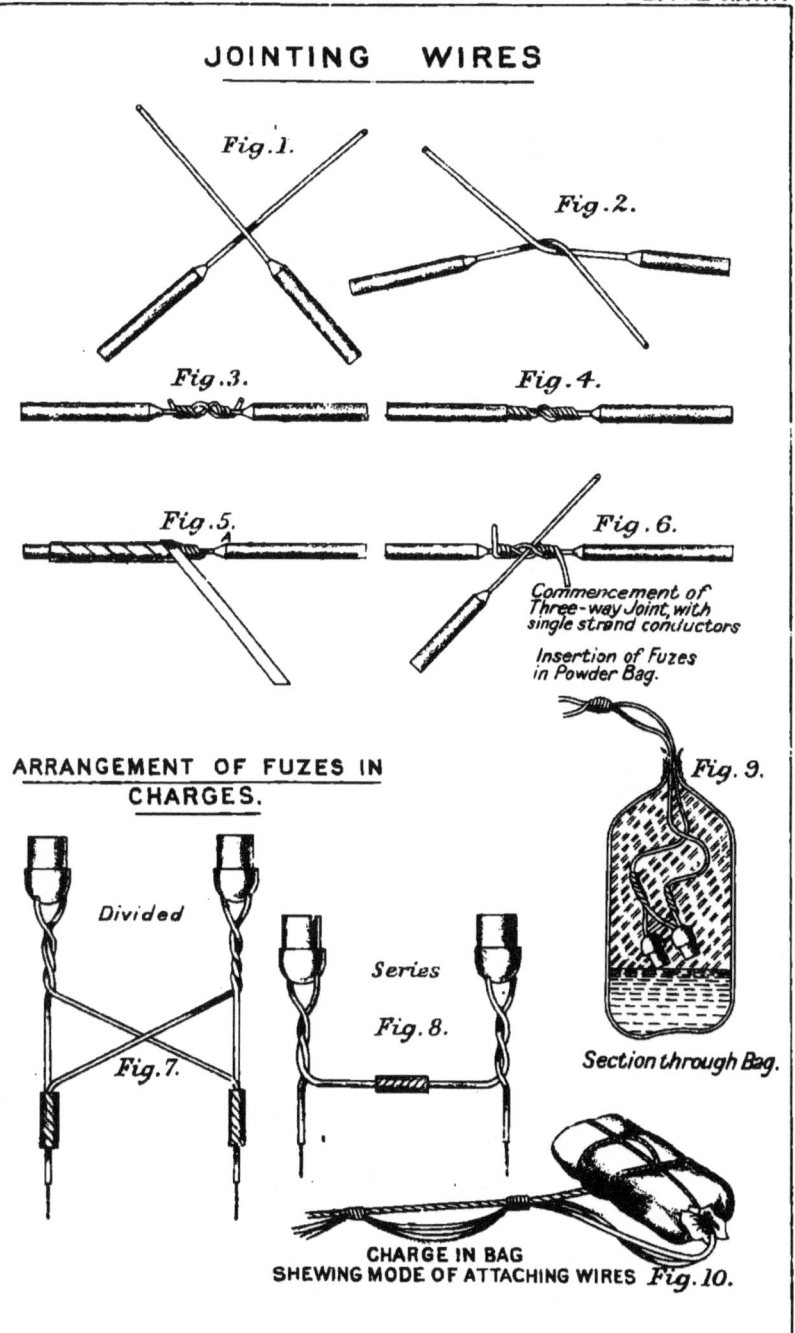

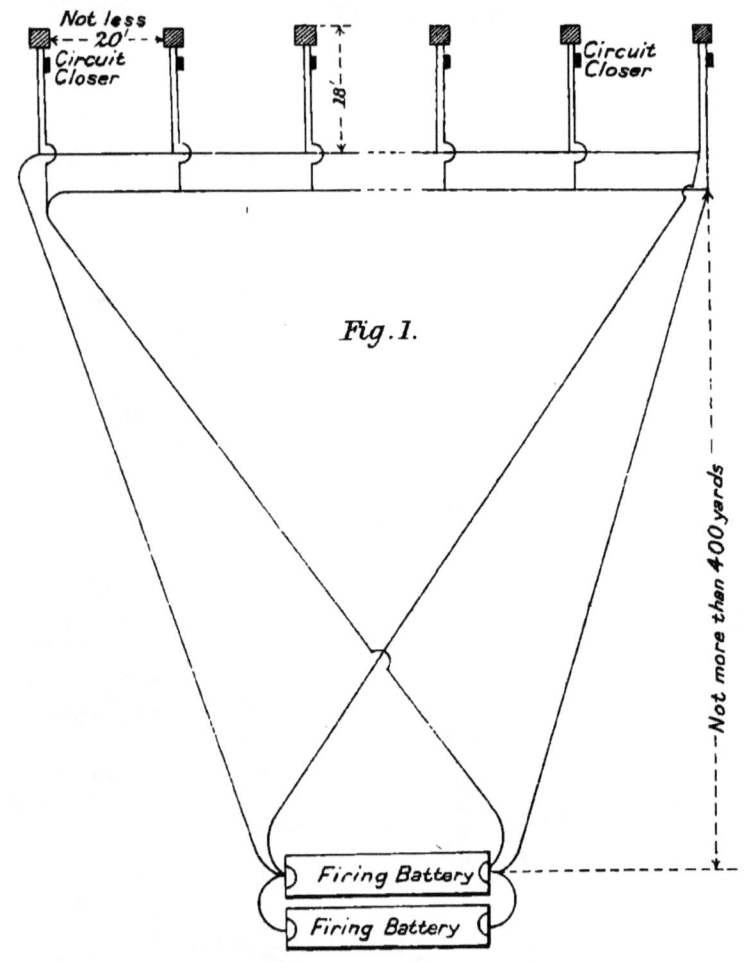

PLATE XXV.

FIRING MINES WITH BATTERY.

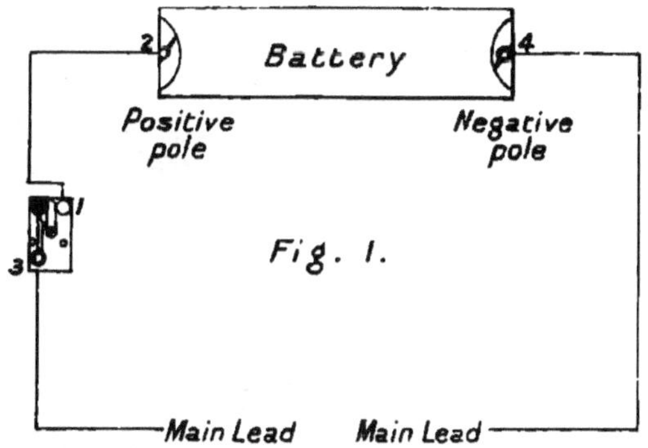

Fig. 1.

Battery
Positive pole
Negative pole
Main Lead — Main Lead

NOTE:— If either main lead is earthed it should be this one.

FIRING BY SUCCESSIVE CONTACTS.

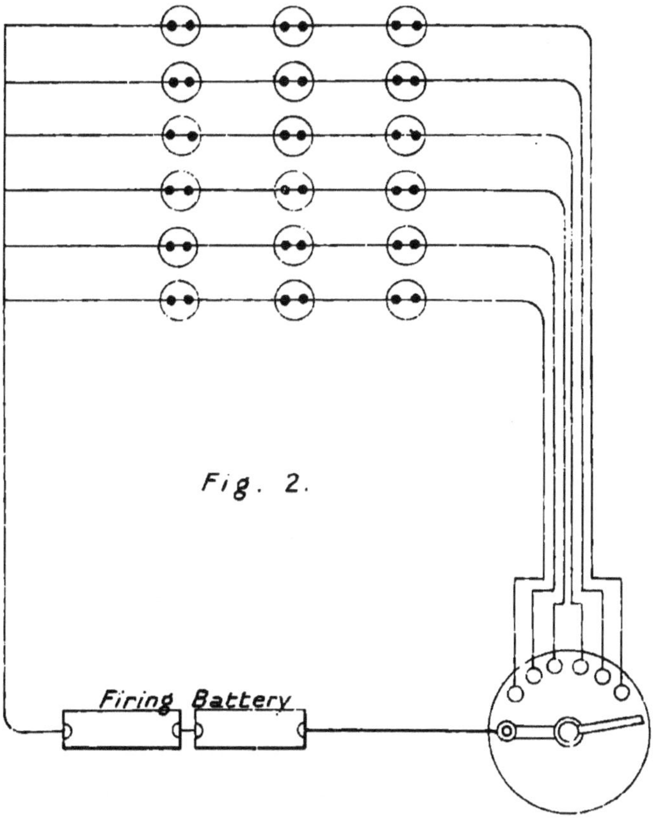

Fig. 2.

Firing Battery

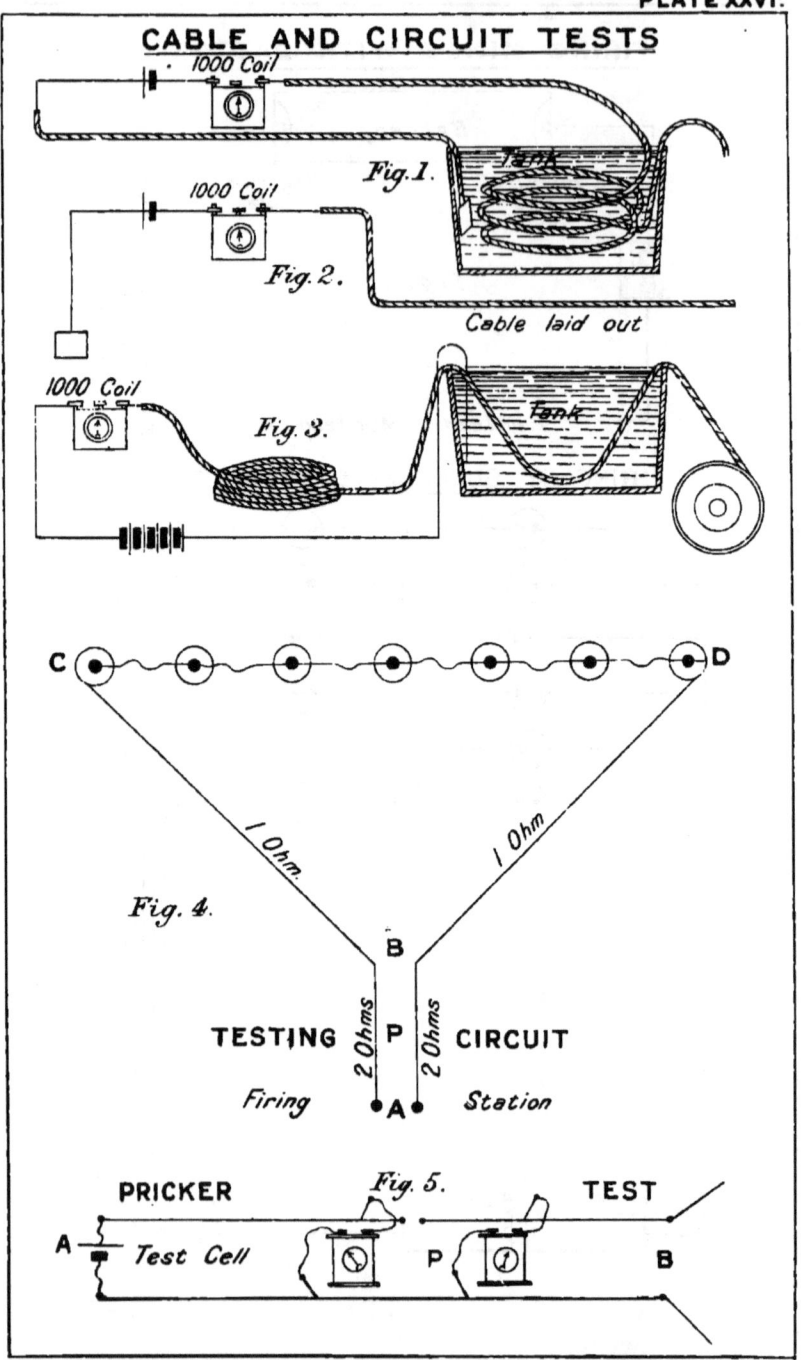

PLATE XXVII.

EXPLODER, DYNAMO, ELECTRIC QUANTITY.
Mark V.

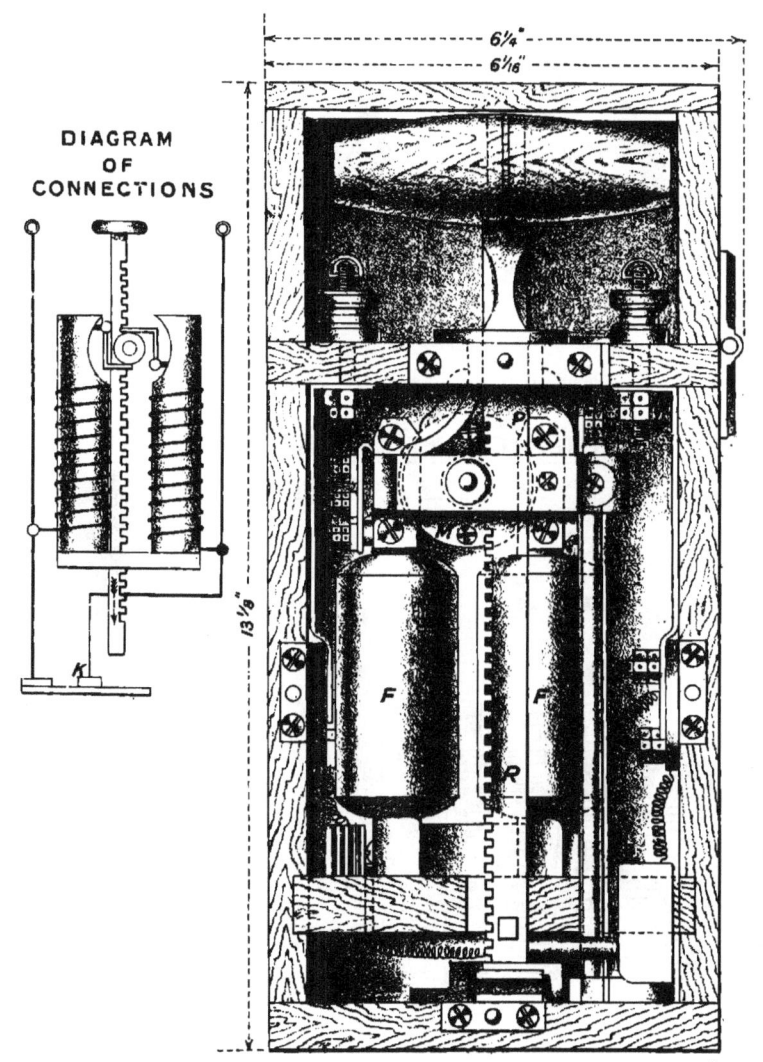

Elevation (near side removed.)

PLATE XXVIII.

CLIFF ROADS.

Fig. 1. Fig. 2.

Section of Cliff Roads.

BORING AND BLASTING
Position of Boreholes.

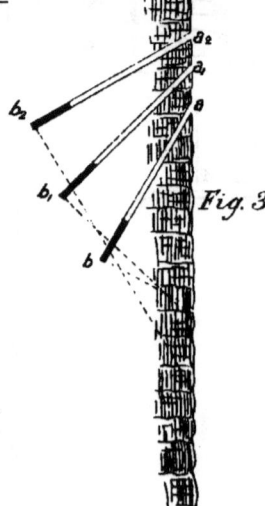

Fig. 3.

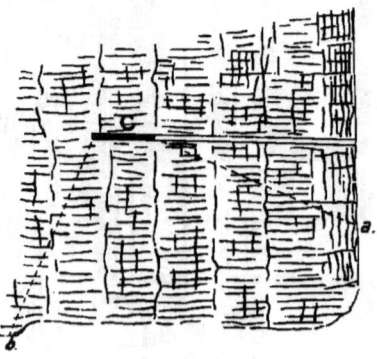

Fig. 4.

PLATE XXIX.

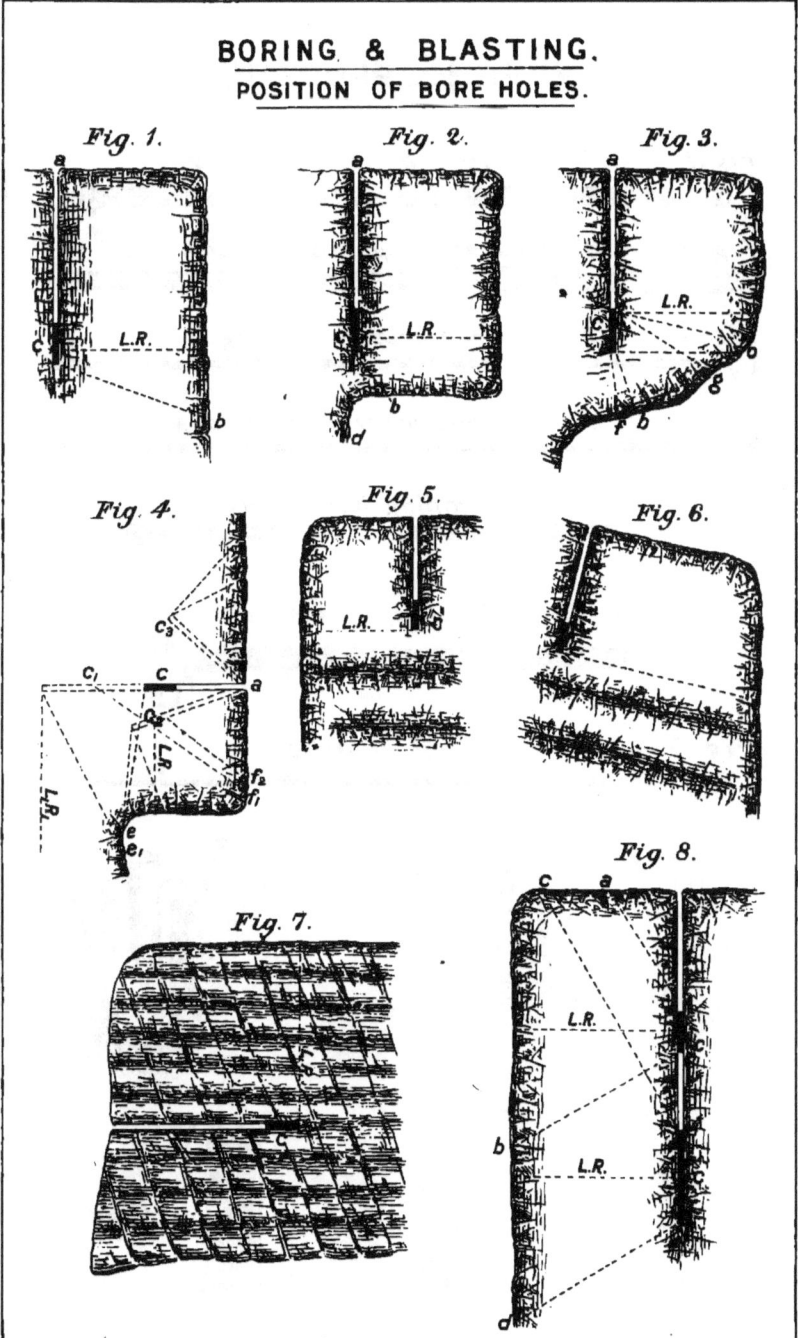

PLATE XXX

BORING & BLASTING.

Fig. 1.   3" hole steel boring bar 4' long.

Fig. 2.   3" hole steel jumping bar 7' long.
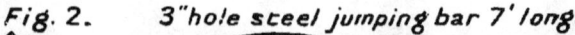

Fig. 3.   3" hole drag or worm 7' long.
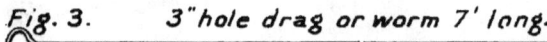

Fig. 4.   3" hole scoop or scraper 6'.6" long.

Fig. 5.   3" hole tamping bar 7' long.

Fig. 6.   14 lb: sledge hammer.

Fig. 7.   priming needle

Fig. 8.
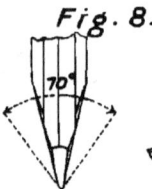

Fig. 9.
plug & feathers

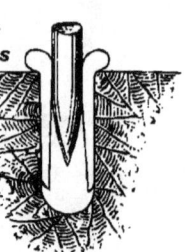

Fig. 10.

Fig. 11.

Fig. 12.

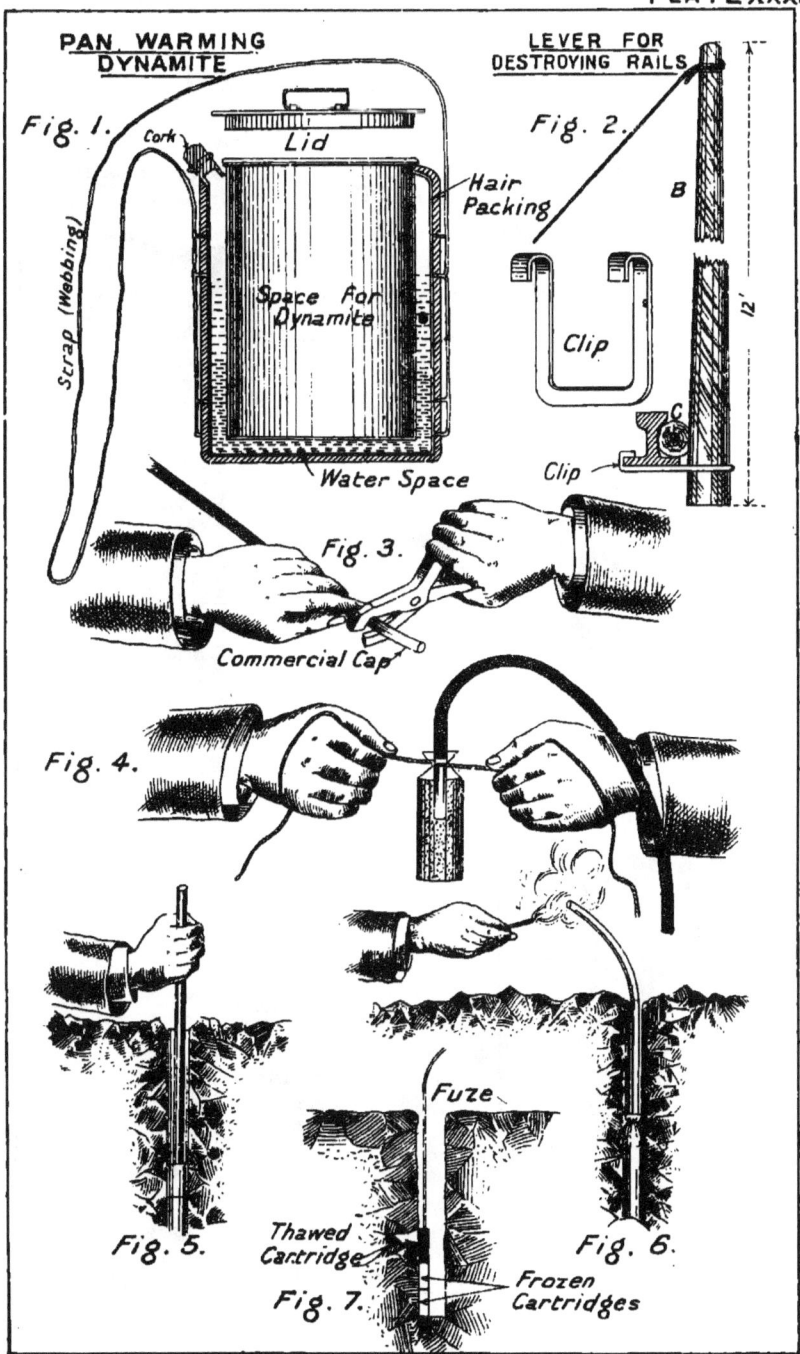

PLATE XXXII.

DEMOLITION OF REVETMENTS.

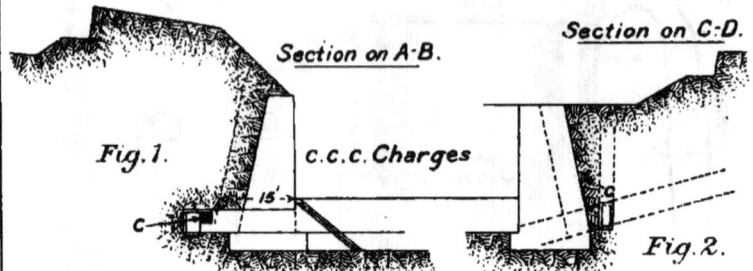

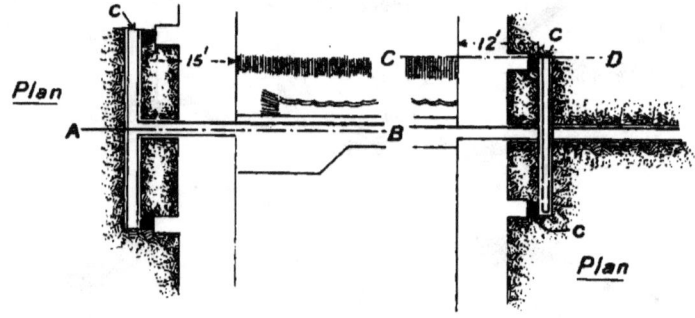

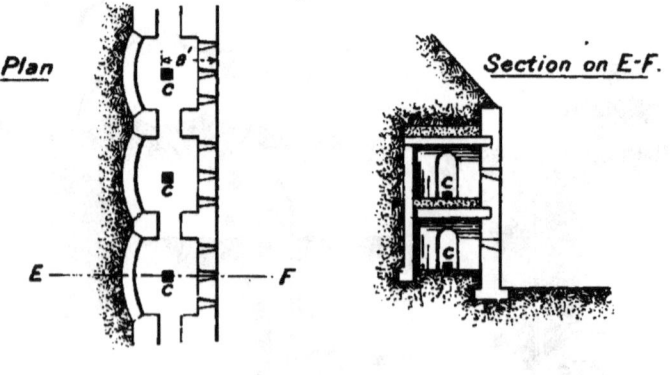

Scale 30' to 1 inch.

PLATE XXXIII.

DEMOLITION OF BUILDINGS & BRIDGES.

Fig. 1.

Fig. 2.

Fig. 3.

Fig. 4.

Fig. 5.

Fig. 6.

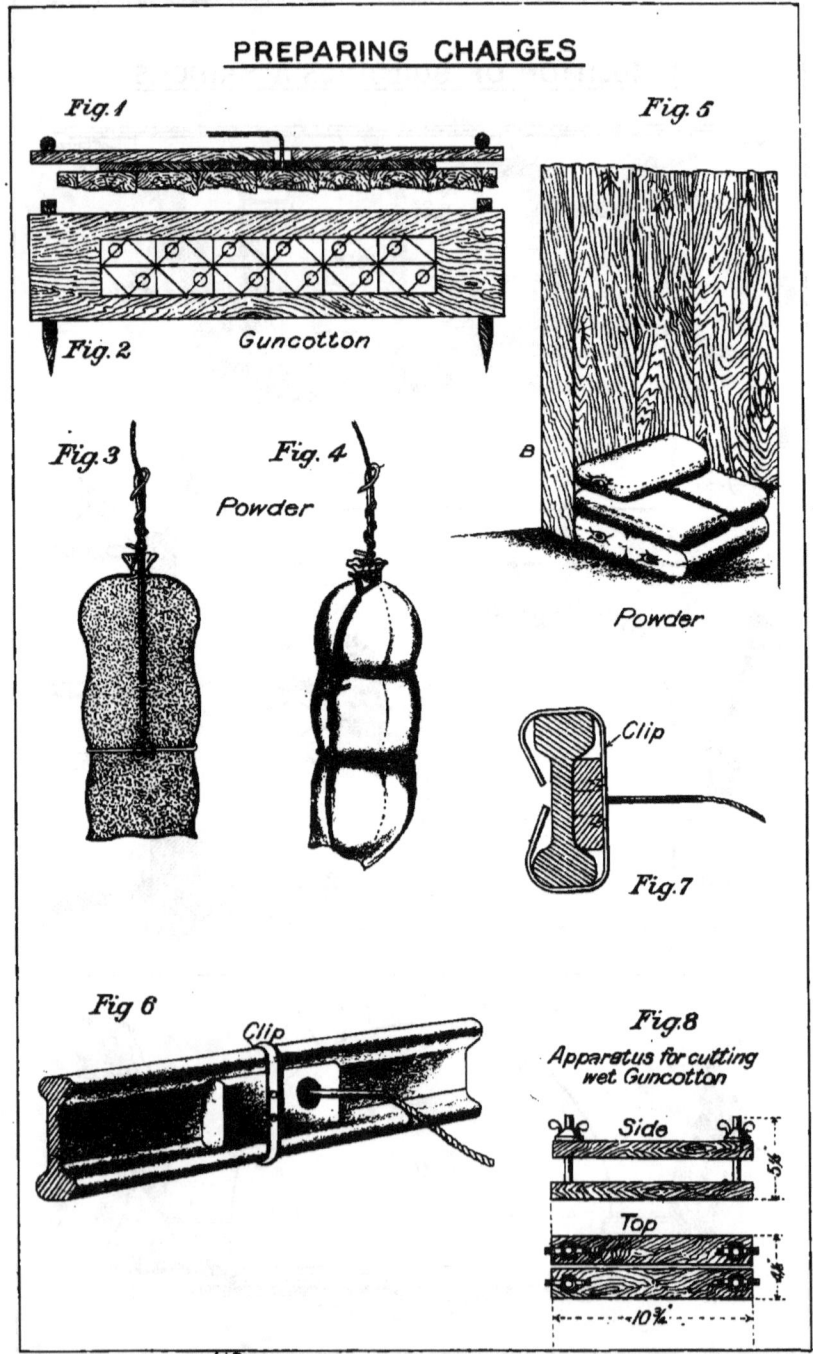

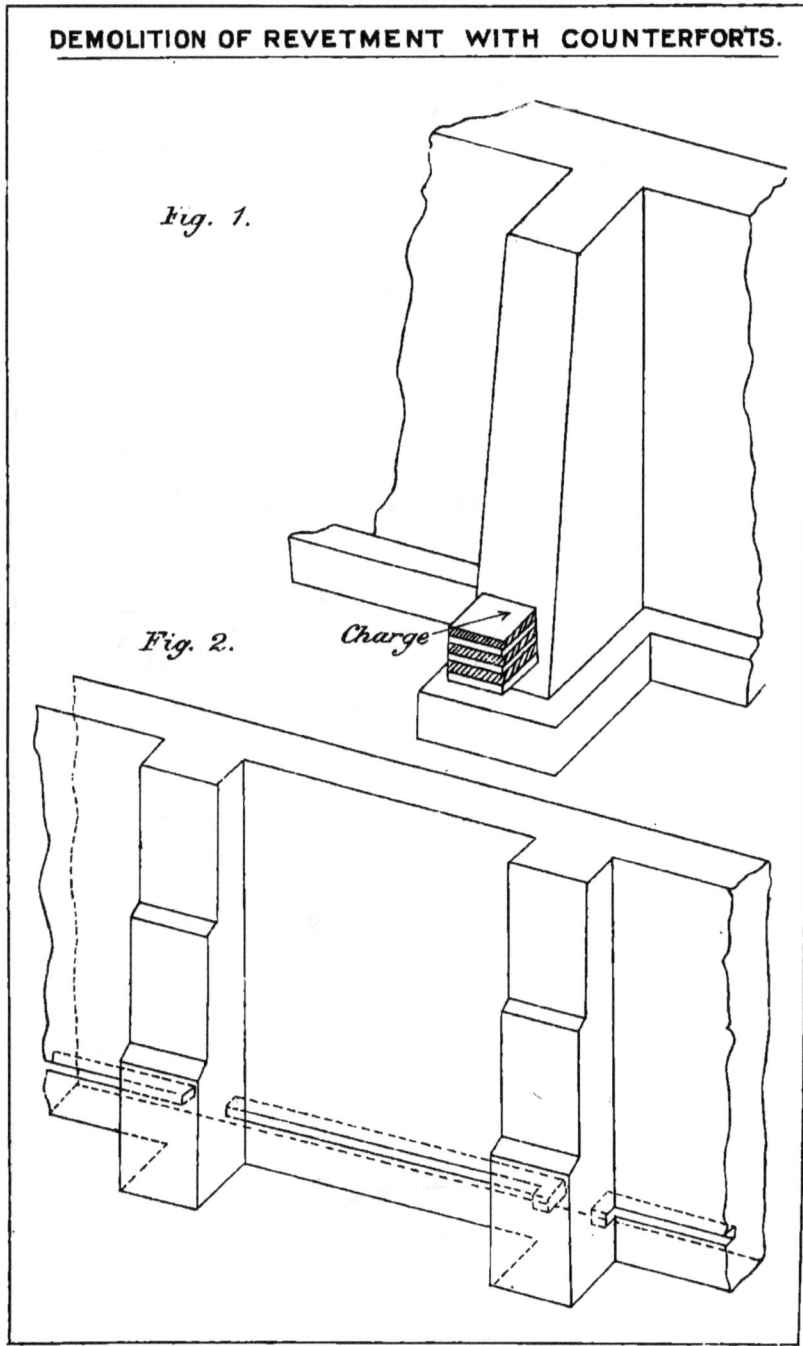

PLATE XXXVI.

DEMOLITION OF IRON GIRDER BRIDGES.

Fig. 1.

Fig. 2.

Fig. 3.

Fig. 4.

Fig. 5.

Fig. 6.

Fig. 7.

Fig. 8.

PLATE XXXVII.

DEMOLITION WITH GUNCOTTON.

Fig. 1.

Fig. 2.

Fig. 3.

Fig. 5.

Fig. 4.

Fig. 6.

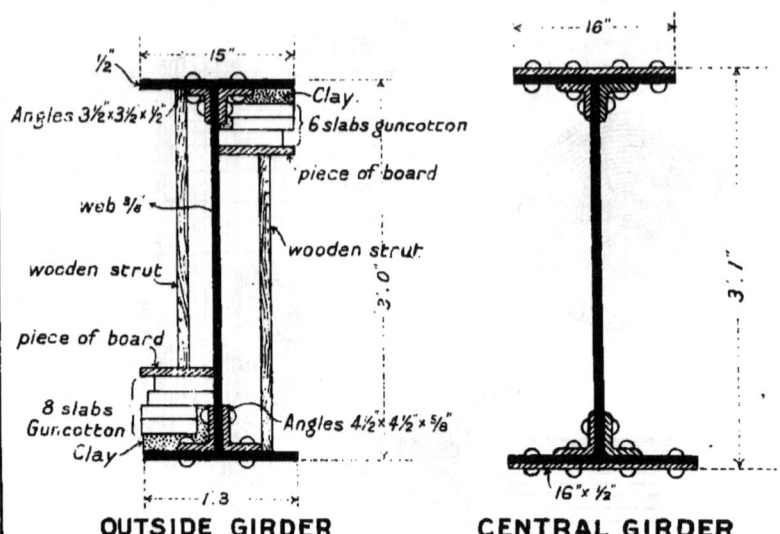

CLEAR SPAN 30', DOUBLE LINE, 4' 8½" GAUGE.

OUTSIDE GIRDER **CENTRAL GIRDER**

The charge for the demolition of the girder shewn in Fig:1. is worked out as follows, using the ordinary formula $\frac{3}{2} Bt^2$:—

Top flange $\frac{3}{2} \times 1\frac{1}{4}$ (breadth) × {$\frac{1}{2}$"(thickness of flange) + $\frac{1}{2}$" (thickness of angle iron) + $\frac{1}{2}$" (height of one rivet head)}^{2}
= $\frac{3}{2} \times \frac{5}{4} \times (\frac{3}{2})^2$ = 4·22 lbs.

Bottom flange $\frac{3}{2} \times 14$" (breadth) × {$\frac{1}{2}$" (thickness of flange) + $\frac{5}{8}$" (thickness of angle iron) + $\frac{1}{2}$" (height of one rivet head)}^{2}
= $\frac{3}{2} \times \frac{7}{4} \times (1\frac{5}{8})^2$ = 4·95 lbs

Web, Top portion $\frac{3}{2} \times \frac{7}{2}$" (breadth) × {$\frac{3}{8}$"(thickness of web) + 2 × $\frac{1}{2}$" (two thicknesses of angle iron) + $\frac{1}{2}$" (height of one rivet head)}^{2}
= $\frac{3}{2} \times \frac{3}{2} \times (1\frac{3}{8})^2$ = 1·32 lbs.

Web, Bottom portion $\frac{3}{2} \times \frac{7}{2}$" (breadth) × {$\frac{3}{8}$"(thickness of web) + 2 × $\frac{5}{8}$"(two thicknesses of angle iron) + $\frac{1}{2}$" (height of one rivet head)}^{2}
= $\frac{3}{2} \times \frac{7}{2} \times (1\frac{5}{8})^2$ = 2·26 lbs.

Web, Central portion $\frac{3}{2} \times \{3' - (2 \times 2\frac{1}{4} + 1\frac{1}{2} + \frac{3\frac{1}{4}}{12})\}$ (breadth) × {$\frac{3}{8}$}^{2} (thickness of web)
= $\frac{3}{2} \times 2\frac{1}{4} \times (\frac{3}{8})^2$.

The total charge is 13·22 lbs: or just 14 slabs. This should be placed as shewn in the figure in two charges of 6 and 8 slabs respectively.

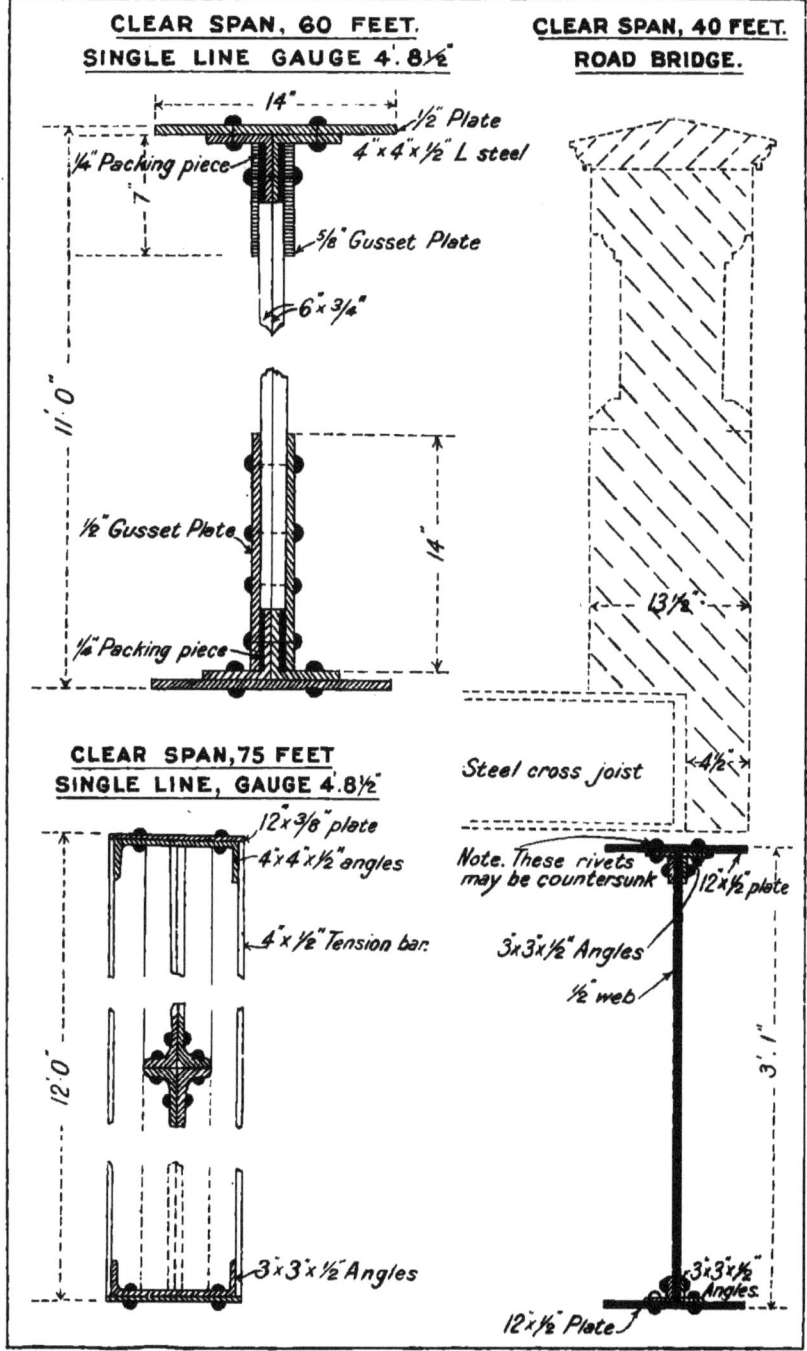

www.ingramcontent.com/pod-product-compliance
Lightning Source LLC
Chambersburg PA
CBHW071004160426
43193CB00012B/1904